IMPROVING SCHOOL ACCOUNTABILITY: CHECK-UPS OR CHOICE

ADVANCES IN APPLIED MICROECONOMICS

Series Editor: Michael R. Baye

Recent Volumes:

Volume 11: Economics of the Internet and E-Commerce

Volume 12: Organizing the New Industrial Economy

Volume 13: Experimental and Behavioural Economics

Volume Edited by John Morgan

ADVANCES IN APPLIED MICROECONOMICS VOLUME 14

IMPROVING SCHOOL ACCOUNTABILITY: CHECK-UPS OR CHOICE

EDITED BY

TIMOTHY J. GRONBERG

Professor of Economics
Texas A&M University

DENNIS W. JANSEN

Professor of Economics
Texas A&M University

ELSEVIER
JAI

Amsterdam – Boston – Heidelberg – London – New York – Oxford
Paris – San Diego – San Francisco – Singapore – Sydney – Tokyo

JAI Press is an imprint of Elsevier

JAI Press is an imprint of Elsevier
The Boulevard, Langford Lane, Kidlington, Oxford OX5 1GB, UK
Radarweg 29, PO Box 211, 1000 AE Amsterdam, The Netherlands
525 B Street, Suite 1900, San Diego, CA 92101-4495, USA

First edition 2006

British Library Cataloguing in Publication Data
A catalogue record for this book is available from the British Library

ISBN-13: 978-0-7623-1351-8
ISBN-10: 0-7623-1351-X
ISSN: 0278-0984 (Series)

For information on all JAI Press publications
visit our website at books.elsevier.com

Printed and bound in The Netherlands

06 07 08 09 10 10 9 8 7 6 5 4 3 2 1

CONTENTS

LIST OF CONTRIBUTORS

Hella Bel Hadj Amor	Institute for Education and Social Policy, Steinhardt School of Education, New York University, New York, NY, USA
Julie Berry Cullen	Department of Economics, University of California San Diego, La Jolla, CA, USA
Jeff DeSimone	Department of Economics, University of South Florida, Tampa, FL, USA and National Bureau of Economic Research, New York, NY, USA
Randall W. Eberts	W. E. Upjohn Institute for Employment Research, Kalamazoo, MI, USA
David N. Figlio	Department of Economics, University of Florida, Gainesville, FL, USA
Lawrence S. Getzler	Department of Planning and Budget, Richmond, VA, USA
Stephen Gibbons	Centre for the Economics of Education and Centre for Economic Performance, London School of Economics, London, UK
Timothy J. Gronberg	Department of Economics, Texas A&M University, College Station, TX, USA
Kevin M. Hollenbeck	W. E. Upjohn Institute for Employment Research, Kalamazoo, MI, USA
George M. Holmes	Cecil G. Sheps Center for Health Services Research, University of North Carolina, Chapel Hill, NC, USA
Dennis W. Jansen	Department of Economics, Texas A&M University, College Station, TX, USA

John T. Jones	Kentucky Legislative Research Commission, Office of Education Accountability, Frankfort, KY, USA
Hamilton Lankford	Department of Economics, University at Albany SUNY, Albany, NY, USA
George S. Naufal	Department of Economics, Texas A&M University, College Station, TX, USA
Randall Reback	Department of Economics, Barnard College, Columbia University, New York, NY, USA
Nicholas G. Rupp	Department of Economics, East Carolina University, Greenville, NC, USA
Amy Ellen Schwartz	Steinhardt School of Education and Robert F. Wagner Graduate School of Public Service, New York University, New York, NY, USA
Olmo Silva	Centre for the Economics of Education and Centre for Economic Performance, London School of Economics, London, UK
Leanna Stiefel	Robert F. Wagner Graduate School of Public Service, New York University, New York, NY, USA
Lori L. Taylor	Bush School of Government and Public Service, Texas A&M University, College Station, TX, USA
Eugenia F. Toma	Martin School of Public Policy & Administration, University of Kentucky, Lexington, KY, USA
James Wyckoff	Rockefeller College of Public Affairs, University at Albany SUNY, Albany, NY, USA
Ron Zimmer	Rand Corporation, Pittsburgh, PA, USA

EDITORS' INTRODUCTION

The existing state of K-12 public education in the United States is perceived as unacceptable by a large number and a wide variety of critics. How to improve upon this state is the subject of much disagreement. The public discussion is heated, and even the academic debate is often sharp. One common thread of argument stresses the need to increase accountability as a strategy for improving the quality of public schools. There are two broad classes of mechanisms for increasing accountability. If the current outcomes are too low, then setting acceptable performance standards is one approach to generating quality improvements. The task becomes one of defining appropriate accountability standards and then establishing a system of incentives to implement those standards. Alternatively, the low current performance may reflect weak productivity incentives traceable to the limited competition, which many school operators face. The suggested remedy is a dose of increased choice either increased public sector offerings, such as charter schools, or increased private sector choice via voucher-type programs.

This volume brings together 10 papers that tackle important economic issues surrounding accountability reforms. The papers bring to bear relevant microeconomic analysis and current microeconometric techniques. The first four papers consider topics relevant to the standards mechanism, which we refer to as the "check-up" approach to improving school accountability. The final six papers address various topics germane to the choice approach.

The volume opens with two papers that address a moral hazard problem in the design of school accountability systems. If schools are rated on the basis of test score performance, schools have an incentive to take actions to alter the test-taking pool in order to boost ratings. Julie Berry Cullen and Randall Reback develop a theoretical model of student exemptions under an accountability system based upon standardized test pass rates. The model yields two testable predictions. The first suggests that the return to increasing exemptions for student groups with expected pass rates below the accountability threshold is greater than for student groups with expected pass rates above the threshold. The focus here is upon subgroups within schools. A second test is based upon shifts in the marginal benefit curve for exemptions across campuses and across years. Exogenous shifts upward in the marginal benefit curve will, for a given marginal cost curve, increase the likelihood of an increase in exemptions from the prior year. Cullen and Reback use data from Texas to test these two predictions. They find support for both. Campuses target exemptions within the campus population where the expected rating returns are highest, and they expand exemption rates, largely by classifying more students as special needs kids, between years in response to increases in exemption incentives.

In a complementary analysis, David Figlio and Lawrence Getzler investigate whether the introduction of accountability testing in Florida via the Florida Comprehensive Assessment Test (FCAT) has affect public school special education assignment decisions. Figlio and Getzler take advantage of a rich data set consisting of student records for six large county-level school districts over a relatively long time period, 1992–1999. These panel data enable the estimation of student-level fixed effect models. The student fixed effects capture time-invariant student-level variation in the probability of disability classification. The authors also control for underlying linear time trends in disability classification. They find that the introduction of the FCAT testing regime is associated with a significant increase in the rate of disability classification.

The findings in these two papers are both important and troubling. At a minimum, they suggest that the information content of the accountability exams is compromised by the gaming responses of schools. Perhaps more importantly, they suggest that the allocation of resources across students is being distorted in ways that do not serve the kids, nor society, well.

The next two papers investigate issues surrounding the choice of performance measures to include in an accountability system. Hella Bel Hadj Amor, Amy Ellen Schwartz, and Leanna Stiefel provide a novel look at the performance measurement question by asking whether high schools that produce high-scoring students on traditional high school measures of success also produce high-performing college students. They use a unique data set that allows them to track a large cohort of New York City public high school students from ninth grade through their high school years and, for a subset of that cohort, into the City University of New York. They estimate student-level regressions with school fixed effects and controls for a number of student characteristics. The school fixed effects generate average value-added measures for each campus for each performance measure. A key finding is that the correlations among the high school measures and between the high school value-added and the college GPA value-added rankings are low.

Do high ratings based upon traditional performance measures go hand in hand with efficiency? Timothy Gronberg, Dennis Jansen, and George Naufel address this question using stochastic production frontier methods. The authors utilize a six-year panel of test score, school input, and school student characteristics data for a sample of 3,000 campuses in Texas. They generate estimates of school-specific efficiency based upon the estimates of the one-sided school-specific error term in a stochastic production frontier model. School rankings on the basis of estimated efficiency are not well correlated with school rankings on the basis of traditional measures of school performance.

These papers also raise red flags for accountability mechanism designers. Schools do not appear to be ranked similarly across various defensible measures of success. Difficult trade-offs in system design need to be considered.

There are a number of different margins that can be affected by the institutional structure of the school market. The remainder of the volume consists of papers that estimate the impact of the choice structure of the school market upon several of these margins.

The most direct impact of expansions in school choice is upon the students who select into the new school options. Randall Eberts and Kevin Hollenbeck examine the evidence of the effect of charter schools upon the performance of charter-enrolling students in Michigan. They have student-level data and from 1996 through the end of the 2000/2001 school year, are able to match same-student test scores in consecutive years from unique student characteristics. This allows estimation of a value-added education production function. They focus on students in fourth and fifth grades, and estimate that charter student performance is 0.2 standard deviations below that of traditional public school students. They then subdivide charter school students into those attending for-profit charter schools and those attending not-for-profit charter schools, and find that students in for-profit charters perform better than students in not-for-profit charter schools. Finally, they report some evidence that charter schools improve with years of operation.

The indirect or systemic competitive effect of expanded school choice is the potential for improved outcomes among the stayers, i.e. students who do not migrate to the new market entrants. George Holmes, Jeff DeSimone, and Nicholas Rupp look for evidence of a competitive effect of charter school entry on the performance of traditional public school student in North Carolina.

North Carolina charter schools did not exist in the 1996/1997 school year, and three years later there were almost 100 charter schools in operation. Holmes et al. examine the potential effect of these new entrants on students in traditional public schools. Did the growth in the number of charter schools leads to increased achievement for students at traditional public schools? They have school-level data on student performance and measure charter competition by distance from the traditional public school to the nearest charter school. They find that the effect of charter competition is positive, that the presence of charter schools does improve the performance of traditional public schools, and that the closer the charter school, the greater the achievement gains. Further, these gains appear significant for policy purposes. On average, achievement at a traditional public school increases about 1 percent when there is a nearby charter school, an increase that is one fourth of a standard deviation of average test-score gains.

In a related piece, Stephen Gibbons and Olmo Silva explain their work on competition and parental choice for primary schools in England. They look carefully at education boundaries and discontinuities in market access at those boundaries. In this way, they hope to isolate localized variation across district boundaries. They utilized a detailed student census with student and school addresses. In this chapter, we have presented a methodology to identify the impact of school competition and choice on pupil outcomes, using discontinuities in market access generated by proximity to administrative boundaries; this allows isolation of exogenous variation in the competitive pressure-faced schools, which can be used to identify the impact of competition on pupil achievements and stratification by attainments. Their measure of competition is the number of alternative schools that students at a given school could have attended given their addresses, the location of nearby schools, and travel patterns. This intuitive measure is meant to capture the notion that the number of alternatives within reasonable travel distance is a measure of competition.

The conclusion from their study of English schools is that competition has no causal effect on the performance of schools. They find correlation between competition and average student achievement, but not causation. They also find some evidence, though not statistically significant, that competition leads to greater stratification by student achievement.

As a follow up to this concern with stratification, the potential segregation impacts of school choice is the focus of the paper by Hamilton Lankford and James Wyckoff. They model the school choice and residential location decisions of white families in eight New York metropolitan areas. After controlling for individual, peer, school, and local government characteristics, they find that the racial composition of schools and neighborhoods has a large influence on school choice decisions and household location decision. Whites when faced with urban public schools containing moderate concentrations of African Americans or Latinos are more likely to choose private schools or suburban public schools. Lankford and Wyckoff draw out the many implications of their results, which extend beyond the direct impact on racial diversity of schools. Policymakers need to understand the full implications and consequences of parental school choice within the current educational system and within proposed alternatives. To cite one example, it is possible that suburban families are in many cases little impacted by the current push for expanded school choice.

The usual focus in the charter school literature has been upon the exodus of students from traditional public schools to charters. Eugenia Toma, Ron Zimmer, and John Jones provide a fresh perspective on the charter sorting effect. They look for action on the public/private margin. In particular, they estimate the extent of migration of students from private schools to charter schools in Michigan. The empirical model relates the percent of a county's enrollment in private schools to the percent enrolled in charters and a number of county and district variables expected to influence enrollments. Their principal finding is that an increase in the proportion of public school students who are in charter schools is negatively and significantly, both statistically and economically, related to the proportion of the total enrollment in private schools. This result has intriguing implications for the net impact of charters on public school spending.

The final paper in the volume also provides analysis of an unexplored marginal impact of school choice. Lori Taylor contributes to the literature on charter schools by investigating the impact of charters on the market for public school teachers. Taylor first outlines two competing models of salary determination in educator markets. In the first model, schools are oligopsonists in the market for teachers; in the second, schools are oligopolists, with teachers as potential recipients of any rents, in the market for seats. The models differ in the comparative statics impact of market concentration on teacher salaries: charter school growth could either raise or lower teacher salaries, depending upon which model best organizes the teacher market outcomes. The analysis suggests that once charter enrollments reach critical mass, increasing competition from charter schools increases salaries for all, but the most experienced teachers.

We hope that you agree that the range of topics and the quality of treatment afforded to each topic make Improving Public School Accountability: Check-ups or Choice is a unique and valuable addition to the growing and controversial literature in this area. This volume is part of the Elsevier series *Advances in Applied Microeconomics*. The purpose of each annual volume in the series is to present relevant frontier research in advance of journals and other outlets. For additional information about this series, either past volumes or planned future volumes, please visit the website of the series editor, Michael R. Baye, at http://www.nash-equilibrium.com.

TINKERING TOWARD ACCOLADES: SCHOOL GAMING UNDER A PERFORMANCE ACCOUNTABILITY SYSTEM☆

Julie Berry Cullen and Randall Reback

ABSTRACT

We explore the extent to which schools manipulate the composition of students in the test-taking pool in order to maximize ratings under Texas' accountability system in the 1990s. We first derive predictions from a static model of administrators' incentives given the structure of the ratings criteria, and then test these predictions by comparing differential changes in exemption rates across student subgroups within campuses and across campuses and regimes. Our analyses uncover evidence of a moderate degree of strategic behavior, so that there is some tension between designing systems that account for heterogeneity in student populations and that are manipulation-free.

☆The title is inspired by *Tinkering toward Utopia : A century of public school reform* (Tyack & Cuban, 1995), a book describing the evolution of U.S. public schooling during the 20th century.

Improving School Accountability: Check-Ups or Choice
Advances in Applied Microeconomics, Volume 14, 1–34

ISSN: 0278-0984/doi:10.1016/S0278-0984(06)14001-8

1. INTRODUCTION

Advocates of elementary and secondary education reform believe that the current system does not provide adequate checks and incentives to ensure that teachers and school administrators maximize student learning. Increased accountability is seen as a necessary condition for improving the quality of public schools. The two leading current reform movements to improve accountability involve expanding the educational choices of students and establishing performance standards. In this paper, we examine a problematic design issue associated with the latter type of reform by analyzing behavioral responses to incentives to exempt students from taking exams under Texas' system during the 1990s. While the goal of establishing standards is to improve school efficiency and student outcomes, standards are inevitably imperfect instruments.

Performance-based incentive systems are not new to the public sector and there is a well-developed literature addressing the potential pitfalls.[1] First, public agencies typically pursue multiple goals, of which only some produce measurable outcomes. Since rewards are necessarily tied to measurement, agents may divert resources toward these and away from other valuable outcomes. This issue may be particularly problematic in the education setting where teachers multi-task and where desirable outcomes, such as social adjustment, are often not easily measured.

Second, when outcomes do have empirical counterparts, the performance measures may only be weakly correlated with progress toward program goals. For example, by teaching specifically to the content of high-stakes exams, measured achievement may improve in the absence of general improvements in knowledge and ability in those subject areas.[2] Further, most states base school ratings on pass rates, so that schools may achieve higher ratings by targeting instruction to near-failing students, while not necessarily improving the performance of other students (Reback, 2005).

Finally, the performance measures themselves are often flawed, so that agents can improve reported performance without making progress on actual performance. We refer to behaviors that fall under this final potential pitfall as "gaming," and the form of gaming that we focus on is the exclusion of low-achieving students from the test-taking pool.[3] When bureaucracies use heterogeneous inputs, as in the education sector, there is inevitably a trade-off between designing an accountability system that is "fair," in terms of accounting for this heterogeneity, and "manipulation-proof," in terms of ensuring that measured performance represents real accomplishment. For example, some students with pre-existing academic limitations should be legitimately excluded from high-stakes exams, or at least given alternative treatment. On the other hand, when an accountability system allows student exemptions from exams, schools are then able to improve measured performance by manipulating the composition of students taking the exams. Officials at a strategic school might classify additional students in exempt categories, such as special education or limited English proficient, misreport students' statuses, or "encourage" absences primarily to improve aggregate outcomes.

Although the potential for this dysfunctional response is well recognized, there has been relatively limited systematic analysis of the link or its practical relevance.[4] Haney (2000) and Deere and Strayer (2001a) provide descriptive evidence by documenting increases in special education classification rates particularly for minority and low-achieving students, respectively, following the introduction of the Texas policy. In the presence of strong secular upward trends in special education placements,[5] Deere and Strayer (2001b) present more convincing evidence by showing a reversal in the growth in the rate at which special education students sit for achievement exams following a recent policy change that counts scores of special education test-takers. More recent studies use within-state and within-school control groups. For example, Figlio and Getzler (2002) find that schools at risk of failing reclassify previously low-performing students as disabled at higher rates following the introduction of the testing regime in Florida,[6] and Figlio (2005) finds that schools also alter the test-taking pool by strategically assigning long suspensions to low-performing students subject to disciplinary action near the test-taking period – and in both cases the behavior is stronger for students in tested grades.[7,8]

Our paper differs from prior studies in that it exploits the specific structure and evolution of the performance targets of the Texas system to formulate more precise school-level incentives. We begin by developing a model of the marginal benefits to administrators from exempting students in order to increase the probability that their schools attain higher ratings. We then conduct empirical tests of two theoretical predictions that arise from the model. First, given that the pass rate standards apply not only to all students but also separately to students within race/ethnicity and economic disadvantage subgroups, we analyze changes in exemptions rates among subgroups within the same schools. We predict that exemption rates should increase most for groups whose pass rates are expected to be below the required threshold, because these groups are most likely to constrain the school from attaining the next-highest rating. Our findings confirm this prediction; exemption rates are inflated by up to 7 and 14 percent for

Hispanic and Black students, respectively, in years when these students are under-performing relative to peers in the same campus. Although the requirements for separate subgroups are meant to ensure that schools target improvement efforts toward all students, this policy also appears to encourage targeted exemptions.

In our second test, we use student-level test score data to explicitly compute the marginal benefit to a school from exempting additional students between consecutive years. Using these explicit incentives, we analyze whether changes in the level of exemptions at the same school during consecutive years are related to changes in incentives. Strong short-run incentives to exempt additional students are found to raise the likelihood that a school has a one-year increase in the fraction of students classified as exempt by 11 percent. This finding for overall exemptions appears to be driven by more aggressive special education placements and higher absenteeism.

The remainder of the paper proceeds as follows. In the next section, we provide detailed information about the Texas accountability system. Section 3 then presents a conceptual framework for measuring variation in schools' incentives to exempt students that arises from the structure of the accountability system. Sections 4 and 5 describe our empirical strategies and results, respectively. Section 6 offers a brief set of implications and conclusions.

2. TEXAS ACCOUNTABILITY SYSTEM

2.1. Background

The Texas accountability system originally applied only at the student level in the form of exit exams required for graduation. School-level accountability began in 1993, with schools classified into four rating categories based on student pass rates.[9] The rating categories are low performing, acceptable, recognized, and exemplary.[10] The same base indicators for determining ratings were used through 2000, after which the number of tests and grades tested were expanded and an entirely new set of assessments were introduced in 2003.[11] During our sample period, a school's rating depends on the fraction of students who pass Spring Texas Assessment of Academic Skills (TAAS) achievement exams in reading, mathematics, and writing. The reading and math exams are given in grades 3–8 and 10, while the writing exams are given only in grades 4, 8, and 10.[12] For the tested grades combined, all students and four separate student subgroups (White, Hispanic, Black, and economically disadvantaged) must demonstrate pass rates that exceed year-specific standards for each category.[13] In addition, prior year dropout rates must be below and prior year attendance rates must be above threshold levels.

Table 1 displays the year-specific standards for each category for the years 1993–1998. There was a planned phase-in of the pass rate standards for the acceptable and recognized categories to 50 percent by 2000 and 80 percent by 1998, respectively. Those two categories also depend on improvement in pass rates from the previous year during the phase-in period.[14] Although the thresholds have evolved, the standards for passing have remained the same.

A school's rating can have real consequences. The ratings are easily understood and are made public. The rating a school attains may affect how attractive it is perceived to be, which could affect its student population, property values, and local support for funding.[15] In addition, ratings can affect the regulatory burden placed on schools. Those placed in the lowest category undergo an evaluation process and may be reconstituted or otherwise sanctioned, including an allowance for students to transfer to

Table 1. Key Provisions of the Texas Accountability System.

	Minimum TAAS Pass Rate (%)			Maximum Dropout Rate (%)			Minimum Attendance Rate (%)		
	E	R	A	E	R	A	E	R	A
1993	90.0	65.0	20.0	1.0	3.5	N/A	97.0	95.0	N/A
1994	90.0	65.0	25.0	1.0	3.5	N/A	94.0	94.0	N/A
1995	90.0	70.0	25.0	1.0	3.5	6.0	94.0	94.0	N/A
1996	90.0	70.0	30.0	1.0	3.5	6.0	94.0	94.0	N/A
1997	90.0	75.0	35.0	1.0	3.5	6.0	94.0	94.0	N/A
1998	90.0	80.0	40.0	1.0	3.5	6.0	94.0	94.0	N/A

Notes: Schools are assigned one of four ratings: exemplary (E), recognized (R), acceptable (A), or low performing. Schools are evaluated on three performance measures: current pass rates on the Spring TAAS exams for tested grades, dropout rates for grades 7–12 from the prior year, and the attendance rate for students in grades 1–12 from the prior year. All students and each separate student group (White, Hispanic, Black, and economically disadvantaged) must satisfy the test score and dropout requirements. Except for in 1993 when the requirement applied only to all tests taken combined, the pass rates apply separately to each subject area exam (mathematics, reading, and writing).

The dark shading indicates that there are additional requirements (such as sustained performance or required improvement) that mean a school could achieve the indicated standard and still not obtain the indicated rating.

The light shading indicates that there are alternative provisions (such as required improvement and single group waivers) that mean the minimum standards are not always binding.

better-performing schools inside or outside the district. Schools with the highest rating become exempt from some regulations and requirements. Finally, in most years there have been financial awards for schools that are either high performing or show substantial improvement.

The opportunity for schools to attain a higher rating by gaming this system is related to the way the accountability subset is defined. In order to safeguard schools against the risks of serving disadvantaged populations, there are a number of categories of students that are not included in calculating the school's aggregate pass rates. During our sample period, fiscal years 1993–1998, there are four possible reasons why a student would not be tested at all: (i) the student is in special education with a severe enough handicap to limit the usefulness of testing, (ii) the student is Limited English Proficient (LEP) and the Spanish test was not offered that year, (iii) the student was absent that day, or (iv) some other reason (e.g., illness, cheating). There are three possible reasons why a tested student would not have his/her performance contribute to the school pass rate: (i) the student is tested but is in a special education program, (ii) the student took a Spanish test, or (iii) the student was mobile, i.e., not in the district as of October of the school year. Classifying additional students as special needs or LEP or "helping" them to fall into any of these other categories could improve measured performance if these students would likely fail their tests.

Policymakers and practitioners understand the role that differential exemptions can play in upsetting the validity of the ratings categories. The Texas accountability system has evolved to address these types of concerns. Since 1999, special education and Spanish TAAS test-takers have been included in the accountability subset, and more recently an assessment specifically designed for disabled students has been incorporated to further increase participation. Our analysis is based on data from the years leading up to these reforms when gaming is likely to have been more prevalent.[16]

2.2. Descriptive Trends

Fig. 1a presents mean school pass rates by subject and year. For all subjects, there was a dramatic, steady increase in pass rates between 1994 and 1998.[17] Furthermore, this rise in performance occurred for all of the various accountability subgroups. For example, Fig. 1b reveals that the average White, Hispanic, Black, and economically disadvantaged pass rates on the math exam increased from 71, 52, 41, and 50 percent to 90, 81, 73, and 79 percent, respectively. Though the pass rate thresholds for various

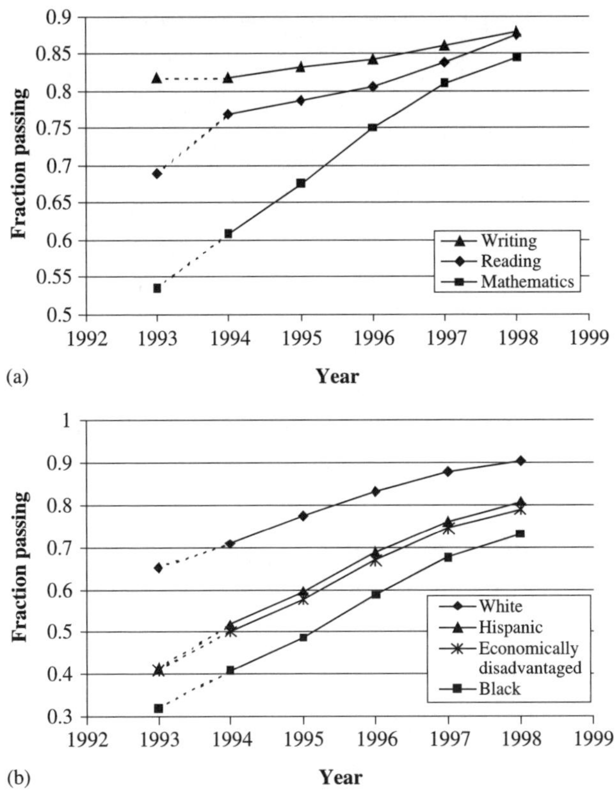

Fig. 1. (a) Mean School TAAS Pass Rate by Subject (b) Mean School Mathematics TAAS Pass Rate by Subgroup.

accountability ratings increased over this period (see Table 1), these pass rate improvements were significant enough to cause an upward trend in school ratings. Fig. 2 displays the distribution of school ratings by year. Since the TAAS exams are supposed to be comparable over time, on the surface, it appears that there has been tremendous academic improvement.

Fig. 3 presents mixed evidence as to whether alterations in the test-taking pool can explain any part of this "miracle." After rising between 1993 and 1995, mean overall exemption rates have since fallen. The fraction of students exempted due to special education placement increased each year, particularly for disabled students who were able to take the test. The fraction LEP exempt also increased rapidly in the early years, before leveling

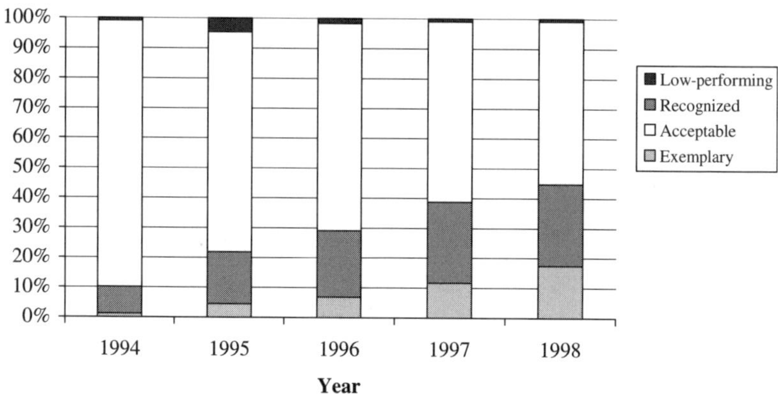

Fig. 2. Percent of Schools Receiving each Rating.

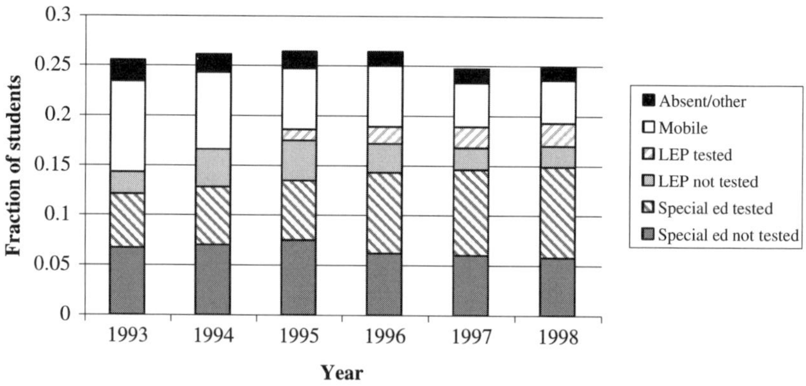

Fig. 3. Mean Share of Students Exempt by Category.

off. The slowing in the rate of growth in each of these categories could be related to the pending inclusion of special education and Spanish test-takers in the accountability system, which started in 1999 and was first announced in 1996. The overall decrease is driven by pronounced declines in the fraction exempted due to mobility status. The drop in mobility exemptions in 1997 was due to a policy change that tightened the process for identifying a student as new to a district.[18] Thus, the overall decrease in exemptions does not dispel the idea that the accountability system, prior to becoming more inclusive, may have led to higher rates of placement in excepted categories than would have otherwise prevailed.

3. CONCEPTUAL FRAMEWORK

3.1. Basic Model

In this section, we develop a simple model of the marginal benefits and costs of exempting students under a pass rate threshold system. We do not model the politics and competing objectives of agents within schools, and treat a school's exemption decisions as being made by a single agent or administrator. Another important simplification is that we treat exemption decisions as depending on current-year incentives, and thus ignore potential dynamic behavioral responses. The framework generates testable predictions that motivate the empirical analyses that we conduct. We focus our theoretical discussion exclusively on the benefits and costs that are directly related to the accountability system, but in our empirical analyses we do control for the important role of fiscal incentives to place students in special programs that arise from the structure of the school finance system (Cullen, 2003).

Though there are three separate subject exams and separate hurdle requirements for student subgroups, start by assuming there is only one exam and that only the overall pass rate matters. Suppose that the administrator at school j takes the current level of exemptions (E_j^0) as given and is deciding how many students to exempt from among the set of students who are in the accountability pool ($N_j - E_j^0$). Define $\hat{P}_{ij}$ to be the administrator's expectation concerning the probability that student i will pass the exam. Let P_{ij} equal 1 if the student passes the exam and 0 if the student fails, so that $P_{ij} = \hat{P}_{ij} + \varepsilon_{ij}$ with $E[\varepsilon_{ij}] = 0$. Assume that the disturbance terms associated with the administrator's predictions are independent, or at least perceived to be independent by the administrator.[19] Then, the administrator's expectation of the overall pass rate is based on the sum of independent binomial outcomes and is approximately normally distributed, with mean equal to the mean student pass probability,

$$\hat{R}_j = \frac{1}{N_j - E_j^0} \sum_{i=1}^{N_j - E_j^0} \hat{P}_{ij}$$

and standard deviation

$$\sigma_j = \frac{\sqrt{\sum_{i=1}^{N_j - E_j^0} \hat{P}_{ij}(1 - \hat{P}_{ij})}}{\left(N_j - E_j^0\right)}$$

The standard deviation of the expected pass rate is greater when the underlying predicted probabilities for students are more uncertain (i.e., closer to 0.5) and when there are fewer test-takers.

The distribution of the expected pass rate determines the potential benefits to reclassifying students or otherwise exempting students from the test-taking pool. Let T equal the closest pass rate threshold to $\hat{R}_j$ (either from above or below) and define Z_j to be the marginal benefit associated with attaining the higher rating. If the administrator has risk neutral preferences, the marginal benefit of an additional exemption equals Z_j times the probability that this exemption causes the aggregate pass rate to be above T. The marginal benefit from increasing exemptions by $\Delta E_j = E_j^1 - E_j^0$ can be written as

$$MB(\Delta E_j) = Z_j \times \left[\Phi\left(\frac{\hat{R}_j\left(N_j - E_j^1\right) - T}{\sigma_j\left(N_j - E_j^1\right)} \right) - \Phi\left(\frac{\hat{R}_j\left(N_j - E_j^0\right) - T}{\sigma_j(N_j - E_j^0)} \right) \right] \tag{1}$$

where Φ is the cumulative standard normal density function. We refer to the term in square brackets as the raw (i.e., non-normalized) marginal benefit.

Both the change in the expected overall pass rate and in its standard deviation will influence the raw marginal benefit from increased exemptions. Assuming that administrators shrink the accountability pool by exempting students with the lowest pass probabilities, the expected pass rate will improve so that $\hat{R}_j(N_j - E_j^1) \geq \hat{R}_j(N_j - E_j^0)$. Selective new exemptions will also typically decrease the standard deviation, which on its own has an ambiguous effect on the probability that the overall pass rate exceeds the required threshold, depending on whether the mean expected pass rate is above or below the threshold. Regardless, changes in the expected pass rate will generally dominate, so that additional exemptions are beneficial.

In order to provide intuition for when incentives for additional exemptions are likely to be greatest, it is helpful to graph the marginal benefit curve under different scenarios. Consider an example where an administrator expects 68 percent of the accountability pool to pass this year's exam. Suppose the nearest pass rate threshold is 70 percent, so that the school is deemed "recognized" if the pass rate is at least that high. If the administrator exempts an additional (approximately) 2 percent of students in tested grades, and these students all had near-zero probabilities of passing, then the likelihood of reaching the next highest rating increases to 50 percent. Fig. 4a shows the shift in the distribution of the expected pass rate, with the associated increase

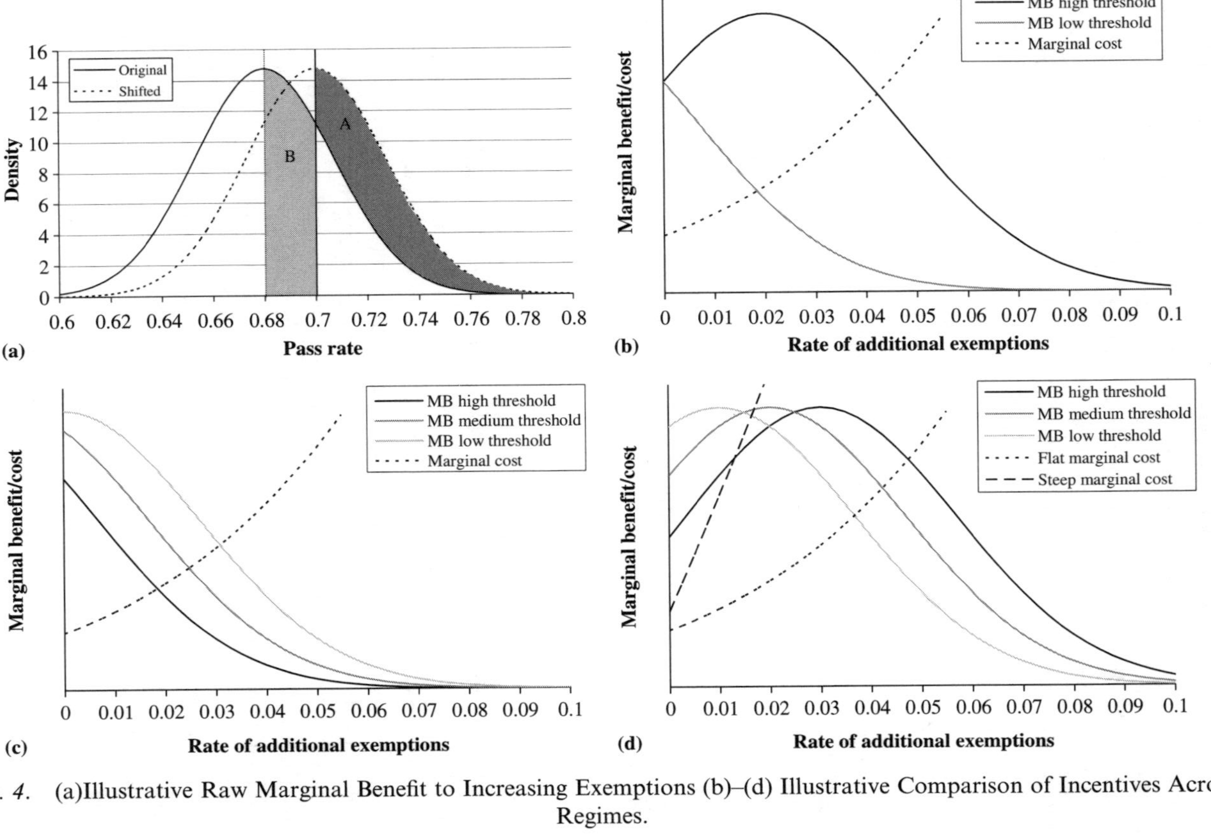

Fig. 4. (a)Illustrative Raw Marginal Benefit to Increasing Exemptions (b)–(d) Illustrative Comparison of Incentives Across Regimes.

in the probability of meeting the criterion represented by shaded area A. Note that, abstracting from evolutions in the standard deviation that accompany additional exemptions, the experiment could equivalently be carried out by hypothetically sequentially shifting the threshold down. From this perspective, as the administrator increases exemptions starting from the status quo, the raw marginal benefit curve would track the original pass rate distribution curve in reverse starting from where it crosses the relevant pass rate threshold, and the two shaded areas in the figure are identical.

Fig. 4b illustrates marginal benefit curves for a school under two pass rate regimes. In Fig. 4b, the x-axis shows the percentage point increase in the exemption rate (as a fraction of total enrollment), starting at the status quo. These illustrations are derived from the notion established above that the raw marginal benefit curve is closely related to the initial probability density function for the expected overall pass rate, adjusted for changes in the standard deviation as additional students are exempted and scaled by Z_j. As shown, the marginal benefit to exempting additional students when the initial pass rate is above the threshold (e.g., a threshold of 0.66) will generally be steadily decreasing. In contrast, the marginal benefit schedule when the initial pass rate is below the threshold, as in the case shown in Fig. 4a, will at first increase and then decrease.

In order to determine how many students a given school would optimally choose to exempt, the marginal benefits have to be traded-off against marginal costs. We presume that marginal costs are likely to be an increasing function of the level of exemptions, although the testable predictions that we develop in the next section do not depend on this. Exempting additional students likely involves short-run costs associated with reclassification, as well as long-run costs associated with providing a different type of service to the student. Schools are discouraged from classifying students as special education or LEP on test day without actually assigning special services by the threat of audit if the number exempted exceeds service caseloads. The state also threatens to audit schools with excessively high absenteeism relative to annual attendance rates or high rates of "other" exemptions.

Fig. 4b also depicts a representative marginal cost curve. In order to interpret the marginal cost curve appropriately, realize that the x-axis equivalently indexes the overall number of exemptions, with the origin set to the current exemption rate. In the example that is depicted, the marginal benefit to additional exemptions exceeds the marginal cost regardless of whether the threshold is high or low. The administrator will in one case want to improve the chances of attaining the higher rating, and in the other reduce the risk of receiving the lower rating. If the thresholds are equidistant from the mean expected pass rate across the two regimes, the administrator will generally behave more aggressively in the high-threshold regime. Obviously, administrators will also often have incentives to decrease exemptions, which in this framework would occur when policy or other changes cause marginal costs to exceed marginal benefits at the existing level of exemptions.

3.2. Testable Predictions

Our first empirical test uses within-school variation in whether subgroup pass rates are expected to be above or below the closest relevant threshold. Consider the case where there are two mutually exclusive subgroups in a campus. If one group's expected rate is above the threshold (group A) while the other's is below (group B), exempting students in the former group is associated with muted benefits. The reduction in the risk that group A falls below the threshold translates into only a fractional reduction in the risk that the school is rated in the lower category.

For example, suppose a school's rating is only influenced by the pass rates of these two mutually exclusive subgroups. Using the notation developed above, the marginal benefit of exempting more students in g, given that there is another group h, is

$$MB_{gj}(\Delta E_{gj}) = Z_j \times \left[\Phi\left(\frac{\hat{R}_{gj}(N_{gj} - E^1_{gj}) - T}{\sigma_{gj}(N_{gj} - E^1_{gj})}\right) - \Phi\left(\frac{\hat{R}_{gj}(N_{gj} - E^0_{gj}) - T}{\sigma_{gj}(N_{gj} - E^0_{gj})}\right)\right] \times \Phi\left(\frac{\hat{R}_{hj}(N_{hj} - E^0_{hj}) - T}{\sigma_{hj}(N_{hj} - E^0_{hj})}\right) \quad (2)$$

The last term represents the probability that the school satisfies the pass rate requirement for the other group. The marginal benefit to increasing exemptions for group B by a given amount will be greater than for group A as long as $\phi(k_{Bj})/\phi(k_{Bj}) > \Phi(k_{Aj})/\Phi(k_{Aj})$, where $k_{gj} = (\hat{R}_{gj} - T)/\sigma_{gj}$ and ϕ is the standard normal probability density function. If the variances are the same, this condition always holds whenever $k_{Bj} < k_{Aj}$., since log-concavity of the normal density and distribution implies the hazard function $(\phi/(1-\Phi))$ is everywhere increasing. We empirically test the prediction that, controlling for factors related to the variance of the test score distribution and to the cost of exempting students on the margin, there should be larger increases in exemption rates for student groups with expected pass rates below the relevant threshold ($k_{Bj} < 0$) than for student groups with expected pass rates exceeding this threshold ($k_{Aj} > 0$).

Our second empirical test uses student-level data to explicitly calculate shifts in schools' marginal benefit curves between years. Figs. 4c and 4d illustrate the relationship between changes in marginal benefits and changes in exemption levels. Fig. 4c shows three different potential marginal benefit curves for a school where the mean expected pass rate is in all cases above the relevant threshold, and each curve is associated with a threshold of differing stringency. These marginal benefit curves do not cross, so that one can readily determine whether incentives have increased or decreased. In Fig. 4d, where similar curves are shown for a campus with the mean expected pass rate below the threshold values, which regime induces the greatest increase in exemptions depends on the school's cost function. If there are steep marginal costs associated with higher exemption levels, then schools may increase exemptions by less when their expected pass rate is relatively far from the required threshold.

We structure the empirical analysis in order to test predictions that are robust to these underlying ambiguities. First, we characterize the marginal benefit curve local to the observed exemption level in the prior year, and then determine whether the curve shifts up or down over a range of incremental exemptions. Assuming that marginal cost curves are fairly stable across consecutive years, schools with local upward shifts in the marginal benefit curve should be more likely to increase exemption rates than schools with local downward shifts. Further, the greater the upward shift, the greater is the likelihood of an increase in exemptions from the prior year. Although we also estimate the relationship between changes in the level of exemptions and these changes in incentives, the predictions for the continuous outcome measure are not similarly independent of the shape of the marginal cost curve.

4. DATA AND EMPIRICAL STRATEGIES

4.1. Data

We combine several administrative data sets, each collected and provided by the Texas Education Agency. These data sets include school- and student-level panel data. The school-level data for the years 1993 through 1998 come from the Academic Excellence Indicator System (AEIS), and are publicly available for download from the Texas Education Agency (http://www.tea.state.tx.us/perfreport/aeis/). The AEIS data are used to determine school ratings and include overall and student subgroup pass rates, attendance and dropout rates, and exemption rates broken down by type of exemption and student subgroup. These data also include a wide variety of campus demographic and financial variables. We purchased the restricted-use student-level data from the Public Education Information Management System (PEIMS) for the same years. These data include test scores, exemption status, and basic demographics for all students in tested grades. Individual students can be tracked across years and campuses through student- and campus-specific identifiers.

The total number of schools in Texas during our sample period ranges from 6,184 in 1993 to 7,053 in 1998. We analyze the 88 percent of schools (representing 97 percent of students) that are rated based on the standard accountability system and their own test scores. Schools that are excluded from our analysis fall into three categories: (i) campuses that are not rated because they do not serve students in grades 1–12 (e.g., pre-kindergarten centers and special education schools), (ii) alternative education campuses that are evaluated under a different system, and (iii) schools that are assigned the test score performance of the school with which they have a feeder relationship since they do not serve students in tested grades (e.g., K-2nd grade and 9th grade centers). Although information from the early years is used in the calculation of incentives for other years, our regression samples exclude 1993, since not all of the relevant grades were tested in that year, and exclude 1994, to allow us to model changes in exemption rates from the prior year.[20]

4.2. Comparison of Subgroups within Schools

Our first empirical analysis focuses on schools in which there is heterogeneity in the achievement of student subgroups relative to the relevant pass rate standard. As previously shown, we would generally expect a strategic school administrator to increase exemptions by more (or decrease exemptions by less) for groups that are predicted to perform below the threshold. We test this proposition by investigating whether these groups exhibit greater one-year changes in exemption rates than other groups within the same school and year.

Since actual student performance is endogenous with respect to exemptions, we determine overall and subgroup-specific expected pass rates by using the prior year performance of students and adjusting for upward trends in achievement. In particular, we find the statewide percentile associated with the lowest-scoring student in a given grade who passed during year *t*, and then calculate the fraction of students in that grade in each school (and each subgroup at the school) that scored at that percentile or better in year t–1. School administrators and teachers likely expect an achievement distribution similar to that of the previous year's cohort, adjusted for upward trends in achievement.

Given these expected pass rates, we then determine the target rating for each school by identifying the lowest rating for which at least one relevant pass rate is expected to be below the standard required threshold. We classify a group as "under" if the subgroup contributes to the school's rating and its expected pass rate (on either reading or math) is below this threshold and fails to satisfy any alternative less-binding criteria (such as required improvement).[21] Subgroups that are not classified as "under" either have expected pass rates that satisfy the requirements for the relevant ratings category or are not held separately accountable because there are too few students represented in the group.[22]

A campus may have up to three mutually exclusive race/ethnicity subgroups: White, Hispanic, and Black. For those campus-years with multiple subgroups and across-subgroup variation in "under" status, we estimate the following baseline regression model:

$$\Delta e_{gjt} = \alpha_{jt} + \delta_g + \theta_1 \times \text{Under}_{gjt} + \theta_2 \times d_{gjt-1} + \theta_3 \times d_{gjt-1} \times \text{Under}_{djt} + \mathbf{T}_{gjt-1}\mathbf{\Omega} + \mathbf{X}_{gjt}\mathbf{\Gamma} + \varepsilon_{gjt} \quad (3)$$

where g, j, and t denote the subgroup, school, and year, respectively. The dependent variable is the change in the exemption rate from the prior year. Under_{gjt} is a dummy variable equal to one if the group's pass rate is expected to hold the campus back from attaining the next highest rating. To incorporate any differential incentives to exempt economically disadvantaged students and differing degrees of overlap between this subgroup and the race/ethnicity subgroups, we include the fraction of the subgroup that is economically disadvantaged in the prior year (d_{gjt-1}), and an interaction between this fraction and an indicator for whether the economically disadvantaged subgroup is predicted to be "under" (Under_{djt}). Importantly, the specification includes campus-year fixed effects (α_{jt}), so that the model identifies the effect of "under" status relative to other student groups in the same campus and year.

The remaining variables included in the control set attempt to eliminate the potential for confounding factors that may be correlated with a group's expected status. First, groups that are "under" will tend to have relatively low academic ability, so that there may be secular differences in exemption patterns for this reason. Also, campuses may face differential marginal costs of exemptions through special program placements for students from different race/ethnicity subgroups for unrelated reasons. To address these concerns, we control for the fraction of students in the subgroup in the prior year with math and reading test scores in various failing ranges ($\mathbf{T}_{gjt-1}$) and subgroup fixed effects (δ_g).[23] The distribution of prior scores also helps to control for differences in the standard deviations of the expected pass rates across groups, as do the control variables related to the relative and absolute size of group g included in the vector $\mathbf{X}_{gjt}$.[24]

Although our baseline model controls for any shared school-wide changes in exemptions between years, since we include controls for campus-year, we also report specifications that allow random growth that differs by subgroups within schools. In these cases, the effect of being below the threshold is identified by subgroups that are "under" in some years and not in others.

4.3. Relationship between Changes in Campus-Level Exemption Rates and Incentives

Our second empirical test explores whether schools are more likely to increase exemptions when the potential impact on the likelihood of attaining the relevant rating from additional exemptions increases between back-to-back years. Our approach is to first estimate the raw marginal benefit curve associated with additional exemptions in t–1. Then, artificially holding the set of students in the accountability subset fixed, we simulate the raw marginal benefit curve in t by adjusting predicted pass probabilities for statewide upward trends and allowing the accountability rules to update. This allows us to isolate exogenous variation in changes in incentives for the same school that arises from changes in the required pass rate thresholds and the general upward trend in student performance over time.

We begin by describing how we estimate the raw marginal benefit curve associated with additional exemptions in t–1. First, each student in the accountability subset in t–1 is assigned a pass probability for each exam equal to the statewide fraction of students with the same test score in t–2 who actually pass the exam in t–1.[25] Second, we calculate the expected pass rate for all students and each student subgroup on each exam ($\hat{R}_{gj}$), as well as the standard deviation in these rates (σ_{gj}), in t–1 by aggregating the student-level pass probabilities.

If these performance measures were independent, we could readily calculate the probability that a school meets the relevant targets for each rating by calculating the probability each student group exceeds the requirement for each subject and then multiplying these probabilities across subjects and groups. However, shocks to a student's performance may be correlated across exams, and all students contribute to the overall pass rate as well as possibly to that of a race/ethnicity and/or the economically disadvantaged subgroup. For tractability, we assume that math and reading performance are independent, but assume that writing requirements will always be satisfied if reading requirements are satisfied.[26] In aggregating across groups, we use the lowest of the following three probability measures for math and reading: (1) the product of the probabilities that each accountable racial subgroup meets the required threshold, (2) the product of the probabilities that the economically disadvantaged subgroup and the White subgroup, if accountable, meet the required threshold,[27] and (3) the probability that the overall campus pass rate meets the required threshold.[28] We are implicitly assuming that whenever the most binding subset of indicators satisfies the requirements, so will the remaining indicators. For example, if it is less likely that a school meets the required pass rate for all race/ethnicity subgroups than for the overall student population, then we presume that the overall pass rate exceeds this threshold in the event that the pass rates for all race/ethnicity subgroups do.

Given this method of using individual student pass probabilities to determine the likelihood that a school obtains a certain rating, we can easily calculate the change in this likelihood if one additional student becomes exempted. We determine the most advantageous exemption for each campus as that which generates the greatest increase in the probability of attaining any of the three ratings, and identify the ratings category most relevant to the campus as the one associated with the maximum increase. We then treat that student as exempted, determine which subgroups continue to meet the minimum size requirements, adjust the expected pass rates and standard deviations, re-calculate the probabilities that the school meets the relevant performance standards, and use these probabilities to determine the new likelihood that the school will obtain the rating. We repeat this process until we have traced out the raw marginal benefit to a campus for exempting various numbers of additional students.

We follow the same process in order to simulate the raw marginal benefit curve in the following year, t. We start with the accountability subset in t–1 as before, and the only differences are that we adjust the student-level predicted pass probabilities for statewide trends and update the policy parameters.[29]

Fig. 5 illustrates our resulting measures of the change in incentives for an example case. We determine whether the raw marginal benefits to exempting an additional one, two, and three percent of students in tested grades have all either increased or decreased.[30] We can also measure the amount by which the marginal benefit curve has shifted, shown by areas a, b, and c in

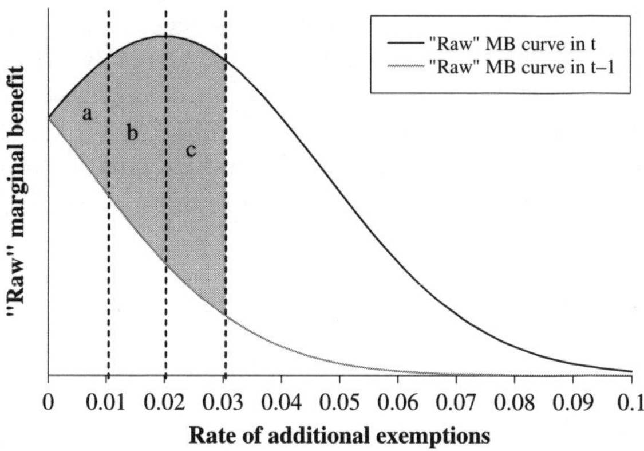

Fig. 5. Illustrative Increase in the "Raw" Marginal Benefit Curve.

the figure. Assuming that the marginal costs of exempting additional students and the marginal benefits to attaining the next highest rating (Z_j) remain relatively constant across consecutive years; schools should be more likely to increase exemptions from the prior year when the raw marginal benefit has shifted up in the directly relevant range, as compared to when it has shifted down.

The baseline regression model that we estimate is

$$y_{jt} = \beta_1 \times 1_{jt}^{\text{inc}} + \beta_2 \times 1_{jt}^{\text{ambig}} + \lambda_{ct} + \eta_{ct-1} + \mathbf{X}_{jt}\mathbf{\Pi} + T_{ijt} \times \delta_t + u_{jt} \quad (4)$$

where j and t denote the school and year, respectively. The dependent variable is either a dummy variable indicating whether exemptions increased or the change in the exemption rate from the prior year.[31] Our key incentive measure is a dummy variable indicating that the raw marginal benefit curve is higher at all three levels of additional exemptions in the second year of the comparison (1_{jt}^{inc}). If schools behave strategically, then we expect $\beta_1 > 0$. The specification also includes an indicator for cases where the curve shifts up at some points and down at others (1_{jt}^{ambig}), so that the reference group includes cases where the curve shifts everywhere down. To account for the fact that the relevant ratings category varies across campuses and perhaps from the prior year, we include dummies indicating the ratings category predicted to be relevant in the current (λ_{ct}) and prior year (η_{ct-1}). Because our incentive measure is based on simulated changes in the raw marginal benefit curve, we also present results where the sample is restricted to campus-years when the relevant ratings category (and hence Z_j) is predicted to be the same as the prior year.

The vector $\mathbf{X}_{jt}$ includes a variety of campus-level control variables related to the size and demographic composition of students that may affect the marginal costs of exempting students.[32] The predicted overall math and reading pass rates based on the accountability subset in $t-1$ are also included to allow for heterogeneity in trends in exemptions related strictly to average performance, so that the variation across campuses in the increase in incentives comes from more subtle variation in the distribution of test scores and heterogeneity across student subgroups. Finally, we include year-specific tax base quintile effects to capture secular time effects and schools' fiscal incentives to place students in exempt categories, particularly special and bilingual education, that arise from the structure of the school finance system (Cullen, 2003).

In addition to estimating Eq. (4), we also present results from models that add campus fixed effects to allow for campus-specific random growth in exemptions. This model identifies strategic responses from differential behavior on the part of campuses across years when incentives have increased and years when they have decreased. Finally, we also estimate a variation that adds an interaction between the indicator for an increase in incentives and the magnitude of the increase, to test whether campuses are more likely to react when there is a greater upward shift in the marginal benefit curve.

5. RESULTS

In this section, we present the empirical results for our two tests. The first test explores whether campuses broadly target exemptions to subgroups for which exemptions are most advantageous from the perspective of attaining or maintaining a higher rating. The second test considers strategic behavior at a finer level – whether campuses respond to short-run increases in incentives to exempt more students that are determined by expected positioning relative to the phased-in pass rate targets.

5.1. Comparison of Subgroups within Schools

The sample for this analysis includes campus-years that have variation in the "under" status of race/ethnicity subgroups over the period 1995 through 1998. We lose 36 percent of observations for which either only one subgroup is held separately accountable or all are predicted to exceed the less restrictive requirements for the most relevant rating. We exclude an additional five percent of observations for campuses that have variation across years in the set of race/ethnicity subgroups that are represented (i.e., at least five students in the subgroup in tested grades). This leaves us with 11,026 campus-year observations, representing 59 percent of regular education campuses in those years.[33]

Table 2 presents the summary statistics for this sample. White and Hispanic subgroups are represented at most campuses in our analysis sample, while Black subgroups are represented at only 72 percent of campuses. The disparities in achievement shown in Fig. 1b across subgroups underlie the differences in the rates at which the various subgroups are predicted to be holding the campus back from the next highest rating. When present, White, Hispanic, and Black students are predicted to be "under" 24, 64, and 54 percent of the time, respectively. Although Hispanics tend to outperform Blacks, Black subgroups are more likely to be too small to be separately accountable. When White students are "under" they are most commonly in a school with Hispanic and Black peers that are not necessarily outperforming them, but that are not separately accountable. For the majority of cases where the Hispanic and Black subgroups are classified as "under," the White subgroup is predicted to exceed the ratings requirements.

Table 3 presents the regression results for the independent variables of most interest from estimating variants of Eq. (3). In all cases, the dependent variable is the change in the subgroup's exemption rate from the prior year and the control set includes campus-year fixed effects. The findings confirm our hypothesis that campuses target exemptions toward student subgroups when they are likely to prevent the campus from earning a higher rating. The estimates presented in the first column suggest that membership in a subgroup that is "under" (i.e., a subgroup whose pass rate is expected to be below the required threshold) is associated with a statistically significant 0.6 percentage point increase in exemptions. However, there does not appear to be a differential effect on exemptions for subgroups that have a high-fraction low income when the low-income subgroup is predicted to be "under." There is also evidence of a secular trend toward relative decreases in exemptions for Hispanic and Black subgroups.[34] This underlying tendency may have been partly due to aforementioned longitudinal changes in the feasibility of certain types of exemptions; mobility exemptions became more difficult in the middle of the sample period and schools knew that limited English proficiency exemptions would disappear with the introduction of Spanish exams after our sample period.

Column 2 is a more demanding specification that adds fixed effects for subgroups by campus. These estimates are identified from the relative changes in exemptions, as compared to peers in the same campus, across years when

Table 2. Summary Statistics for Analysis of Race/Ethnicity Subgroups.

Variable	Student Subgroup		
	White	Hispanic	Black
Exemption rate	0.211	0.310	0.272
	(0.089)	(0.153)	(0.109)
Change in exemption rate	−0.003	−0.003	−0.003
	(0.072)	(0.103)	(0.104)
Subgroup's enrollment share (for tested grades)	0.466	0.381	0.225
	(0.262)	(0.277)	(0.208)
Number of students in tested grades in subgroup	184	163	92
	(174)	(192)	(112)
Fraction of students low-income in subgroup	0.309	0.683	0.643
	(0.208)	(0.213)	(0.227)
Fraction scoring 0–49 on the math exam in the prior year	0.038	0.096	0.144
	(0.051)	(0.087)	(0.115)
Fraction scoring 50–59 on the math exam in the prior year	0.064	0.121	0.153
	(0.056)	(0.082)	(0.094)
Fraction scoring 60–64 on the math exam in the prior year	0.048	0.077	0.088
	(0.040)	(0.056)	(0.064)
Fraction scoring 65–69 on the math exam in the prior year	0.068	0.096	0.103
	(0.046)	(0.059)	(0.067)
Fraction of campus-years:			
Subgroup is represented	0.957	0.948	0.724
Subgroup's pass rate is below the standard	0.233	0.605	0.392
When subgroup's pass rate is below the standard:			
White subgroup's pass rate is above the standard	0	0.669	0.741
White subgroup's pass rate is below the standard	1	0.093	0.055
White subgroup is not separately accountable	0	0.219	0.121
Hispanic subgroup's pass rate is above the standard	0.030	0	0.178
Hispanic subgroup's pass rate is below the standard	0.242	1	0.387
Hispanic subgroup is not separately accountable	0.617	0	0.366
Black subgroup's pass rate is above the standard	0.003	0.015	0
Black subgroup's pass rate is below the standard	0.093	0.250	1
Black subgroup is not separately accountable	0.565	0.402	0
Number of observations	10,552	10,449	7,983

Notes: There are 11,026 campus-years from 1995–1998 that have variation across subgroups in their expected performance compared to the relevant standard. For these campus-years, at least one subgroup's expected pass rate is below the standard, and at least one other subgroup either is expected to exceed the standard or has too few students to be separately accountable. Each column in the table reports statistics for the campus subgroup indicated in the column heading. There are a total of 28,984 campus-year-subgroup observations, with the number of observations contributed by each race/ethnicity subgroup indicated in the final row. The top panel shows the mean (and standard deviation in parentheses) for the variable indicated by the row heading. The bottom panel shows the fraction of campus-years represented by alternative combinations of relative performance for each subgroup.

Table 3. Ordinary Least-Squares Regression Results for Analysis of Race/Ethnicity Subgroups.

Independent Variable	Dependent Variable = Change in Exemption Rate					
	(1)	(2)	(3)	(4)	(5)	(6)
Subgroup is "under"	0.006** (0.001)	0.017** (0.003)	−0.001 (0.002)	0.002 (0.005)	−0.001 (0.002)	0.006 (0.006)
Subgroup is Hispanic and "under"	—	—	0.012** (0.004)	0.021** (0.007)	—	—
Subgroup is Black and "under"	—	—	0.013** (0.004)	0.037** (0.008)	—	—
Share low income in subgroup × low-income subgroup is "under"	−0.003 (0.007)	0.018 (0.012)	−0.002 (0.007)	0.015 (0.012)	−0.008 (0.009)	0.002 (0.017)
Share low income in subgroup × subgroup is "under"	—	—	—	—	0.004 (0.007)	0.008 (0.013)
Share low income in subgroup × subgroup is "under" × low-income subgroup is "under"	—	—	—	—	0.013** (0.006)	0.019* (0.010)
Subgroup is Hispanic	−0.013** (0.002)	—	−0.017** (0.003)	—	−0.015** (0.002)	—
Subgroup is Black	−0.014** (0.003)	—	−0.019** (0.003)	—	−0.016** (0.003)	—
Share low income in subgroup	0.006 (0.009)	−0.010 (0.027)	0.007 (0.009)	−0.008 (0.027)	0.005 (0.010)	−0.003 (0.028)
Includes campus × year fixed effects	Yes	Yes	Yes	Yes	Yes	Yes
Includes campus × subgroup fixed effects	No	Yes	No	Yes	No	Yes

Notes: The sample is restricted to campus-years for which there is variation across subgroups in their expected performance compared to the relevant standard. There are 28,984 observations defined at the level of the campus, year, and race/ethnicity subgroup for the years 1995–1998. Each column presents the results from a separate ordinary least-squares regression. The dependent variable in each case is the change in the exemption rate from the prior year for the subgroup. Standard errors that are robust to unspecified correlation across observations from the same campus are shown in parentheses. In addition to the variables shown, all specifications include the share of students in the subgroup scoring in various failing ranges on the math and reading exams in the prior year (the measures included for reading are for the same ranges as for the math exam), the change in the share low-income from the prior year, the prior level and change in the subgroup's enrollment share, and the prior level and change in the number of students in tested grades (measured by a five-part spline with cut-points defined by quintiles of the size distribution). All specifications also include campus-year fixed effects, and the specifications in the even columns add campus-subgroup fixed effects.

*Significance at the 10 percent level;

**Significance at the 5 percent level.

the subgroup is predicted to be holding the campus back and years when there is not an incentive to target exemptions to that subgroup.[35] Here the effect of being "under" rises to a 1.7 percentage point (or more than a five percent) increase in exemptions that is also highly statistically significant.

Columns 3 and 4 consider whether the effect varies by race/ethnicity subgroup, with the second set of estimates from the specification that includes campus-subgroup fixed effects. There is strong evidence of strategic targeting for Hispanic and Black students, but no similar shifting to White subgroups when the subgroup is "under." The net increases for Hispanic and Black subgroups are 1.1 and 1.2 percentage points, respectively, in the model without campus-subgroup fixed effects, and 2.3 and 3.9 percentage points when those are included. These statistically significant one-year changes are equivalent to 0.15 and 0.36 standard deviations of their respective mean exemption levels. Incentives related to subgroup performance appear to negate schools' underlying tendency to shift exemptions away from Hispanic and Black students and toward White students over our sample period.

The final two columns of Table 3 test for an exacerbating effect on subgroups that are predicted to be low performing, and that also have a high-share low income in campus-years when the low-income group is predicted to be "under." In these cases, exempting members of a particular race/ethnicity group may be particularly beneficial. This prediction appears to hold, particularly when the model includes campus-subgroup fixed effects. Consider a racial subgroup that has 50 percent of its students in the low-income category, which is approximately the mean rate. The estimates in column 6 imply that, compared to cases in which neither this race/ethnicity subgroup nor the low-income subgroup is "under," when both are "under" exemptions increase by 2.1 percentage points, an effect that is 1.25 times as large as our baseline estimate in column 2.

In results that are not shown, we find that the estimates are quite similar if we split the sample into two periods: pre- and post-1997. We also find that the results are robust to the inclusion of race-year fixed effects. We also do not find any evidence of differential responsiveness depending on whether subgroups are holding the campus back from escaping a low rating or from attaining a high rating.

5.2. Relationship between Changes in Campus-Level Exemption Rates and Incentives

The sample for this analysis is based on campuses for the years 1996 through 1998. We lose observations from 1995 since this is the first year for which there are two years of prior data available for calculating incentives (we require information on 8th graders in *t*–2), and this year serves as the basis for determining whether incentives have increased or not in 1996. After excluding five percent of observations where the relevant ratings category does not remain constant as we trace out the raw marginal benefit curve for increasing exemptions by up to three percentage points, 16,567 campus-year observations remain.

Table 4 presents summary statistics for this sample. On average, 25.3 percent of students are excluded from the accountability subset, and the majority of these students are exempt due to special education placement. Slightly less than half of campuses increase exemptions between years. The incentives to exempt students on the margin are also predicted to have increased from the prior year nearly half of the time. Conditional on increasing, the mean magnitude of the increase is 22.1 percentage points. To interpret this value, recall that we calculate the raw marginal benefit as the change in the probability that the campus meets the requirements for the most relevant rating associated with exempting an additional three percent of students, and that this variable captures the change in this marginal benefit from the prior year.

Table 5 presents ordinary least squares regression results from specifications based on Eq. (4). Each cell in the table reports the estimated coefficient on an indicator for whether incentives increased from the prior year from a separate regression. The top panel shows results for the full sample, while the bottom panel restricts the sample to campus-years when the relevant ratings category is predicted to remain the same as in the prior year. For the latter sample, there is less uncertainty about whether marginal benefits including the scaling factor Z_j have increased conditional on determining that the raw marginal benefit curve has shifted up.

The results in column 1 are based on specifications where the dependent variable is a binary indicator signaling whether the exemption rate increased from the prior year. In the full sample, campuses with increased incentives are 1.6 percentage points more likely to increase overall exemptions. The effect is larger in the sample with no change in the relevant ratings category. Here, the increase is 3.4 percentage points, or approximately seven percent of the sample mean. These effects for overall exemptions appear to be driven by special education exemptions and exemptions due to absences and other miscellaneous reasons. The specifications in column 2 control for campus fixed effects, allowing for differential growth rates across campuses. Although the point estimates are somewhat attenuated, the loss of statistical significance is primarily explained by loss of precision. Only slightly more

Table 4. Summary Statistics for Campus-Level Analysis.

Variable	Mean	Variable	Mean
Dependent variables		*Student characteristics*	
Fraction of students exempt	0.253	Fraction Hispanic	0.347
	(0.103)		(0.316)
	[0.461]	Fraction Black	0.135
Fraction special education	0.146		(0.199)
exempt	(0.058)	Fraction low income	0.491
	[0.562]		(0.269)
Fraction LEP exempt	0.044	Fraction in tested grades	0.580
	(0.090)		(0.263)
	[0.274]	Enrollment in tested grades	351
Fraction mobility exempt	0.049	(3–8,10)	(269)
	(0.027)	Predicted overall math pass	0.816
	[0.395]	rate	(0.090)
Fraction absent/other exempt	0.014	Predicted overall reading	0.744
	(0.019)	pass rate	(0.126)
	[0.402]		
Raw marginal benefit		*Relevant ratings category*	
Increased from prior year	0.477	Acceptable	0.066
Decreased from prior year	0.398	Recognized	0.667
Ambiguous change	0.125	Exemplary	0.267
Magnitude conditional on an	0.221	District per pupil tax base	192
increase	(0.260)	wealth in prior year	(223)
		(thousands of 1998 $)	

Notes: The summary statistics are based on the sample of regular schools for the fiscal years 1995 through 1998 described in the text, and includes a total of 15,657 campus-year observations. (We exclude the five percent of campus-year observations where the most relevant ratings category changes as we trace out the marginal benefits to exempting an additional three percent of students.) We show the mean for the variable indicated in the row heading, with the standard deviation in parentheses. For the exemption variables, the fraction of campuses with increases from the prior year is also shown in square brackets. The predicted pass rates are based on the accountability subset in the prior year, accounting for statewide increases in pass rates between the prior and current year as described in the text. The relevant ratings category is the one we predict to be the "nearest" from either above or below given the predicted overall and subgroup pass rates.

than half of the campuses in our sample experience both years with increased incentives and years with decreased incentives.

The dependent variable in column 3 is the change in the exemption rate. While the point estimate is not statistically significant in the full sample, increased incentives lead to a statistically significantly 0.41 percentage point increases in overall exemptions in the restricted sample. Again, the effect can

Table 5. Estimated Relationships between One-Year Changes in Exemptions and Incentives.

Sample and Exemption Type	Dependent Variable			
	Indicator for Exemptions Increased		Change in Exemptions	
	(1)	(2)	(3)	(4)
Full sample ($N = 15{,}657$)				
Total exemptions	1.55*	1.27	0.16	0.08
	(0.91)	(1.22)	(0.10)	(0.14)
Special education exemptions	1.52*	0.84	0.13*	0.08
	(0.93)	(1.22)	(0.07)	(0.10)
LEP exemptions	0.14	−0.76	−0.06	−0.10
	(0.77)	(0.98)	(0.06)	(0.08)
Student mobility exemptions	0.02	0.14	0.01	0.04
	(0.89)	(1.20)	(0.06)	(0.08)
Absent/other exemptions	1.48*	1.77	0.07**	0.06
	(0.92)	(1.26)	(0.04)	(0.05)
No change in relevant ratings category from prior year ($N = 12{,}847$)				
Total exemptions	3.40**	3.22**	0.41**	0.32**
	(1.02)	(1.50)	(0.11)	(0.17)
Special education exemptions	2.00*	1.43	0.23**	0.17
	(1.05)	(1.50)	(0.08)	(0.12)
LEP exemptions	1.15	−0.17	0.02	0.02
	(0.89)	(1.24)	(0.07)	(0.10)
Student mobility exemptions	0.40	0.47	0.07	0.10
	(0.99)	(1.47)	(0.06)	(0.10)
Absent/other exemptions	1.79*	1.55	0.08**	0.04
	(1.04)	(1.56)	(0.04)	(0.06)
Includes campus fixed effects	No	Yes	No	Yes

Notes: Each cell presents the coefficient (multiplied by 100) on an indicator for an increase in incentives from the prior year from a separate ordinary least-squares regression. The top panel shows results for the sample of regular schools for 1995–1998 described in the notes to Table 4. The bottom panel shows the results for the sub-sample with "no change in ratings category" that excludes the 18 percent of campus-year observations where the ratings category that is relevant for calculating incentives changes from the prior year. The rows indicate the type of exemption the dependent variable is based on. The first two columns present results when the dependent variables are defined to be indicators for whether the relevant exemption rate increased from the prior year. Columns 3 and 4 present results when the dependent variables are expressed as changes in the rate from the prior year. Columns 2 and 4 also control for campus fixed effects. Standard errors (mulitiplied by 100) that are robust to unspecified correlation across observations from the same campus are shown in parentheses. All specifications include the prior level and change in the student demographic characteristics shown in Table 4 (with enrollment in tested grades captured by a five-part spline with cut-points defined by quintiles of the size distribution), the prior level and change in the grade distribution of students in tested grades, predicted overall math and reading pass rates, indicators for the relevant ratings category in the prior and current year, prior year per pupil tax base wealth quintile interacted with an indicator for the year, and an indicator for an ambiguous change in incentives from the prior year.

*Significance at the 10% level;

**Significance at the 5% level.

be attributed to special education and absences, which increase by 0.23 and 0.08 percentage points, respectively. Only the statistical significance of the overall exemption rate survives the inclusion of campus fixed effects in column 4. These effects are relatively small, ranging from 0.04 to 0.08 standard deviations of the distribution of annual changes. Recall that the theoretical prediction for the size of the change in the level of exemptions is not as clear as for the likelihood that exemptions increase.

Table 6 presents results from specifications that add an interaction term between the indicator for an increase in incentives and the magnitude of the

Table 6. Estimated Relationships between One-Year Changes in Exemptions and Incentives.

Sample and Dependent Variable	Independent Variable			
	1^{inc}	$1^{inc} \times \Delta MB$	1^{inc}	$1^{inc} \times \Delta MB$
	(1a)	(1b)	(2a)	(2b)
Full sample ($N = 15{,}657$)				
Indicator for total exemptions increased	0.59	4.46*	−0.74	8.94**
	(1.03)	(2.37)	(1.41)	(3.14)
Change in total exemptions	0.11	0.21	−0.01	0.39
	(0.11)	(0.19)	(0.16)	(0.27)
No change in ratings category ($N = 12{,}847$)				
Indicator for total exemptions increased	2.14*	5.93**	0.94	10.44**
	(1.18)	(2.70)	(1.72)	(3.81)
Change in total exemptions	0.36**	0.24	0.29	0.17
	(0.13)	(0.23)	(0.19)	(0.33)
Includes campus fixed effects	No		Yes	

Notes: The top panel shows results for the sample of regular schools for 1995–1998 described in the notes to Table 4. The bottom panel shows the results for the sub-sample with "no change in ratings category" that excludes the 18 percent of campus-year observations where the ratings category that is relevant for calculating incentives changes from the prior year. The rows indicate whether the dependent variable is an indicator for an increase in exemptions or the change in exemptions. Columns 1a and 1b present estimated coefficients on an indicator for an increase in incentives from the prior year (1^{inc}) and that indicator interacted with the size of the increase ($1^{inc} \times \Delta MB$) in specifications that include the full set of control variables describe in the notes to Table 5. Columns 2a and 2b present the same results from specifications that add campus fixed effects as well. Standard errors that are robust to unspecified correlation across observations from the same campus are shown in parentheses. All coefficients and standard errors have been multiplied by 100.

*Significance at the 10 percent level.

**Significance at the 5 percent level.

increase to the control set. A larger increase is associated with a greater probability of increasing exemptions between years. To interpret the magnitude of these estimates, compare two administrators: one that has no increase in incentives from the prior year, and one for whom the likelihood of meeting the ratings criteria through additional exemptions has increased by 50 percentage points (one standard deviation above the mean increase). The estimates for the full sample in columns 1a and 1b imply that the overall exemption rate would be 2.8 percentage points more likely to increase at the school where the administrator faces enhanced incentives. For the restricted sample, the predicted increase in the likelihood is 5.1 percentage points (or 11 percent). The estimated responsiveness is slightly larger for the second specification that controls for campus fixed effects.

Table 6 also reveals that there are no statistically or economically significant relationships between the magnitude of the change in incentives and the change in the level of exemptions. Although exemptions are more likely to increase when there is a large upward shift in the marginal benefit curve associated with incremental exemptions, relatively strong incentives measured locally do not systematically lead to relatively large increases in exemptions.

6. CONCLUSIONS

Given the difficulties associated with designing an accountability system that is both fair and manipulation proof, we investigate the extent to which administrators appear to exploit loopholes that allow for exemptions for students that are at an academic disadvantage. We first develop a simple model of the incentives to exempt marginal students in order to secure more favorable ratings under the system that was in place in Texas during the mid-1990s. The model generates two testable predictions that motivate our empirical analyses. In our first empirical test, we find that, regardless of whether incentives to exempt additional students increase or decrease from the prior year, campuses actively preserve or increase those exemptions that are most advantageous. This leads to a targeting of exemptions toward low-performing Hispanic and Black students. In the second test, we find that campuses respond to short-run increases in incentives to expand exemption rates between consecutive years by classifying more students as special needs and encouraging absences.

The gaming that we observe involves potential real costs – costs to the schools that expend resources to engage in this activity, and costs due to decisions that are made based on distorted measures of performance. To the extent the accountability ratings reflect arbitrary differences in classification practices, these misleading ratings can lead to inefficiencies such as misguided educational policy decisions, misguided enrollment decisions, and unwarranted changes in property values. There may be unintended, real (positive or negative) effects on student outcomes if the induced changes in classifications change the type of instruction a student receives or the student's label. The social welfare implications of classifying additional students in special programs depend on the level of pre-existing distortions. Cullen (2003) finds that financial incentives under the school finance system already likely lead to excessive classifications, so that the accountability system exacerbates rather than corrects existing distortions.

Texas' accountability program served as the blueprint for the *No Child Left Behind Act of 2001* (*NCLB*), a federal law requiring all states to adopt standardized testing for students in grades 3 to 8 and to use student proficiency rates in order to rate schools. A key difference between current state systems and the early Texas system is the presence of a minimum participation requirement of 95 percent of students in the tested grades. Critics of this participation requirement are concerned that schools serving high fractions of high needs students are at a disadvantage, but sacrifices in vertical equity may be warranted if the more comprehensive participation requirement under *NCLB* reduces the inefficiencies described above.

NOTES

1. Ladd (2001) provides an overview of the theoretical issues associated with designing effective performance standards in the school accountability context.
2. There is mixed evidence whether improvements on the test instruments used for accountability are matched by parallel gains on other exams (e.g., Hanushek & Raymond, 2005; Jacob, 2005; Klein, Hamilton, McCaffrey, & Stecher, 2000).
3. Jacob and Levitt (2003) find evidence that the accountability system in place in Chicago has led to a more direct form of gaming – cheating, likely by both students and teachers.
4. The most extensive previous literature on an analogous form of caseload manipulation under performance-based incentive systems has examined "cream-skimming" of participants by local job training agencies (e.g., Heckman, Heinrich, & Smith, 2002; Heckman, Smith, & Taber, 1996; Anderson, Burkhauser, & Raymond, 1993).
5. Hanushek and Raymond (2005) caution against drawing strong inferences from pre- and post-analyses in this setting, and do not find any relationship between special education classification rates and the introduction of strong state accountability policies in a state-level panel analysis that accounts for flexible time trends.

6. Even when controlling for time trends, Figlio and Getzler (2002) find that the introduction of high-stakes testing led to about a 50 percent increase in the rate that students from low-income families were exempted from test-taking due to special education classifications.

7. Jacob (2005) also finds evidence of strategic special education placements using a similar triple-differences strategy that compares trends in special education classification rates for low- versus high-performing students in low- versus high-performing schools in Chicago before and after the high-stakes testing policy.

8. In addition to students enrolled in tested grades being exempted, low-achieving students can be excluded by being retained in untested grades or encouraged to drop out. Jacob (2005) reports higher retention rates in untested grades following the implementation of the accountability system in Chicago. Haney (2000) reports a similar finding for minorities in Texas, although Carnoy, Loeb, and Smith (2001) show that this trend was pre-existing. The literature linking testing standards to dropout rates has focused on the negative impact of grade retention and failure on completion (e.g., Reardon, 1996; Kreitzer, Madaus, & Haney, 1989), rather than on the interaction with school incentives.

9. Throughout, we refer to school years by the year associated with the final term, or the fiscal year. That is, we refer to school year 1993–1994 as year 1994.

10. Districts are also assigned one of four ratings, based on identical indicators defined at the district level. Throughout, we focus on campus-level incentives, since incentives at both levels are likely to be closely aligned and the kinds of behaviors that could affect exemptions occur at the school level.

11. Detailed accountability manuals are available for each year at http://www.tea.state.tx.us/perfreport/account/.

12. There is little interaction between student and school incentives under the accountability system – student performance on the high-stakes tests does not directly affect retention decisions, and graduation requirements can be met by passing end-of-course exams or eventually passing the exit-level TAAS exam.

13. In the first year of this system, 1993, the subgroups were not held separately accountable. In all years, subgroup pass rates only count when the number of students contributing scores exceeds specified minimum levels. Economically disadvantaged students are those who are eligible for free- or reduced-price lunch or for other public assistance.

14. The ability to substitute a minimum amount of growth in pass rates for a minimum pass rate level could, in theory, introduce important dynamics to schools' incentives. However, this more lenient alternative is only available for the acceptable category and, as Fig. 3 shows, only a handful of campuses are ever unable to meet the standards for that ratings category.

15. Figlio and Lucas (2004) find empirical evidence that the arbitrary distinctions made by Florida's school report card system are capitalized into housing values, particularly in the short run.

16. Although it would be revealing to track gaming before and after the tightening of restrictions on exemptions, the student-level data that underlie our analysis are not available to us for these more recent years.

17. The 1993 pass rates are not directly comparable since students were tested in fewer grades in that year.

18. A student's information reported on the Spring test document was no longer required to perfectly match Fall enrollment data for the student to be identified as having been in the district. For instance, prior to 1997, a student would have been classified as mobile if his name was entered as Juan Garcia in the Fall and as John Garcia on the Spring exams.

19. This assumption, $Cov(\varepsilon_{rj}, \varepsilon_{sj}) = 0 \forall r, s \in \{1, N_j - E_j^0\}, r \neq s$, affects the specific shape of the marginal benefit curve and facilitates the simulation of incentives in our empirical work. It is possible that the surprises to students' pass rates are not independent, such as if students in an entire classroom are not prepared to correctly answer certain questions. Generalizing the framework to account for correlated disturbances would lead to the same basic predictions unless the individual error terms are correlated with each other in such a way that the distribution of the expected overall pass rate becomes severely skewed or multi-peaked.

20. In 1993, only students in grades 4, 8, and 10 were tested.

21. We ignore writing since only rarely do subgroups fail to satisfy that requirement if the reading requirement is met. Math is almost always the binding subject, and in only 10 percent of cases does the subgroup meet the math requirement but fall short of the reading requirement.

22. Pass rates for student subgroups with either fewer than 30 students tested or fewer than 200 students tested and less than 10 percent of all tested students do not factor into campus ratings under the Texas system. A subgroup is predicted to fail minimum size requirements based on its status in t–1.

23. For both math and reading, we include the fraction of students in the group scoring in the following failing ranges (i.e., scores below 70) during the prior year: below 50, 50–59, 60–64, and 65–69.

24. The vector X_{gjt} includes prior year level and changes in the subgroup's share of enrollment in tested grades and the number of students in tested grades (measured by a five-part spline with cut-points defined by quantiles of the size distribution). Also included is the change in the share of students economically disadvantaged.

25. All of the calculations are done separately by grade. For grades 4 through 8, we group students who earned identical scores in the prior year on the math, reading, or writing exam, depending which is the outcome of interest. If students are missing prior year scores for certain subjects, we use prior year scores on the other subjects if available. If all prior year scores are missing, we assign the average estimated probability of passing among students who earned the same score in the current year. For grade 10, since students are not tested in grade 9, we group students based on scores in grade 8 (two years earlier), and then apply the same procedures as for the other grades. A few 10th grade students automatically count as passing the exam, because they passed the exam previously, and we set these students' pass probabilities equal to one. For grade 3, since this is the first grade of testing and prior scores are never available, we assign the same pass probability to all students within a school, based on the scores of the previous year's cohort within that school. We use the same method for third graders as described in the previous section: finding the statewide percentile associated with the lowest-scoring third-grade student who passed in the current year and calculating the fraction of students in each school's third grade that scored at that percentile or better in the prior year.

26. This assumption holds very well in the data; in 95 percent of the cases in which the reading pass rate threshold is met, the writing pass rate threshold is also met.

27. While nearly two-thirds of minority students are economically disadvantaged, less than one-third of White students are. Given that there is far less overlap, it is reasonable to treat the White subgroup as distinct.

28. We also account for dropout and attendance rates – setting the probability of attaining any given rating to zero if these criteria (which are based on prior year outcomes) are not satisfied.

29. We assign each student a predicted pass probability for each exam in *t* by upgrading the pass probability used in the prior calculations to that at the same percentile of the statewide distribution of predicted pass probabilities (calculated in exactly the same way as for students in *t*–1) for students in year *t*.

30. We chose to consider exemptions up to an additional three percent since that is the increase at the 75th percentile of the distribution of one-year changes in exemptions.

31. We estimate both models using ordinary least squares to facilitate the inclusion of campus fixed effects in some specifications. We have estimated the models with the binary variable as the dependent variable that do not include campus fixed effects using a Probit specification as well. The estimated marginal effects evaluated at the mean are nearly identical to the point estimates that we report for our key variables from the linear model.

32. We control for the prior year level and change in the following variables: the fraction of students who are in one of the tested grades, the grade and race/ethnicity distribution of students across tested grades, and a five-part spline measuring the number of students in tested grades at the school.

33. Although we analyze a restricted sample, the mean rates at which students in the three race/ethnicity subgroups are exempted are nearly the same as in the full sample.

34. Point estimates reveal similarly sized (although statistically insignificant) negative trends in exemption rates for Hispanic and Black students in the sample of 355 campus-years for which there are no differential incentives to exempt low-performing students from any particular subgroup (i.e., no student subgroup is large enough to be separately accountable).

35. Approximately one-third of campuses have variation across years in the status of at least one group.

ACKNOWLEDGMENTS

The authors would like to thank the Communications and Student Assessment Divisions of the Texas Education Agency for providing the student-level longitudinal test documents data, as well as the Office of Tax Policy Research and the Department of Economics at the University of Michigan for providing funding for data acquisition. We also thank Nora Gordon and Jim Ziliak for particularly helpful discussions.

REFERENCES

Anderson, K. H., Burkhauser, R. V., & Raymond, J. E. (1993). The effect of creaming on placement rates under the Job Training Partnership Act. *Industrial and Labor Relations Review*, *46*(4), 613–624.

Carnoy, M., Loeb, S., & Smith, T. L. (2001). *Do higher state test scores in Texas make for better high school outcomes?* Consortium for Policy Research in Education Research Report RR-047.

Cullen, J. B. (2003). The impact of fiscal incentives on student disability rates. *Journal of Public Economics*, *87*(7–8), 1557–1589.

Deere, D., & Strayer, W. (2001a). *Putting schools to the test: School accountability, incentives, and behavior*. Private Enterprise Research Center Working Paper 114. Texas A&M University.

Deere, D., & Strayer, W. (2001b). *Closing the gap: School incentives and minority test scores in Texas*. Mimeo: Texas A&M University.

Figlio, D. N. (2005). *Testing crime and punishment*. National Bureau of Economic Research Working Paper 11194. Cambridge, MA.

Figlio, D. N., & Getzler, L. S. (2002). *Accountability, ability, and disability: Gaming the system*. National Bureau of Economic Research Working Paper 9307. Cambridge, MA.

Figlio, D. N., & Lucas, M. E. (2004). What's in a grade? School report cards and the housing market. *American Education Review*, *94*(3), 591–604.

Haney, W. M. (2000). The myth of the Texas miracle in education. *Education Policy Analysis Archives*, *8*(41) (http://epaa.asu.edu/epaa/v8n41/).

Hanushek, E. A., & Raymond, M. E. (2005). Does school accountability lead to improved performance? *Journal of Policy Analysis and Management*, *24*(2), 297–327.

Heckman, J. J., Heinrich, C. J., & Smith, J. (2002). The performance of performance standards. *Journal of Human Resources*, *37*(4), 778–811.

Heckman, J. J., Smith, J. A., & Taber, C. (1996). What do bureaucrats do? The effects of performance standards and bureaucratic preferences on acceptance into the JTPA program. In: G. Libecap (Ed.), *Advances in the Study of Entrepreneurship, Innovation, and Growth* (Vol. 7, pp. 191–218). Greenwich, CT: JAI.

Jacob, B. A. (2005). Accountability, incentives and behavior: Evidence from school reform in Chicago. *Journal of Public Economics*, *89*(5–6), 761–796.

Jacob, B. A., & Levitt, S. D. (2003). Rotten apples: An investigation of the prevalence and predictors of teacher cheating. *Quarterly Journal of Economics*, *118*(3), 843–877.

Klein, S. P., Hamilton, L. S., McCaffrey, D. F., & Stecher, B. M. (2000). What do test scores in Texas tell us? *Education Policy Analysis Archives*, *8*(49) http://epaa.asu.edu/epaa/v8n49/.

Kreitzer, A. E., Madaus, G. F., & Haney, W. M. (1989). Competency testing and dropouts. In: L. Weis, E. Farrar & H. G. Petrie (Eds), *Dropouts from school: Issues, dilemmas, and solutions*. Albany, NY: State University of New York Press.

Ladd, H. F. (2001). School-based educational accountability systems: The promise and the pitfalls. *National Tax Journal*, *54*(2), 385–400.

Reardon, S. (1996). Eighth grade minimum competency testing and early high school dropout patterns. Presented at the annual meeting of the American Educational Research Association, New York, NY.

Reback, R. (2005). *Teaching to the rating: School accountability and the distribution of student achievement*. Unpublished working paper.

Tyack, D., & Cuban, L. (1995). *Tinkering toward Utopia: A century of public school reform*. Cambridge, MA: Harvard University Press.

ACCOUNTABILITY, ABILITY AND DISABILITY: GAMING THE SYSTEM?[☆]

David N. Figlio and Lawrence S. Getzler

ABSTRACT

This paper utilizes highly detailed student-level data to examine whether the initiation of a high-stakes test for accountability purposes affected Florida public schools' decisions regarding whether to assign students to special education. Using student-level fixed effects models, we find that schools systematically placed students from low socio-economic status backgrounds and historically low-performing students into special education categories that were at the time exempt from the accountability system. High-poverty schools are significantly more likely to reclassify low-achieving students than are more affluent schools. These results provide important implications for the design of school accountability systems.

INTRODUCTION

Education is currently at the forefront of the nation's political agenda: everyone, regardless of political persuasion, wants to see an improvement in the

[☆] Paper prepared for "Economics of Education: Choice and Accountability," Elsevier *Advances in Microeconomics*, D. Jansen and T. Gronberg (Eds).

Improving School Accountability: Check-Ups or Choice
Advances in Applied Microeconomics, Volume 14, 35–49

ISSN: 0278-0984/doi:10.1016/S0278-0984(06)14002-X

performance of U.S. schools. This consensus ends abruptly, however, when it comes to determining how to effect such a change in performance. One popular approach is to increase the accountability of schools to the public, by assessing schools on the basis of improvements in students' performance on standardized examinations and by offering remedies, such as increased choice (either within the public sector or through vouchers for private schools), reconstitution, or closure, in the event of persistent identified failure of a school to improve. Accountability measures have been proposed or implemented in dozens of states and going forward will be required in all the states.

On January 8, 2002, President Bush signed into law the reauthorization of the Elementary and Secondary Education Act, also known as the *No Child Left Behind Act of 2001* (NCLB). A centerpiece of this education reform involves implementing a system of school accountability. States must design systems of school report cards based on the fraction of students demonstrating proficiency in reading and mathematics. Under NCLB, if students do not make adequate yearly progress, schools and districts face consequences such as mandatory public school choice and the possibility of complete school restructuring as well as the redirection of federal funds; states risk the loss of federal administrative dollars. Additionally, the classifications or grades formally assigned to schools may affect the attractiveness of the local area to potential and current residents and the perceptions of local officials by the public. Figlio and Lucas (2004) provide evidence that housing markets are highly responsive to introduction of government-provided school report cards. Thus, the grading of schools using student test data provides numerous incentives for schools to "game the system."

Schools may react to these incentives by increasing class time spent on subjects and topics that are emphasized in the accountability exams, while decreasing class time on subjects and topics either not in or not emphasized in the exams. It should be noted that this type of strategy may be perceived by policy makers as precisely the desired response to the accountability system rather than as a "gaming" of this system. Significant class time may also be taken on test-taking strategies. Schools may even be less inclined to discourage poorer students from dropping out. For example, a Virginia school district superintendent said that the state's accountability exam system "actually encourages higher dropout rates ... It is actually to the school's advantage to drop slow learners and borderline students from the school, because they are usually poor test-takers" (Borja, 1999). In part, because of the newness of school accountability systems, we know of few serious attempts to quantify school responses to these incentives.[1]

Another potential reaction to the incentives created by accountability systems involves the classification of students into special education categories exempt from taking the tests used for school grading.[2] Schools could potentially improve their state-assigned grade or classification by taking their poorest-performing students out of the testing pool by classifying them into the special education categories exempt from taking the tests.[3] Additionally, the schools could potentially improve their state-assigned grade or classification by refraining from classifying better-performing students into the special education categories exempt from taking the tests. The American Institutes for Research's (AIR) new national study on special education costs helps demonstrate the potential flexibility and opportunity that school decision makers have in determining in which, if any, special education category to place students. AIR finds very wide variation in costs and services within single special education categories. In fact, they find less than 10 percent of the variation in special education costs in carrying out Individualized Education Plans can be explained by the exceptionality categories in the federal/state indicator record (Chambers, Parrish, Shkolnik, & Perez, 2002). This implies that there may be significant discretion in how to classify individuals with specifically identifiable needs.

In this paper, we use highly detailed student-level data to examine whether the initiation of the Florida Comprehensive Assessment Test (FCAT) has affected Florida public schools' decisions on special education assignments. Using student-level fixed effects models, we find that following the introduction of the FCAT testing program low-performing students and students from low socio-economic backgrounds were significantly and substantively more likely to be reclassified into disability categories exempted from the accountability system. These differences persist even after controlling for a rich set of time trends in disability classification. We also find that high-poverty schools are significantly more likely to reclassify low-achieving students than are more affluent schools.

While ours is the only paper to apply student-level fixed effects models to this topic, we know of two other current working papers that describe similar issues. Jacob (2005), looking at the effects of test-based accountability in Chicago, shows that low-achieving students in struggling schools are the most likely to be placed in special education, a finding similar to ours. While Jacob does not estimate student fixed-effects models, he does control for prior achievement test scores and background characteristics. Cullen and Reback (2002), using aggregate data and a clever identification strategy, exploit the discontinuity in rewards in the Texas accountability system to show that schools respond to incentives to shape the test pool. These two papers, taken together with ours, present complementary evidence – in three states and with three very different identification strategies – that schools respond to the incentive to classify marginal students into special education.

HIGH-STAKES TESTING IN FLORIDA

Beginning in the 1996–1997 school year, students in certain grades began to take the FCAT in reading and mathematics for the purpose of evaluating schools' performance in fostering educational achievement.[4] The FCAT tests were designed to align closely with the Sunshine State Standards, a set of basic and applied skills that students in particular grades are expected to know. Students in fourth, eighth, and tenth grades were tested in reading and writing, while students in fifth, eighth, and tenth grades were tested in mathematics; since 2001, students in third through tenth grades were tested annually in reading and mathematics. The tests are challenging, and are generally accepted to be among the more comprehensive state-level student assessments. These tests were initially used by the state as a tool to assess individual students and schools, and beginning in 1999 were used to grade schools on an explicit A through F scale, though this new grading regime was not fully known at the time of our last year of testing in the present analysis. However, after Jeb Bush's election to the Governorship in 1998, schools recognized that there would very likely be an increase in accountability associated with the FCAT, given that education reform and accountability were major policy platforms of Governor Bush's election campaign. While scores were not publicly reported in the first year of the testing program, 1996–1997, there could have been some anticipatory responses given that students were taking the examination and it was well known to educators that scores would be reported in subsequent years.

Prior to 1999, schools still faced serious accountability pressure under the FCAT. Although schools were not explicitly rewarded or sanctioned on the basis of aggregate performance on the FCAT, scores were publicly reported and prominently reported in the mass media. For instance, each of the 10 highest-circulation newspapers in Florida gave front-page coverage to FCAT results each year, even prior to 1999, and each newspaper annually presented tables with school-level FCAT scores reported. In addition, real-estate agents routinely provided school-level FCAT scores for prospective homebuyers.

All regular education students are required to take the FCAT examinations, but students in only a small number of disability classifications are required to take the exam. Specifically, all speech or language impaired or hospital/homebound students are required to take the FCAT. But in all other disability categories (educable or trainable mentally handicapped, orthopedically impaired, deaf or hard of hearing, visually impaired, emotionally handicapped, specific learning disabled, profoundly mentally handicapped, dual-sensory impaired, autistic, severely emotionally disturbed, traumatic brain injured, or developmentally delayed) FCAT test participation is determined by school personnel and the student's parents in the student's Individualized Education Plan, and test scores of all the students in these categories are exempted from school accountability programs. While some of these disability categories are clearly more mutable than others, it is certainly possible that marginal students may be classified (or declassified) from some of the exempted categories as a result of the testing regime.

IDENTIFICATION STRATEGY AND DATA

We are interested in investigating the effects of the testing regime on disability classification probabilities. Owing to the numerous potential omitted variables problems in this application, we utilize panel data and estimate models with *student-level fixed effects* to capture any time-invariant student-level variation in the probability of disability classification. Therefore, we draw our identification from students whose timing of classification switches coincides with the timing of the testing regime. Since some students may be classified in anticipation of testing policy changes and others may experience delays in testing-related classification changes, this strategy yields *conservative* estimates of the effect of testing on disability classification. Student fixed effects are only necessary if the composition of the student body is changing over time; in a dynamic state such as Florida, this is a reasonable fear. It turns out ex post that the inclusion of student fixed effects does not substantively change the estimated effects of the introduction of high-stakes testing on disability classifications.

Because of the possibility that different types of students have become more likely to be reclassified into special education over time for reasons unrelated to the FCAT, we also control for *linear time trends in disability classification*. We estimate these linear trends using data from before the introduction of the FCAT, and project the trends through the FCAT period. We estimate a simple model in which we assume that the classification probabilities for all students trend together over time. In more highly parameterized models, we allow linear trends in classification probabilities to vary across different types of students or schools. This strategy should also serve to generate conservative estimates of the effects of testing on disability classification, because some of the change in disability classification associated with the testing regime would almost surely be captured by a time trend. We also have estimated models that include both attribute-specific linear time trends and year effects (to capture any non-linear time trend in overall classification patterns). By this, we mean that we estimate linear time trends separately for different student subgroups, such as free lunch eligible students. In these models, we cannot estimate an overall testing effect, because the testing regime began at the same time for the entire sample. However, we can still estimate the coefficients on the interaction terms between the testing regime and student or school attributes. In each case, these estimated interaction terms are virtually identical to those reported in the paper; therefore, we do not report two sets of regression results, and instead report only the set of results where it is possible to estimate an overall testing effect.

Our data come directly from the student records of six large herein-unidentified county-level school districts, each among the 100 largest school districts in the United States.[5] Students in these school districts are more likely to be urban and are somewhat more likely to be racial or ethnic minorities than would a cross-section of Florida in general, but are large and diverse enough to have vast quantities of students of all socio-economic backgrounds, and schools at all levels of the socio-demographic spectrum.

School districts in Florida have uniform reporting requirements, and students are merged over time based on social security number, and in the event of no match by social security number, by first name, sex, race, and birth date. Students who change school districts over the study period remain in the study provided they relocated to another district included in the project. For the period from 1991–1992 through 1998–1999, we follow every student in kindergarten through eighth grade for all six counties. School district records include free lunch status, grade, and disability status. In addition, in two of these counties, we observe the student's Stanford 9 (or equivalent) standardized test score for nearly every student in each year from 1994–1995 through 1998–1999. (Counties vary from year to year in which students are tested. In one county, students were tested beginning in grade one in some years and grade two in other years; in the other, students were tested beginning in grade two in some years and grade three in other years.) All told, our dataset consists of 4,334,284 student-year observations. We observe student background characteristics in 4,171,752 cases, and prior year Stanford 9 test scores in 907,577 cases. (Note that we have substantially fewer observations on prior test scores not because of sample attrition – 94 percent of students in the two relevant counties have test score data – but rather because we only have Stanford 9 (or equivalent) test scores for two of the six counties, and then for a shorter time window.) Owing to the likelihood of error correlation at the school level, we adjust all standard errors for heteroskedasticity and clustering at the school level.

Table 1 shows the changes in disability classification rates in our population over time. We observe that the overall rate of disability classification increased over the period is covered by this study. At the beginning of the study period, 7.3 percent of students were classified as disabled in categories that would eventually be test-exempt. By the end of the period, however, this classification rate had increased to 10.8 percent. While most of the increase in disability classification generally occurred following the introduction of the testing regime, there is an apparent trend in classification occurring prior to the testing period, implying that our decision to control for time trends is a prudent one. (Of course, some of the pre-testing run-up in disability classification could be in anticipation of the introduction of the testing system.) Table 1 also presents these figures for free lunch eligible students (a proxy for likelihood of performing poorly on the FCAT examination) and those who are not free lunch eligible. In the case of the free lunch eligible, classification rates increased from 8.7 percent to 10.6 percent in the period prior to the introduction of the testing regime, while in the case of more affluent students, classification rates remained relatively stable in starting at 6.1 percent and ending at 6.2 percent. After the introduction of the testing regime, the test-excluded disability classification rates increase substantively for both groups.

Table 1. Over-Time Changes in Test-Excluded Disability Classification Rates, Six Florida Counties.

School Year	Overall Classification Rate (%)	Classification Rate of Free Lunch Eligible Students	Classification Rate of Non-Free Lunch Eligible Students
1991–1992	7.3	8.7	6.1
1992–1993	7.8	9.3	6.1
1993–1994	8.1	9.5	6.5
1994–1995	7.8	9.7	5.2
1995–1996	8.8	10.6	6.2
Introduction of testing regime			
1996–1997	9.4	11.0	7.6
1997–1998	9.6	11.8	7.1
1998–1999	10.8	13.2	7.4

The left panel of Table 2 describes the transitions into disability classification, by grade, before versus after the introduction of the testing regime. The vast majority of students enter special education during the elementary grades, but one might reasonably expect that if the increase in reclassification is occurring as a result of the testing regime as opposed to general trends toward increased classification that the third-to-fourth-grade transition would see the largest spike in classification following the introduction of high-stakes testing, as fourth grade is the first year of testing with consequences for schools. We observe that there is no statistically significant or economically meaningful change in classification transitions from grade-to-grade after versus before the testing program's introduction in any of the elementary school-grade transitions, *except for the transition into fourth grade.* In this transition, we observe increased propensities for students to be reclassified into test-exempt special education categories following the introduction of the FCAT testing program. This difference is significant at the 1 percent level when standard errors are adjusted to account for clustering of errors within schools.

The right panel of Table 2 breaks these transitions out separately for free lunch eligible students and more affluent students. We observe that the post-FCAT increase in disability classification during the third-to-fourth-grade transition is entirely due to increases in classification of low-income students. On the other hand, at no other transition does the post-FCAT effect on reclassification ever approach statistical significance for either low-income or more affluent students. This provides some suggestive evidence that schools may be responding to incentives to reclassify certain students as disabled in order to reduce their contribution to aggregate measures of test performance. Of course, whether these effects are causal remains to be seen.

Table 2. Grade-to-Grade Transitions in Test-Exempt Disability Classification, Before versus After Testing Regime Introduction.

Among Students NOT Classified as Disabled in Grade	Percentage of Students Classified in a Test-Exempt Category in the Following Grade								
	General Population			Free Lunch Eligibles			Non-Free Lunch Eligibles		
	Pre-FCAT	Post-FCAT	Robust *p*-Value of Difference	Pre-FCAT	Post-FCAT	Robust *p*-Value of Difference	Pre-FCAT	Post-FCAT	Robust *p*-Value of Difference
1	3.0	3.0	0.699	3.5	3.5	0.968	2.3	2.3	0.945
2	3.2	3.2	0.987	4.0	4.0	0.817	2.2	2.3	0.267
3	2.7	2.9	0.007	3.3	3.8	0.000	1.9	1.9	0.276
4	2.0	2.0	0.608	2.5	2.6	0.466	1.3	1.3	0.455

REGRESSION RESULTS

Table 3 describes the estimated effects of the introduction of high-stakes testing on test-excludable disability classification. Specification 1 reports the estimated mean effects of the introduction of testing, in a model controlling for student- and grade-level fixed effects, but no time trends. We observe that the introduction of FCAT test is associated with an increase in the likelihood that a student will be classified as disabled by 5.6 percentage points. This estimated effect is statistically significant at any reasonable level; it is also economically significant as 8.9 percent of the sample of students are identified as having a test-excludable disability, implying that the introduction of FCAT testing is associated with a more than 50 percent higher rate of disability classification in the six counties in question.

While schools have a financial incentive to classify students as disabled regardless of background, this incentive should be particularly strong for students whom the school views as at risk of performing poorly on the standardized examination. Given that low-income students tend to do more poorly on standardized examinations than do higher-income students, one proxy for this screen might be free lunch eligibility. Therefore, the second specification of Table 3 includes an interaction term between testing and free lunch eligibility. We observe that while post-FCAT, the classification of more affluent students increased by an estimated 3.6 percentage points, the estimated change in classification associated with the change in testing

Table 3. Estimated Effects of Testing on Disability Placement, by Socio-Economic Status (Robust Standard Errors in Parentheses beneath Coefficient Estimates).

Specification	1	2	3	4	5	6	7	8
Student fixed effects	Yes	Yes	Yes	Yes	Yes	Yes	Yes	Yes
Grade fixed effects	Yes	Yes	Yes	Yes	Yes	Yes	Yes	Yes
Standard errors adjusted for school-level clustering	Yes	Yes	Yes	Yes	Yes	Yes	Yes	Yes
General time trend included	No	No	Yes	Yes	No	No	Yes	Yes
Separate trends for low- and high-income students	No	No	No	Yes	No	No	No	Yes
Coefficient on testing	0.056	0.036	0.010	0.009	0.046	0.027	0.002	0.012
	(0.001)	(0.001)	(0.001)	(0.001)	(0.001)	(0.001)	(0.001)	(0.001)
Coefficient on testing × free lunch eligible		0.038	0.039	0.039		0.034	0.034	0.016
		(0.002)	(0.002)	(0.002)		(0.002)	(0.002)	(0.002)
Number of counties	6	6	6	6	2	2	2	2

regime is twice as large for free lunch eligible students. Specification 3 adds a time trend to the model; here, we observe that while the estimated effect of the testing regime for more affluent students falls considerably, the estimated difference in the effects for free lunch and non-free lunch students remains virtually the same, and is still statistically significant at any reasonable level of significance. Specification 4 controls for separate time trends for low- and higher-income students, and again the results clearly indicate that low socio-economic-status students are most likely to be reclassified in response to the testing policy, even after controlling for a rich set of time trends.

Specifications 5 through 8 from Table 3 present the results from these same four regressions, but only for the two counties where we also have Stanford 9 test scores. We observe that while the results are the same as those reported above, in terms of being strongly statistically significant, the estimated magnitudes of the results, though still quite large, are more modest than in the six-county case. This suggests that the models that follow, which look at testing effects by prior test scores rather than socio-economic status, may also generate relatively conservative estimates of the responses to the testing regime. However, we have no way of knowing for certain whether this is true.

Specification 9 from Table 4 presents the results from the parallel model to Table 3's Specification 6. Here, all variables are interacted with the student's Stanford 9 mathematics test score from the prior year rather than with free lunch eligibility. As with Specification 6, this specification does not control for time trends. The drawback of this exercise is that, due to data limitations, we can only observe one pre-testing year of data. But we still observe results that yield similar conclusions as the free lunch interactions do: the lower the last year's test performance, the more likely a student is to be classified as disabled. Specifications 10 and 11 repeat the same model, but in turn add a general time trend, then a time trend interacted with the prior year's mathematics test score. We see that in both of these specifications, schools tended to increase disability classification post-testing disproportionately for students who performed poorly on the prior year's test.

Specification 12 from Table 4 presents the identical model as Specification 11 (all fixed effects and past-performance-specific trends), but changes the dependent variable to look only at a very specific classification decision. In this model, students are included in this specification only if they are either classified as learning disabled or have another disability *that does not automatically exclude them from testing on the FCAT*. This model is extremely

Table 4. Estimated Effects of Testing on Disability Placement, by Prior Mathematics Test Performance (Robust Standard Errors in Parentheses beneath Coefficient Estimates).

Specification	9	10	11	12	13	14
Sample	Full Population	Full Population	Full Population	Learning Disabled or Test-Included Disabled Students	Full Population	Full Population
Student fixed effects	Yes	Yes	Yes	Yes	Yes	Yes
Grade fixed effects	Yes	Yes	Yes	Yes	Yes	Yes
Standard errors adjusted for school-level clustering	Yes	Yes	Yes	Yes	Yes	Yes
General time trend included	No	Yes	Yes	Yes	Yes	Yes
Separate trends for low- and high-performing students	No	No	Yes	Yes	No	Yes
Separate trends for high- and low-poverty schools	No	No	No	No	Yes	Yes
Student performance-based separate trends for high- and low-poverty schools	No	No	No	No	No	Yes
Coefficient on testing	0.028 (0.003)	0.012 (0.003)	0.009 (0.002)	0.019 (0.004)	0.016 (0.002)	0.004 (0.003)
Coefficient on testing × prior year math score	−0.029 (0.006)	−0.039 (0.006)	−0.018 (0.004)	−0.043 (0.008)		−0.012 (0.005)
Coefficient on testing × high-poverty school					0.011 (0.003)	0.009 (0.003)
Coefficient on testing × high-poverty school × prior year math score						−0.013 (0.005)
Number of counties	2	2	2	2	2	2

highly parameterized, and because of the fixed effects included in the model, identifies the effects of testing entirely on the basis of approximately 2,000 students whose classification switches between learning disabled, and therefore test-excluded and non-excluded disabilities. Even in this specification, which we present as corroborative evidence, the results stay consistently strong in magnitude and statistical significance, indicating that schools are more likely to switch low performers from a test-included to a test-excluded disability, following the introduction of the testing regime. Because of the relatively small number of classification switchers, however, the remainder of the paper focuses on disability classification more generally, rather than this very specific type of classification decision.

Specifications 13 and 14 from Table 4 report the results of models in which students are grouped by school type, with the notion that certain schools might be more sensitive to a school accountability system than are others. We identify schools as "high poverty" if the school has more than the district-wide median fraction of free lunch eligible students. Specification 13 controls for separate time trends for high- and low-poverty schools, while Specification 14 further controls for prior-test-score-specific separate time trends for high- and low-poverty schools. We observe that high-poverty schools are significantly more likely to reclassify students than are their relatively low-poverty counterparts. As Specification 14 demonstrates, these results are particularly concentrated for previously low-performing students. In summary, schools that ex ante are likely to be more threatened by a test-based accountability system, because they have a larger fraction of students likely to perform poorly on the examination, tend to be more aggressive in reclassifying previously low-performing students as disabled in an apparent response to the introduction of the high-stakes testing program.

DISCUSSION

We have estimated that the introduction of the high-stakes FCAT testing is associated with a dramatically higher rate of disability classification. We have also determined that the probability that a low-performing student or a student from a low socio-economic background would be reclassified into a disability category exempted from the accountability system increased significantly after the introduction of the high-stakes FCAT examinations. In addition, we found that high-poverty schools are significantly more likely to reclassify students than more affluent schools.

Altering decisions on special education classification for students reduces the accuracy of the grades or classifications given to schools based on the accountability exams and profoundly affects the educational experience of individual students. Reduced accuracy in the grades or classifications given to schools based on the accountability exams reduces the potential effectiveness of public policy based upon that data.

The incentive to place the students likely to perform worst on the state tests into special education classes may cause schools to place in special education students whom they believe would be better off in other classes. Since many states have laws that limit the number of students per special education teacher, the placement of those students into special education classes who otherwise would not have been so placed may require that students who would benefit more from special education be prevented from taking special education classes.

Also, the cost of providing special education far exceeds the cost of traditionally educating a student. According to a new study by the American Institutes for Research, the ratio of spending per special education student to spending per regular education student is 1.90 on average(Chambers et al., 2002). Thus, funds could be inappropriately spent on special education for students who may be better off in less costly traditional classrooms; schools could potentially spend those funds more productively if the incentives to alter special education assignments did not exist.

The NCLB Act requires that students that are classified into special education categories participate and be counted. Specifically, under the NCLB Act, all students in each defined subgroup[6] must meet or exceed the state's proficient level of academic achievement by the end of the 2013–2014 school year. The legislation specifies intermediate goals for meeting this objective. These include each state establishing "statewide annual measurable objectives" that include a "single minimum percentage of students who are required to meet or exceed the proficient level on the academic assessments." These minimum percentages apply separately to each subgroup of students, but not all subgroups must make adequate yearly progress each year. The subgroups that do not meet or exceed the minimum percentage still must decrease their percentage of students that are below proficiency by 10 percent when compared with the preceding year.[7]

Despite the requirement under the NCLB Act that all subgroups, including students with disabilities, be included in the accountability testing system, incentives to game the system through special education classification will remain. First, NCLB does permit testing accommodations for students with disabilities. Accommodations, such as additional time, can potentially aid any student's performance, including those students without legitimate or clear-cut disabilities. Thus, the incentive to over-classify[8] low-performing students and students from low socio-economic backgrounds into special education remains. Also, since all subgroups, including students with disabilities, will be required to have the same minimum percentage of members meeting proficiency or at least decrease the percentage of non-proficient students by 10 percent annually, schools will have the incentive to place "ringers" in the students with disabilities category. In other words, since it will likely be particularly difficult to have the students with disabilities subgroup reach the minimum percentage, schools will have a strong incentive to add students to that category who are likely to achieve proficiency. For example, schools would likely improve their probability of attaining adequate yearly progress for all subgroups if they were to place relatively high-achieving students with mild dyslexia into the students with disabilities subgroup, who would not have otherwise been so classified.

NOTES

1. Papers that discuss these types of incentives include Elmore, Abelmann, and Fuhrman (1996), Goldhaber (2002), Ladd (2001), and Koretz (1996). However, these are not empirical studies of school responses to incentives. A few recent academic papers describe school responses to incentives embedded within accountability systems, other than the response described in this paper. Figlio (in press) finds that the introduction of accountability exams in Florida has resulted in fewer and shorter disciplinary suspensions for poor-performing students during the "cram period" prior to accountability exam testing dates. Figlio and Winicki (2005) show that Virginia schools threatened with sanctions tend to alter their nutrition programs during testing periods, and substantially increase nutrients clinically shown to boost short-term cognitive performance. Jacob (2005) and others present evidence that schools subject to accountability systems may respond by retaining marginal students.

2. The NCLB Act will require special education participation, but for reasons mentioned in the Discussion section of this paper, incentives to game the system through the classification of students into special education categories will remain.

3. States may have other incentives to over-classify students into special education categories. For example, Cullen (2003) found that fiscal incentives could explain nearly 40 percent of the growth in student disability rates in Texas.

4. Students had previously taken the Florida Writes! writing assessment.

5. Counties participating in this study wish to remain unidentified.

6. Students with disabilities are one of several defined subgroups.

7. *Source: The No Child Left Behind Act of 2001.*

8. Some may be of the opinion that prior to the accountability exams not enough students were receiving special education. If this opinion is accurate, then perhaps this incentive results in some students being better off. Still, as described earlier in this paper, this will likely cause schools to place in special education at least some students who would be better off in other classes. And since many states have laws that limit the number of students per special education teacher, the placement of those students into special education classes who otherwise would not have been so placed may require that students who would benefit more from special education be prevented from taking special education classes.

ACKNOWLEDGEMENTS

We are grateful to Sheila Murray, Richard Rothstein, and Jim Wyckoff as well as seminar participants at Iowa State University, the National Bureau of Economic Research, Stanford University, University of California-Davis, and University of Florida, and participants at the APPAM and AEFA meetings for helpful comments and suggestions, to the National Science Foundation for research funding, and to six undisclosed school districts for generously providing us with the confidential data employed in this study. Any remaining errors are our own. The opinions expressed herein are those of the authors and do not necessarily reflect the positions of their employers.

REFERENCES

Borja, R. (1999). Comments: SOLs raise concern, little support/change tests, use multiple criteria, speakers say. *Richmond Times-Dispatch*, December 1.

Chambers, J., Parrish, T., Shkolnik, J., & Perez, M. (2002). A report on the 1999–2000 special education expenditures project. Special session presented at the annual research conference of the American Education Finance Association, March, Albuquerque, NM.

Cullen, J. (2003). The impact of fiscal incentives on student disability rates. *Journal of Public Economics*, *87*(7–8), 1557–1589.

Cullen, J., & Reback, R. (2002). *Tinkering toward accolades: School gaming under a performance accountability system*. Working Paper. University of Michigan.

Elmore, R., Abelmann, C., & Fuhrman, S. (1996). The new accountability in state education reform: From process to performance. In: H. Ladd (Ed.), *Holding schools accountable* (pp. 65–98). Washington, DC: The Brookings Institution.

Figlio, D. (in press). Testing, crime and punishment. *Journal of Public Economics.*

Figlio, D., & Lucas, M. (2004). What's in a grade? School report cards and the housing market. *American Economic Review*, *94*(3), 591–604.

Figlio, D., & Winicki, F. J. (2005). Food for thought? The effects of school accountability plans on school nutrition. *Journal of Public Economics*, *89*(2–3), 381–394.

Goldhaber, D. (2002). *The reauthorization of the Elementary and Secondary Education Act (ESEA): What might go wrong with the accountability measures of the 'No Child Left Behind Act?* Policy Memo. Thomas B. Fordham Foundation.

Jacob, B. (2005). The impact of high-stakes testing on student achievement: Evidence from Chicago. *Journal of Public Economics*, *89*(5–6), 761–796.

Koretz, D. (1996). Using student assessments for educational accountability. In: E. Hanushek & D. Jorgenson (Eds), *Improving America's schools: The role of incentives*. Washington, DC: National Academy Press.

Ladd, H. (2001). School-based educational accountability systems: The promise and the pitfalls. *National Tax Journal*, *54*(2), 385–400.

DO GOOD HIGH SCHOOLS PRODUCE GOOD COLLEGE STUDENTS? EARLY EVIDENCE FROM NEW YORK CITY

Hella Bel Hadj Amor, Amy Ellen Schwartz and Leanna Stiefel

ABSTRACT

We examine variation in high school and college outcomes across New York City public high schools. Using data on 80,000 students who entered high school in 1998 and following them into the City University of New York, we investigate whether schools that produce successful high school students also produce successful college students. We also explore differences in performance across sex, race, and immigration, and we briefly explore selection issues. Specifically, we estimate student-level regressions with school fixed effects, controlling for student characteristics, to identify better and worse performing schools based on state mandated exams, graduation, and college performance.

Improving School Accountability: Check-Ups or Choice
Advances in Applied Microeconomics, Volume 14, 51–80

ISSN: 0278-0984/doi:10.1016/S0278-0984(06)14003-1

1. INTRODUCTION

While education has long been a pathway to economic success, since the 1980s the premium in earnings for college versus high school education has grown almost continuously. Yet in order to enter – let alone *succeed* in – college, a student must earn a high school diploma and gain adequate high school preparation. This pivotal role for high schools in determining enrollment and success in college is receiving increasing attention from researchers as well as policymakers. While much of the attention focuses on using testing for high school accountability, there is increasing interest in the relationship between high schools, college going and success.

As an example, although the *No Child Left Behind Act* of 2001 (NCLB) currently requires testing only in grades 3–8 and one high school grade, in January 2005 President Bush announced his desire to expand the law to include more high school tests as well as high school graduation rates (e.g., Kornblut, 2005). Perhaps more interesting, the state of Michigan recently decided to replace the state high school exams with the American College Test (ACT) plus five other subject exams that "would be accepted by colleges and universities for entrance and placement purposes."[1]

In New York State, students will soon be required to pass exams in five subject areas (the long-standing "Regents" exams") in order to graduate from high school. In the past, Regents' exams were taken by far fewer than most of the states' high school students, and those taking the exams were probably the most academically accomplished as well as the most likely to attend college. Since in the near future all students will be required to pass Regents' exams to graduate from high school, the Board of Regents' seems to intend to broaden the pool of college-ready students.

Even if more policies focus on the success of schools at turning 8th graders into graduates or into graduates ready for college, insufficient attention is being paid to whether these "successes" actually do translate into successful college students. While some researchers have looked at the high school characteristics of individual students (e.g., grade point average) when assessing college success, very few have studied how high schools perform as organizations per se. Yet in a world of increasingly stringent accountability for organizational outcomes, such research is crucial in order to understand if there is conflict or congruence between the various missions high schools are asked to achieve, and more specifically between the ways these missions are measured. The primary purpose of this paper is to begin to fill this gap by examining the extent of variation in high school and college outcomes across New York City public high schools and to investigate whether high schools that produce students who do well on high school measures of success also produce students who do well on college measures of success.

Note that this is early evidence because the requirement to obtain five passing grades on Regents' examinations is not yet fully implemented and because we do not yet have college persistence or graduation information for our sample of students. Nevertheless, it is important to assess whether success is likely from early evidence and to ascertain whether there are conflicts between traditional measures of successful high schools (such as graduation rates or passing scores on high school exams) and less traditional measures of successful high schools (such as college application or matriculation or grades).

We use data on 80,000 New York City (NYC) public high school students who entered 9th grade in 1998, follow them through their high school years and, where relevant, into the City University of New York (CUNY). We investigate whether schools with high graduation rates and test scores also produce students who earn high grade point averages (GPAs) at CUNY. Specifically, we estimate student-level regressions with school fixed effects, controlling for student characteristics, to rank high schools along a number of different indicators, including state mandated high school exams, graduation rates, Scholastic Aptitude Tests (SAT) scores, and college performance. The school fixed effects capture the average value added by the school to its student performance. We then compare high school success along these different dimensions. Results will be useful in devising accountability measures for high schools. If high schools are ranked similarly on all indicators of success, then the need to evaluate trade-offs may be mitigated. Otherwise, policymakers will need to better align measures of success or at least be attentive to the choices of outputs for which the schools are held accountable.

The paper is organized as follows. In Section 2, we review the relevant literature to provide background for the study. In Sections 3 and 4, we describe the data and the methodology, respectively. In Section 5, we present results on the relationships between various indicators of high school performance and in Section 6 we conclude with a summary and discussion of the implications of our results for policies on accountability.

2. LITERATURE REVIEW

2.1. The Transition from High School to College

There is not a great deal of research on the relationship between how well high schools perform and how successful their students are in college.

Nonetheless, within this scant literature, two strands emerge, one that examines the relationships between high school outcomes and college outcomes, and another that examines the relationships between specific policies and college entrance exams and outcomes.

In the first strand are papers that estimate straightforward multivariate models of college GPAs, controlling for high school outcomes (e.g., high school GPA, class rank, receipt of general equivalency diploma (GED), and SAT scores), and a limited set of student characteristics. For example, Cohn, Cohn, Balch, and Bradley (2004) estimate such models with a sample of about 500 South Carolina students, focusing on race and sex differences in the likelihood of success in college, eligibility for statewide scholarships, and retention of scholarships after enrollment. Bailey and Weininger (2002) compare credits earned and college attainment of foreign- and native-born students, while Horowitz and Spector (2005) examine the impact of private versus public high school attendance on the college GPAs of 15,000 Indiana undergraduates.

A second strand of literature analyzes the effect of policies, such as state-required graduation exams (e.g., Marchant & Paulson, 2005) or state high-stakes tests (e.g., Ehlert & Podgursky, 2005), on college entrance exams and outcomes. Again using straightforward multivariate regression, Marchant and Paulson (2005) model graduation rates and SAT scores, at the state and student levels, controlling for a few demographic characteristics and, in the SAT models, for high school GPA and an indicator for whether the state requires a standardized test for graduation. A different approach is taken in Ehlert and Podgursky (2005), who assess whether low-stakes state high school performance assessments are reliable measures of true school performance. Their methodology differs entirely from the other papers, however, as the authors eschew regression analysis and instead use an array of correlations between performance levels on proficiency exams and ACT scores, as well as distributions of these measures and of college enrollment, credits, and GPA.

Three important differences exist between our study and those in the literature. First, our interest lies in high schools per se rather than individual students, and more specifically, in whether high schools with high value added on high school measures of success also have high value added on college measures of success. Thus, we not only estimate models of college GPAs (and SATs), but also models of high school outcomes (graduation and performance on New York State high school Regents' exams) and we do this with a focus on high school performance rather than individual student performance. Second, in some models, we do not control for students' high school outcomes, but rather for the quality of students at high school intake, using their 8th grade test scores, thus allowing us to compare the "total" high school effect with one that is mediated by intermediate student high school outcomes. Third, for readers who wish to analyze the effect of individual student characteristics, we drastically reduce omitted variable bias on coefficients of those characteristics by including high school fixed effects and by controlling for a much wider array of student demographics than most papers cited, except perhaps Bailey and Weininger (2002). We include sex (as in Bailey & Weininger, 2002; Cohn et al., 2004; Horowitz & Spector, 2005), race (as in Bailey & Weininger, 2002; Cohn et al., 2004; Marchant & Paulson, 2005), age (as in Bailey & Weininger, 2002; Horowitz & Spector, 2005), poverty status (Bailey & Weininger, 2002, use measures of household income), immigrant status (the variable of interest in Bailey & Weininger, 2002), as well as language ability and special education status.[2]

Our fixed effects specification follows Betts and Morell (1999), who include school fixed (or random) effects in a model of college GPA, although their focus is not on high school effects but rather on the other variables in the models such as family background, high school resources and peer characteristics. Interestingly, the authors obtain similar results when they substitute random effects for school fixed effects. In addition, while the authors indicate the possible presence of selection bias (because some schools send their best students to the University of California at San Diego, while other schools send their second-best students), they argue that their study contributes to the literature because it is an early study that includes student, school, and neighborhood characteristics.[3] In the same vein, our paper serves as an early study of the congruence between high school success on high school and on college outcomes.

2.2. Successful High Schools

By estimating models of both high school and college success, we draw on and expand the literature on high school effectiveness, as well as literature linking high schools to college. Using our unique New York City student-level database, we add to the high school literature, which has drawn in large part on the National Education Longitudinal Study of 1988 (NELS:88). For example, Goldhaber and Brewer (1997) estimate an education production function, modeling the math achievement of 5,000 10th graders as a function of individual and family characteristics, as well as school, teacher, and classroom variables. They expand their analyses by also estimating models with random and fixed effects (both school and teacher), and regressing teacher effects on teacher characteristics.

Other studies start with more complicated models, nesting students within schools in a hierarchical linear framework. Lee and Smith (1997), for example, are ultimately interested in the effect of high school size on the average test score gains of students in schools with varying representations of poor and minority students. Warren and Edwards (2003) use a similar setup to investigate the effects of high-stakes graduation test requirements on high school attainment.

In this work, we estimate high school fixed effect models of student performance and use the fixed effect coefficients to compare high school performance across indicators of high school and college success. In other words, we compare the average value added of high schools to assess the extent to which high schools that exhibit high value added on the high school outcomes are similarly successful on the college outcomes.

2.3. Performance Measurement

There are two common ways that economists measure organization performance in general and school performance in particular. In previous work, we have labeled one method "adjusted performance measures" (APMs). To measure the performance of elementary and middle schools in New York City and Ohio, for example, Stiefel, Schwartz, Bel Hadj Amor, and Kim (2005) use residuals from school-level, multiple-regression equations in which raw performance indicators are the dependent variables. We call these APMs because they adjust the output measure (e.g., the percentage of students passing tests) for student and school characteristics beyond the control of an individual school, such as student educational need and school resources. A lagged performance measure is included as an independent variable to approximate the value added of achievement over the school year.

While using residuals to measure and compare an organization's performance, especially for schools, is not new (other examples include Gramlich, 1976; Ladd & Walsh, 2002; Rubenstein, Schwartz, & Stiefel, 1998; Stiefel, Rubenstein, & Schwartz, 1999, 2003), few papers perform such analyses for high schools. Rumberger and Palardy (2005) is an exception. These authors investigate the relationship between several different indicators of high school performance, in an effort to answer a question similar to ours: Are schools that are effective in raising test scores also effective in reducing dropout rates, transfer rates, and attrition rates? The authors use the residuals from a set of student-level models that control for student characteristics and a rich set of school characteristics to measure and compare school effectiveness.

School fixed effects are an alternative way to measure and compare organizational effectiveness (e.g., Bartelsman & Doms, 2000; Stiefel, Bel Hadj Amor, & Schwartz, 2005). They can be included in student-level models of school performance as long as the included school-level variables are time-variant. Fixed effects are superior measures because residuals include an array of random components, while fixed effects capture the schools' time-invariant, unobserved characteristics, and can be interpreted as the schools' average value added to their students' performance.[4] In this paper, we use the school fixed effects from student-level regressions to rank high schools.

3. DATA

3.1. New York City Students

We use data on a high school cohort of approximately 80,000 students who were expected to graduate from the New York City high schools in 2001. The New York City Department of Education (NYCDOE) provided data on high school students, their demographic characteristics (including race, sex, and immigrant status), their performance on New York State Regents' high school exams, Regents' Competency Tests, 8th grade reading and math tests, the schools they attended throughout their high school career, and whether they graduated high school within four years, and if so, with what type of degree.[5] CUNY provided additional information on high school graduates, their SAT scores, as well as application and enrollment information, including GPAs.

The analysis sample includes nearly 50,000 of the 80,000 students. We exclude 14,000 students who were at one point part of the class of 2001, but who were discharged from New York City high schools (usually to another district or a private school) before graduation.[6] In addition, 2,700 students graduated with a GED and 260 with a special education certificate. The behavior of these latter two groups is unlikely to be captured by the same models that describe the students who have a regular high school experience, i.e., students who, after four years, are still enrolled, graduate with local or Regents' diplomas, or drop out. In addition, in very small schools, the averages of the variables of interest will be very sensitive to the presence of outliers. To avoid the resulting potentially skewed results, we limit the sample to students in schools with more than 10 students.[7] Accordingly, the models restricted to CUNY *enrollees* use students in high schools with more than 10 enrollees. Further, estimating reliable fixed effects for high schools requires a minimum number of students in each high school who have data on the dependent variables of interest. We drop from the remaining sample students from high schools with five or fewer students who enroll in CUNY and have GPA, SAT scores, and English and math Regents' scores. The resulting sample has 50,494 students in 148 high schools. This sample includes 31,453 high school graduates and 13,342 CUNY enrollees. Descriptive statistics are presented in Table 1.

The NYC high school student population in our sample is non-white and poor (Table 1, columns (1), (2), and (3)). Indeed, only 18% of the students are white, while about a third each is Black and Hispanic and 16% are Asian. Seventy-eight percent of the students for whom we have 8th grade school lunch data (69% of the sample) are eligible for a free lunch, and an additional 6% are eligible for a reduced-price lunch. There are fewer males than females (48% and 52%, respectively) and, while the average age of the students in 2001 is about 17, age varies from as low as 14 to as high as 24 years. The diversity in the student population is evident in its racial distribution and in other attributes as well: 23% of the students were born in a foreign country and 50% speak a language other than English at home. A much smaller percentage, 12%, is English language learners. This is not entirely surprising, as the vast majority of the students (91%) entered the NYC school system before the 9th grade.[8] Five percent of the students in the sample received part-time special education services when they were in 8th grade.

There is a wide range in student performance in our sample. While average performance in reading and math on the 8th grade tests is about 0.15 standard deviations above the mean across all students in the original dataset, it deviates from the mean by almost 3 standard deviations in both directions. Disparities are large in high school as well, and scores on the English and math Regents' exams ranges from 1 to 100, averaging about 68. Students usually took the English Regents' exam in 2000 and the math exam in 1998 or later. Only two-thirds of the students graduated high school after fours years (62%).[9]

Enrollees in CUNY look somewhat different from the students as a whole (Table 1, columns (4), (5), and (6)). The share of female is larger (59%), as are the shares of white and Asian students (23% and 20%, respectively). The difference in poverty is small, with 83% of poor and near-poor students among the enrollees, versus 84% for the whole sample. There are higher shares, among the enrollees, of students who are foreign-born (27%), were English language learners in high school (13%), and speak a language other than English at home (55%). This suggests that these students partly overcome language and cultural handicaps, if any, by the time they reach college.

Table 1. Descriptive Statistics, Student Level, 2001 High School Cohort.

	All High School Students			CUNY Enrollees		
	(1) Mean	(2) Minimum	(3) Maximum	(4) Mean	(5) Minimum	(6) Maximum
Student is a high school graduate, in four years	0.62	0.00	1.00	1.00	1.00	1.00
Student applied to CUNY	0.42	0.00	1.00	1.00	1.00	1.00
Student enrolled in CUNY	0.26	0.00	1.00	1.00	1.00	1.00
First semester CUNY GPA	2.57	0.07	4.00	2.57	0.07	4.00
Verbal SAT CUNY applicants[a]	439.76	200.00	800.00	430.55	200.00	800.00
Math SAT CUNY applicants	471.97	200.00	800.00	461.18	200.00	800.00
English Regents' score	68.91	1.00	100.00	73.06	2.00	100.00
Sequential 1 Regents' score	67.55	1.00	100.00	68.90	22.00	99.00
Student is female	0.52	0.00	1.00	0.59	0.00	1.00
Age as of 2001	17.33	14.00	24.00	17.24	14.00	24.00
Student is White	0.18	0.00	1.00	0.23	0.00	1.00
Student is Black	0.34	0.00	1.00	0.28	0.00	1.00
Student is Hispanic	0.32	0.00	1.00	0.28	0.00	1.00
Student is Asian	0.16	0.00	1.00	0.20	0.00	1.00
Student is native American	0.00	0.00	1.00	0.00	0.00	1.00
Student is eligible for free lunch	0.78	0.00	1.00	0.76	0.00	1.00
Student is eligible for reduced-price lunch	0.06	0.00	1.00	0.07	0.00	1.00
Student is not eligible for school lunch	0.15	0.00	1.00	0.17	0.00	1.00
Student is foreign-born	0.23	0.00	1.00	0.27	0.00	1.00

Table 1. (*Continued*)

	All High School Students			CUNY Enrollees		
	(1) Mean	(2) Minimum	(3) Maximum	(4) Mean	(5) Minimum	(6) Maximum
Student is native-born	0.77	0.00	1.00	0.73	0.00	1.00
Student entered the system before 9th grade	0.83	0.00	1.00	0.82	0.00	1.00
Student entered the system in the 9th grade or later	0.09	0.00	1.00	0.09	0.00	1.00
Student is an English language learner	0.12	0.00	1.00	0.13	0.00	1.00
Student speaks English at home	0.50	0.00	1.00	0.45	0.00	1.00
Student receives part-time education services	0.05	0.00	1.00	0.03	0.00	1.00
8th grade reading z-score	0.15	2.94	2.98	0.32	2.94	2.98
8th grade math z-score	0.16	2.65	2.16	0.35	2.51	2.16
LAB percentile (8th grade)	19.79	1.00	99.00	23.90	1.00	99.00

Notes: In columns (1), (2), and (3), $N = 50{,}494$, except student applied to CUNY and student enrolled in CUNY ($N = 31{,}020$), first semester CUNY GPA ($N = 11{,}718$), verbal SAT ($N = 16{,}335$), math SAT ($N = 16{,}336$), English Regents' score ($N = 40{,}283$), Sequential 1 Regents' score ($N = 39{,}952$), race ($N = 50{,}402$), eligibility for school lunch ($N = 34{,}995$), time of entry into the system ($N = 46{,}152$), 8th grade reading z-score ($N = 34{,}663$), 8th grade math z-score ($N = 36{,}454$), and 8th grade LAB percentile ($N = 6{,}083$). See data section of paper for description of how the sample is derived.

In columns (4), (5) and (6), $N = 13{,}342$, except first semester CUNY GPA ($N = 11{,}718$), verbal SAT ($N = 10{,}423$), math SAT ($N = 10{,}424$), English Regents' score ($N = 13{,}150$), Sequential 1 Regents' score ($N = 12{,}726$), race ($N = 13{,}340$), eligibility for school lunch ($N = 9{,}290$), time of entry into the system ($N = 12{,}020$), 8th grade reading z-score ($N = 9{,}111$), 8th grade math z-score ($N = 9{,}555$), and 8th grade LAB percentile ($N = 1{,}612$).

[a]SAT scores are reported for CUNY applicants only.

However, differences in average performance across the two groups are striking: the average reading and math 8th grade *z*-scores are 0.32 and 0.35 (versus 0.15 and 0.16 in the whole sample). While the average English Regents' score is only about one point higher than it is with the whole sample (68.90), the average math Regents' score is four points higher than it is with the whole sample (73.06). Close to the full range of college GPAs is observed, with an average at 2.57.

There is some evidence that the highest-achieving graduates do not enroll in CUNY, as average performance is lower for the enrollees than it is for the graduates on the 8th grade reading test (0.32 versus 0.46) and the 8th grade math test (0.35 versus 0.49).

3.2. New York City High Schools

To illustrate the great variety in New York City high schools, we aggregate the student-level data to the school level and complement it with data from the NYCDOE Annual School Report (ASR) and School-based Expenditure Report (SBER) databases. The ASR database includes student demographic and performance information as well as teacher characteristics. The SBER database provides expenditure data for each school.[10] Table 2 provides descriptive statistics on the sample schools.

Table 2 shows that the 148 high schools in the sample vary widely in their characteristics. While the average school enrolls a little over 1,750 students, there are very small schools (151 students) and very large schools (4,631 students). There is also much variety in student performance, as attested by the wide ranges in the Regents' scores and percentage of students who took the exams. None take them in some schools while all of the students take them in others. While about 57% of the students graduate within four years, some schools graduate all of their students in that timeframe while that number is as low as 14% in other schools. Two-thirds of the students apply to CUNY on average, with much variation in this percentage and in the applicants' SAT scores. In the average school, 42% of the students enroll in CUNY, and this percentage can be as low as 6% and as high as 66%.

There is also great variation in the demographic characteristics of the students, although the average school enrolls a majority of non-white students and poor students. Some schools have populations that are entirely foreign-born, and others have no students who are new to the system. As expected, some high schools receive much higher-performing incoming classes than others; indeed, the 8th grade *z*-scores range from less than 1 to over 2.

Table 2. Descriptive Statistics, New York City High School Level, 2001.

Variable	Mean	Minimum	Maximum
Enrollment (SBER)	1769	151	4631
Performance			
First semester GPA	2.52	1.44	3.33
Recentered SAT verbal score	419.61	300.71	677.52
Recentered SAT math score	440.85	339.29	720.59
English Regents' score	65.43	36.63	95.02
Sequential 1 Regents' score	65.96	55.57	88.83
Percent who took the English Regents' exam	79.49	42.31	100.00
Percent who took the Sequential 1 Regents' exam	79.03	19.05	100.00
Percent who graduated within four years	56.94	13.47	100.00
Percent of graduates who apply to CUNY	67.86	13.60	92.31
Percent of graduates who enroll in CUNY	42.00	6.40	65.77
Demographics			
Percent of female	52.85	4.91	83.95
Percent White	13.20	0.00	79.55
Percent Black	39.76	2.89	97.40
Percent Hispanic	35.25	2.56	92.27
Percent Asian	11.17	0.00	67.14
Percent Native American	0.35	0.00	2.94
Percent free lunch eligible (8th grade)	57.95	22.38	82.38
Percent reduced price lunch eligible (8th grade)	4.46	0.00	10.61
Percent not eligible for lunch (8th grade)	8.77	0.00	43.13
Percent foreign born	20.10	0.00	98.53
Percent native born	79.90	1.47	100.00
Percent who entered the system before 9th grade	84.23	1.10	100.00
Percent who entered the system in 9th grade or later	7.99	0.00	39.56
Percent English language learner	10.33	0.00	90.52
Percent in part-time special education (8th grade)	5.00	0.26	11.76
CTB *z*-score (8th grade)	0.03	−0.69	2.13
CAT *z*-score (8th grade)	0.04	−0.66	2.07
Percent who took ZCTB (8th grade)	70.91	0.00	93.22
Percent who took ZCAT (8th grade)	74.11	0.00	94.59
Resources			
Percent of teachers in this school for more than 2 years	70.94	24.20	100.00
Percent of teachers with more than 5 years of teaching	60.76	14.80	89.50
Percent of teachers fully licensed/permanently assigned	83.86	52.30	100.00
Percent of teachers with a Masters or higher	79.80	50.00	95.20
Total expenditure per pupil	10,171	7,308	39,409

Notes: School means come from aggregated student-level data unless otherwise indicated. $N = 148$, except eligibility for school lunch and 8th grade *z*-scores ($N = 147$), part-time special education ($N = 143$), teachers in the school for more than two years ($N = 135$) and the other teacher variables ($N = 136$).

Teacher characteristics vary greatly across schools as well and, accordingly, so does spending. The average school spends a little over $10,000 per pupil in 2001–2002, and 71% of its teachers have taught in the school for over two years, 61% have been teaching for more than five years, 84% are licensed, and 80% have at least a Masters' degree. Yet some of these percentages are lower than 50% in some schools and reach almost 100% in others.

4. FRAMEWORK AND EMPIRICAL MODEL

High schools with high value added on the high school outcomes may differ from those with high value added on the college outcomes, for two reasons. First, success on high school exams may not be a good indicator of future success in college. Indeed, indicators of high school and college success may measure different abilities and sets of knowledge and have different aims. Thus, high Regents' exams scores, for example, may not imply high SAT scores. This feature may result in unintended consequences for accountability, if the accountability system is based on one test rather than another.[11]

Second, the set of high schools that excel at getting students into college may be a different set of schools than those that do not (e.g., schools that prepare students for the job market). Thus, it is critical to define what a good high school is supposed to do. Since not all students proceed to college, a good school may be defined as one whose students obtain high scores on high school level standardized tests. Such a restrictive definition, however, clearly disadvantages schools whose entering students (though no fault of the high school) are low performers. In this case, a more appropriate definition may take into account that a good high school not only produces students with high test scores, but also enables students to achieve large gains. In such a school, low-performing students who come in from the 8th grade can eventually achieve higher than expected state standardized test scores at the high school level, and graduate with a reasonably high probability. This definition is also more likely to reflect the concerns of policymakers and other stakeholders.

Using this "value added" definition of success reinforces the possibility that schools that produce high school success and those that produce college success differ. Indeed, what would happen if high schools with comparable average high school test scores, regardless of the level of their entering classes, were compared based on how well their students perform in college? High schools that achieve a large value added in high school may deliver students for whom achieving a large value added in college is difficult, while other schools may send students whose high school value added is more marginal, for whom the potential for gains is yet to be depleted. All of these schools are successful on the high school outcomes, but only the second set would be successful on the college outcomes.

The underlying conceptual framework for our analyses is grounded in adjusted performance measures. In order to discern the true contribution of high schools to their students' success, we first purge confounding factors such as the characteristics of the students and the preparation the students bring with them from home and from middle school. The centerpiece of our empirical work is a set of student-level models that remove the influence of student demographic characteristics and prior performance from student outcomes and produce a set of school indicators that capture the remaining contribution of schools.

First, we model the performance of CUNY enrollees at CUNY (their first semester GPA), in a model of adjusted performance:

$$\text{Performance}_{ij} = \alpha_0 + \alpha_1\text{Student}_{ij} + \alpha_2\text{Score8}_{ij} + \varepsilon_{ij} \tag{1}$$

where i indexes students and j high schools. Performance_{ij} represents first semester CUNY GPA.[12] Student_{ij} represents a set of student characteristics, including sex, race, and immigrant status. Including the student's performance on 8th grade exams creates a value-added specification of the model, providing some control for differences in student ability and Score8_{ij} represents performance on these tests.[13] α_0 is the intercept, α_1 and α_2 are slopes that capture the impact of the corresponding variables on the outcome, and ε_{ij} is an error term with the usual properties.

Schools are introduced in this model by adding a set of school fixed effects, η_j, and this is the model we estimate:

$$\text{Performance}_{ij} = \alpha_0 + \alpha_1\text{Student}_{ij} + \alpha_2\text{Score8}_{ij} + \eta_j + \varepsilon_{ij} \tag{2}$$

The school fixed effects capture unobserved characteristics of the schools that affect student outcomes. More specifically, each fixed effect represents the contribution of each school to the student outcome, relative to a reference school, beyond the composition of the student body. The larger the fixed effect, the greater the contribution of that particular school. Thus, school contribution can be measured and compared across schools based on the size of the fixed effects.

Student characteristics include student age and indicators for whether the student is female; Black, Hispanic, or Asian (White is the left-out category); an English language learner; whether they were born in the United States; whether they entered the NYC public school system before the 9th grade; and whether they speak English at home. We use a substitute indicator, when available, for two important student characteristics not reported in high school but reported for 8th graders: student eligibility for free or reduced-price lunch and whether students receive part-time special education services. *Z*-scores on the 8th grade reading and math standardized tests (CTB/McGraw Hill Test of Basic Skills for English language assessment; California Achievement Test (CAT) for math assessment), as well as the 8th grade score on the Language Assessment Battery (LAB), capture past performance. Indicators for missing data are included for race, time of entry into the system, and all 8th grade variables, so as to maintain sample size. Finally, the model includes the number of semesters between high school graduation and CUNY enrollment.

Model (2) is estimated for both college and high school outcomes. College outcome is measured by GPA and high school outcomes include student performance on the state mandated Regents' exams in English and Sequential I (math), their verbal and math SAT scores, and an indicator of whether a student graduates.[14]

Results from Eq. (2) for each outcome provide us with sets of school fixed effects, one for each college and high school outcome. We examine the strength of the relationship between the sets, to determine whether schools that contribute the most to one outcome also contribute the most to the other outcomes.

5. EMPIRICAL RESULTS

5.1. Raw Measures are Poor Indicators of Performance

Adjusting performance for student characteristics and prior performance is a necessary step in evaluating school success. In fact, holding schools accountable for success based on raw measures of performance, such as average graduation rates or Regents' scores, and holding them accountable based on adjusted measures (or value added), i.e., on fixed effects from models of graduation rates or Regents' scores that adjust for student characteristics and prior performance, would lead to very different sets of schools being deemed successful.

To calculate adjusted, fixed effect measures, we estimate models of high school performance, controlling for student characteristics and prior performance. Table 3 shows results for models of the likelihood of graduating and of the English Regents' scores. Coefficients are similar in sign across models, and specific results are described in the appendix.[15]

Table 3. OLS Regression Results: High School Performance of all High School Students.

	English Regents'	Graduated
Female	1.850***	0.083***
	(0.113)	(0.005)
Age as of cohort year	−5.036*	−0.688***
	(2.811)	(0.173)
Age square	0.094	0.017***
	(0.079)	(0.005)
Black	−2.156***	−0.025**
	(0.232)	(0.012)
Hispanic	−1.773***	−0.077***
	(0.208)	(0.008)
Asian	−0.690***	0.016**
	(0.246)	(0.008)
Native American	−2.030**	−0.084**
	(0.824)	(0.035)
Free lunch 8th grade	−0.005	−0.012**
	(0.107)	(0.006)
Reduced lunch 8th grade	−0.112	−0.006
	(0.177)	(0.009)
Native born	1.744***	−0.065***
	(0.398)	(0.016)
Entered system before 9th grade	−0.670*	−0.077***
	(0.387)	(0.016)
Native born* entered system before 9th grade	−2.554***	−0.042***
	(0.383)	(0.015)
ELL	−6.187***	−0.088***
	(0.373)	(0.019)
Native born* ELL	2.432***	0.053**
	(0.506)	(0.021)
Speaks English at home	−0.386***	−0.041***
	(0.145)	(0.007)
PTSE 8th grade	−2.988***	−0.025**
	(0.262)	(0.011)
CTB *z*-score 8th grade	4.636***	0.107***
	(0.119)	(0.005)
CTB *z*-score 8th grade square	−0.231***	−0.023***
	(0.064)	(0.002)
CTB *z*-score 8th grade cube	−0.177***	−0.005***
	(0.022)	(0.001)
CAT *z*-score 8th grade	2.298***	0.145***
	(0.134)	(0.007)
CAT *z*-score 8th grade square	−0.122	−0.021***
	(0.084)	(0.002)

Table 3. (*Continued*)

	English Regents'	Graduated
CAT *z*-score 8th grade cube	−0.237***	−0.016***
	(0.051)	(0.002)
LAB percentile 8th grade	0.030***	0.002***
	(0.005)	(0.000)
Constant	129.732***	6.889***
	(24.564)	(1.514)
Observations	40283	50494
R^2	0.47	0.25
Fixed effects		
Mean	1.05e–08	−4.78e–11
Standard deviation	2.99	0.11
Joint F on fixed effects	26.76***	16.71***

Notes: Robust standard errors are in parentheses. All models include missing dummies for free lunch, time of entry into the system, part-time special education, *z*-scores, and LAB percentile. The Regents' model also includes dummies for the year the Regents' were taken. The number of observations differs across models due to missing data on the Regents'. The graduation model was estimated with the sample of students for whom the Regents' are reported and the results were unchanged.
*Significance at the 10% level;
**Significance at the 5% level;
***Significance at the 1% level.

Using our estimated value-added fixed effects in more detail, we find that even though correlations between the raw and value-added measures of the same outcome are high (close to 0.90), correlations across measures of different high school outcomes are much lower when the value-added measures are compared than when raw measures are compared. This suggests that although the same high schools may at first appear do be doing well (poorly) on all high school measures of success, once measures are adjusted, there are differences that depend on the choice of the indicator of success.

Specifically, comparing raw outcomes suggests that schools that are successful on one high school outcome are generally successful on the others (Table 4, top panel). For example, schools with high Regents' exam scores also have high graduation rates: the Pearson correlations between the outcomes are 0.75 and 0.78, respectively, for English and Sequential 1 (math) Regents' and graduation. This pattern also describes the relationship between the English and Sequential I (math) Regents' scores ($r = 0.79$). Overall, these results suggest that holding schools accountable for one raw high school outcome would lead to roughly the same set of successful

Table 4. Pearson Correlations between High School Outcomes for All Students.

	Graduation	English Regents'	Sequential I Regents'
Raw Measures			
Graduation	1	0.78	0.75
		<0.0001	<0.0001
English Regents'		1	0.79
			<0.0001
Sequential I Regents'			1
Fixed effects			
Graduation	1	0.47	0.50
		<0.0001	<0.0001
English Regents'		1	0.49
			<0.0001
Sequential I Regents'			1

Note: Underlying regressions control for student characteristics.

schools as holding schools accountable for another raw high school outcome.

Caution is warranted, however. Value-added measures of high school outcomes are much less correlated than unadjusted measures (Table 4, bottom panel). Indeed, the correlations among the value-added fixed effects from the graduation and Regents' models fall to around 0.50 (versus close to 0.80 for the unadjusted, raw measures). Thus it is important to consider a range of high school outcomes when assessing the success of a school, and it is critical that these outcomes be adjusted for factors outside the control of schools.

5.2. High School and College Value-Added Outcomes of Enrollees are Not Highly Correlated

Next, we use value-added measures to evaluate how successful high schools are with the students they send to CUNY, on both their high school and college outcomes. Once again, the value-added measures are estimated in a series of student-level regressions with school fixed effects, controlling for student characteristics and prior performance and estimated using a sample restricted to CUNY enrollees (Table 5). Results of these regressions are described in detail in the appendix.

Table 5. OLS Regression Results: High School and College Performance of Enrolled CUNY Students.

	GPA	Verbal SAT	English Regents'
Female	0.200***	−2.428**	1.680***
	(0.015)	(1.209)	(0.140)
Age as of cohort year	−0.374	−78.709***	−2.919
	(0.251)	(27.912)	(3.372)
Age square	0.010	1.762**	0.050
	(0.007)	(0.770)	(0.095)
Black	−0.168***	−17.534***	−1.664***
	(0.027)	(3.178)	(0.259)
Hispanic	−0.158***	−7.183**	−0.961***
	(0.022)	(2.846)	(0.219)
Asian	−0.050**	−12.928***	−0.823***
	(0.022)	(2.950)	(0.226)
Native American	−0.315*	−5.358	−1.961
	(0.188)	(16.040)	(1.276)
Free lunch 8th grade	−0.036	−0.437	0.010
	(0.028)	(2.145)	(0.179)
Reduced lunch 8th grade	−0.068*	0.252	−0.139
	(0.037)	(2.822)	(0.269)
Native born	−0.134***	35.411***	1.674***
	(0.048)	(5.350)	(0.461)
Entered system before 9th grade	−0.044	5.935	−0.308
	(0.050)	(5.132)	(0.436)
Native born* entered system	0.066	−37.138***	−2.225***
Before 9th grade	(0.059)	(6.048)	(0.497)
ELL	−0.012	−67.926***	−4.602***
	(0.040)	(3.672)	(0.407)
Native born* ELL	0.117*	31.643***	2.347***
	(0.070)	(6.844)	(0.515)
Speaks English at home	−0.054***	6.965***	−0.003
	(0.018)	(1.962)	(0.161)
PTSE 8th grade	−0.071	−15.135***	−2.422***
	(0.045)	(5.775)	(0.385)
CTB *z*-score 8th grade	0.130***	57.600***	3.959***
	(0.017)	(1.485)	(0.147)
CTB *z*-score 8th grade square	0.044***	5.314***	0.062
	(0.010)	(1.188)	(0.103)
CTB *z*-score 8th grade cube	−0.023***	−3.849***	−0.182***
	(0.004)	(0.510)	(0.046)
CAT *z*-score 8th grade	0.081***	23.373***	1.895***
	(0.021)	(2.151)	(0.152)
CAT *z*-score 8th grade square	−0.010	1.628*	−0.036
	(0.011)	(0.871)	(0.072)

Table 5. (*Continued*)

	GPA	Verbal SAT	English Regents'
CAT *z*-score 8th grade cube	0.001	−2.798***	−0.156***
	(0.008)	(0.652)	(0.040)
LAB percentile 8th grade	0.001	0.428***	0.033***
	(0.001)	(0.092)	(0.008)
Number of semesters between graduation and enrollment	0.128***		
	(0.016)		
Number of semesters between graduation and enrollment square	−0.011***		
	(0.002)		
Constant	6.424***	1,270.114***	112.014***
	(2.302)	(253.531)	(30.463)
Observations	11,718	10,423	13,150
R^2	0.10	0.56	0.39
Fixed effects			
Mean	2.64e−10	−3.40e−08	3.44e−09
Standard deviation	0.14	23.50	2.36
Joint F for fixed effects	2.12***	6.94***	9.94***

Notes: Robust standard errors are in parentheses. All models include missing dummies for free lunch, time of entry into the system, part-time special education, *z*-scores, and LAB percentile. The Regents' model also includes dummies for the year the Regents' were taken. The number of observations differs across models due to missing data on the Regents' and SAT scores. Models were estimated with the sample of students for whom all three variables are reported ($N = 9{,}292$) and the results were unchanged.

*Significance at the 10% level;

**Significance at the 5% level;

***Significance at the 1% level.

Most of the correlations between the high school and college value-added outcomes of the enrollees are low (Table 6). The GPA fixed effects are somewhat highly correlated with the SAT fixed effects (0.47 with verbal and 0.41 with math), but the correlations drop sharply when the GPA fixed effects are compared to the Regents' scores fixed effects (0.25 with the English Regents' and 0 with the Sequential I (math) Regents').

Cross-tabulations (not reported) of the value-added outcomes divided into three groups of roughly the same size confirm these results. In cross-tabulations of the high school measures of outcome, whether we are looking at high school students or CUNY enrollees, or across the

Table 6. Pearson Correlations between the Fixed Effects from High School and College Outcome Models of CUNY Enrollees.

	English Regents'	Sequential I Regents'	Verbal SAT	Math SAT	GPA
English Regents'	1	0.35 <0.0001	0.54 <0.0001	0.50 <0.0001	0.25 0.00
Sequential I Regents'		1	0.23 0.00	0.43 <0.0001	0.03 0.75
Verbal SAT			1	0.80 <0.0001	0.47 <0.0001
Math SAT				1	0.41 <0.0001
GPA					1

Note: Underlying regressions control for student characteristics.

two samples, close to 50% of the schools, and sometimes as many as 60% of the schools are on the diagonal, i.e., they are in the bottom for both measures, or in the middle for both measures, or at the top for both measures (the numbers are even higher if we examine cross-tabulations of the same outcome across high school students and CUNY enrollees; they can be higher than 90% of the schools). In general, less than 15% of the schools are at the opposite extremes, i.e., are at the top for one measure and the bottom for the other. On the other hand, in cross-tabulations that compare high school to college outcomes, that is fixed effects for the high school outcomes of the enrollees (or the high school students) and for the GPA of enrollees, the percentage of the schools on the diagonal tends to be well below 45% (most often, 36–38%), while the percentage of the schools at the extremes tends to be at least 15% and sometimes over 25%. The SAT and college GPA fixed effects exhibit the highest percentages on the diagonals.

5.3. Focusing on the Enrollees Does Not Bias the Results

High schools may experience different levels of success with the high school outcomes than they do with the college outcomes if the students who enroll in college are systematically different from those who do not. We find, however, that models of high school Regents' performance estimated with

Table 7. Pearson Correlations of Fixed Effects from Outcomes Models for High School Students and CUNY Enrollees.

	Enrollees		
	English	Sequential I	GPA
High school students			
Graduation	0.23	0.29	−0.04
	0.01	0.00	0.61
English	0.89	0.37	0.24
	<0.0001	<0.0001	0.00
Sequential I	0.35	0.88	0.05
	<0.0001	<0.0001	0.51

Note: Underlying regressions control for student characteristics. Enrollees and high school students are different samples.

all high school students are not very different from those estimated with the enrollees (the Regents' are the two outcomes that are available for both subgroups).[16]

Further, Table 7 indicates that the correlation between the fixed effects from the Regents' performance models is very high, 0.89 (using the Sequential I (math) Regents' leads to the same conclusions). This suggests that limiting the sample to the enrollees will not yield misleading conclusions.[17]

5.4. Changing College Performance Models to Control for High School Success Leaves High School Rankings Materially Unaffected

So far, we have compared the fixed effects from models of high school and college performance that control for the performance of students at intake into high school, using their 8th grade test scores. Next, we examine college performance controlling for the high school performance of students (Table 8). Regression results are very similar to those obtained when controlling for 8th grade performance, the one exception being that ELL students have a higher GPA than non-ELL students (this was only true for native-born students when we were controlling for 8th grade performance). The higher the high school scores, the higher the GPA. The fixed effects from this model are extremely highly correlated to the fixed effects from the model of GPA that controls only for 8th grade performance (0.97).

Table 8. OLS Regression Results: Model of College GPA Controlling for High School Success, CUNY Enrollees.

	GPA
Female	0.181***
	(0.015)
Age as of cohort year	−0.185
	(0.241)
Age square	0.005
	(0.007)
Black	−0.111***
	(0.026)
Hispanic	−0.115***
	(0.022)
Asian	−0.068***
	(0.023)
Native American	−0.272
	(0.181)
Free lunch 8th grade	−0.038
	(0.028)
Reduced lunch 8th grade	−0.065*
	(0.036)
Native born	−0.154***
	(0.045)
Entered system before 9th grade	−0.026
	(0.044)
Native born* entered system before 9th grade	0.075
	(0.048)
ELL	0.112***
	(0.041)
Native born* ELL	0.085
	(0.068)
Speaks English at home	−0.049***
	(0.018)
PTSE 8th grade	0.017
	(0.045)
Number of semesters between graduation and enrollment	0.106***
	(0.016)
Number of semesters between graduation and enrollment square	−0.008***
	(0.002)
English Regents' score	0.012***
	(0.001)
Sequential I Regents' score	0.005***
	(0.001)
Verbal SAT	0.001***
	(0.000)
Math SAT	0.000***
	(0.000)

Table 8. (*Continued*)

	GPA
Constant	4.250*
	(2.192)
Observations	11718
R^2	0.14
Fixed effects	
Mean	2.34e−10
Standard deviation	0.12
Joint F for fixed effects	1.84

Notes: Robust standard errors are in parentheses. The model includes missing dummies for free lunch, time of entry into the system, part-time special education, and Regents' and SAT scores. (This model was estimated with the 8th grade scores included as well. Results were almost identical. The one significant difference is that being native born and time of entry into the system have a joint effect on GPA. The correlation between the fixed effects for the two models is 0.9989.)

*Significance at the 10% level;

***Significance at the 1% level.

6. SUMMARY AND DISCUSSION OF RESULTS

6.1. Summary

The roles of U.S. high schools are changing. Toward the middle of the 20th century, American high schools were meant to provide an opportunity to achieve a high school education, but even students who did not or could not avail themselves of this opportunity (that is dropouts) were able to make a decent living. More recently, the public and policymakers seem to have higher ambitions for public high schools, namely to graduate the vast majority of youth. In addition, currently there is considerable discussion of the role of high schools in producing college-ready students, especially since there is some evidence that youths as old as 8th graders overwhelmingly aim to complete college, and additional labor market evidence that even a high school diploma will not land a good job.

Higher ambitions combined with increasingly more stringent accountability standards at the high school level make it important to ascertain if the common measures of high school success are consistent with measures of college success. This paper has presented some early evidence on this issue. We estimate regression-adjusted value-added student outcomes, with high school fixed effects, for a variety of outcomes at both the high school and college levels. In the paper, we report on a subset of these outcomes and find four results.

First, raw unadjusted outcomes of high school success at the high school level (Regents' test results, SAT scores, and graduation rates) correlate well. Second, adjusted, value-added outcomes of high school success at the high school level (Regents' test results, SAT scores, and graduation rates) do not correlate well. Since value-added, adjusted measures are clearly superior to raw outcomes as ways to evaluate the role of a school, this is an unsettling result. Third, when college outcomes (that is college GPAs) are compared to high school outcomes, the correlations with high school SAT scores are around 0.5, but all other correlations are considerably lower. Fourth, these results do not seem to be a product of selection issues, whereby some schools produce college students and others do not.

6.2. Discussion

If policymakers want to measure high school success at producing college students who succeed, they should consider using the already developed and available SAT or ACT test, as has the state of Michigan. A state could pay for all students to take the test and even establish its own criteria for graduation if it desired. This route would use fewer state resources than developing its own tests and would be useful to colleges. High school SAT fixed effects are correlated with college success in our early work and, as reported here, are the best of the alternative ways to assess high school contribution to college success.

If, on the other hand, policymakers want even more from high schools, for example that students not only have aptitude for college work, but also that they have knowledge of a body of material such as how to solve for an unknown in an algebraic equation, or the structure of DNA, or significant events in American history, or identification of important writers etc., then additional tests would be needed. But more tests will be more expensive to administer – to design, implement, and grade – and also more expensive in terms of student, teacher, and other effort. Are they worth it?

If we really do not think all students are capable of completing additional years of education beyond high school, then are measures of college success the right ones on which to base our measures of high school success? Are skills for the marketplace and/or technical training perhaps different than those needed for college success? If they are different, should all high school students be expected to accomplish both types of skills? This will certainly be an expensive proposition if many college students are mechanically or electrically skills "challenged" and, conversely, if many mechanics, repair people, and construction workers are college aptitude "challenged." In order to avoid sorting students by type of work preferred or by aptitude for different kinds of work, how many resources are we willing to expend? This is an old question and harks back to questions of when and if "tracking" should occur and whether technical schools can really prepare students for the workplace or if on-the-job-training is more appropriate. In the U.S., we seem to be headed in the direction of college-ready high school students, but in Europe, this is less true. The advent of stringent accountability for school success may force policymakers and the public to decide if one high school fits all or if there can or should be different kinds of high school education available to students.

The work reported will benefit in the future from additional data on the success of college students, including the majors students choose, their persistence and their graduation rates. In addition, more complete information on college choices that go beyond the CUNY system will be helpful, although 68% of our sample does apply to CUNY and 43% enroll, making the information about CUNY particularly relevant. Knowing the course of study of high school students could be an important measure of high school success since next to the SAT or ACT scores, college admissions offices often claim that the rigor of the course of study predicts admission (and success). Despite all the added information that additional data will provide, however, early evidence indicates that success in college and success on traditional high school indicators are quite different.

NOTES

1. New Exam to Put All Michigan Students on Path to College (2005), Retrieved October 23, from http://www.Michigan.gov.

2. Poverty and special education are included in Marchant and Paulson (2005) in the state-level models.

3. See Rothstein (2004) for an in-depth discussion of selection bias in modeling the relationships between college GPA and SATs.

4. Of course, time invariant unobserved characteristics may represent more than the school's input per se. For example, if parental selection of high schools is unvarying or consistent across schools, and parental characteristics of individual students are not adequately controlled in the fixed effect regression, then the fixed effects will reflect parental selection as well as the school's contribution to value added. We thank Sarah Turner for this insight.

5. New York State currently awards two high school diplomas, a Regents', and a local. The two differ in that receiving a Regents' diploma requires taking additional credits and passing a larger number of Regents' exams.

6. Students are discharged when they leave the NYC public high school system. Most students in this situation (71%) are those who leave the city. Others are

admitted to a parochial or private school or a high school equivalency program, are home-schooled or institutionalized. Some leave the system when they reach 21. Suspension, expulsion, and death are other reasons for discharge.

7. This eliminates 22 schools enrolling a total of 74 students.

8. Note that time of entry into the system is unknown for 9% of the students.

9. This is a higher percentage than that for all New York City students, which is below mid-50 percent, due to the omission of schools and students from our sample as described in previous paragraphs.

10. Note that the ASRs and SBERs provide data for the whole school, while the aggregated student-level data are limited to the students in the 2001 cohort, i.e., students who were expected to graduate in 2001.

11. As noted in the introduction, the Governor of Michigan has announced that all high school students will take the ACT test as a prerequisite for graduation, in part to avoid this disjuncture in measurement.

12. We define as the first semester, the first semester when a student is enrolled in CUNY, takes credits, and earns a GPA.

13. These are only available for students who were in the NYC public school system in the 8th grade (almost 70% of the students). Missing flags are used to maintain the sample size.

14. These models do not include the number of semesters between high school graduation and CUNY enrollment.

15. SAT scores are available for CUNY applicants only, so we cannot estimate these models for all students.

16. Comparing the results from the English Regents' regressions for the enrollees and the high school students, we find only a few cases where a variable that does not affect the enrollees affects high school students. For example, for the latter, the Regents' scores decrease as age increases; they are lower for Native Americans and, surprisingly, for students who speak English at home; and students who entered the system after 9th grade do better than the rest of the students.

17. Note also from the last column in this table that high value added on the high school outcomes when all students are considered seems unrelated to value added on the GPA of enrollees. This may reflect the fact that students who choose to enroll in CUNY are not a random sample of the high school population, where different students enroll in more or less selective colleges, or choose not to enroll.

18. This is also true of the Sequential I Regents' score model (not reported). Other notable results from this model include the fact that Asians outperform the other students, and so do the poor, surprisingly.

19. Models with other dependent variables (math SAT and Sequential I Regents', available from the authors) yielded only slightly different results.

ACKNOWLEDGMENTS

We thank Sarah Turner, Norm Fruchter, Dorothy Siegel and the research workshop of the Institute for Education and Social Policy, New York University, for helpful suggestions. We are solely responsible for the paper's content.

REFERENCES

Bailey, T., & Weininger, E. B. (2002). Performance, graduation, and transfer of immigrants and natives in City University of New York Community Colleges. *Educational Evaluation and Policy Analysis*, *24*, 359–377.

Bartelsman, E. J., & Doms, M. (2000). Understanding productivity: Lessons from longitudinal microdata. *Journal of Economic Literature*, *37*, 569–594.

Betts, J. R., & Morell, D. (1999). The determinants of undergraduate grade point average: The relative importance of family background, high school resources, and peer group effects. *Journal of Human Resources*, *34*, 268–293.

Cohn, E., Cohn, S., Balch, D. C., & Bradley, J. (2004). Determinants of undergraduate GPAs: SAT scores, high-school GPA and high-school rank. *Economics of Education Review*, *23*, 577–586.

Ehlert, M., & Podgursky, M. (2005). What happens if they aren't "proficient?" The predictive validity of a high school state assessment. Paper presented at the Third Research Seminar in Analytic Issues in the Assessment of Student Achievement. The Urban Institute, Washington, DC, May 2.

Goldhaber, D. D., & Brewer, D. J. (1997). Why don't schools and teachers seem to matter? Assessing the impact of unobservables on educational productivity. *Journal of Human Resources*, *32*, 505–523.

Gramlich, E. M. (1976). The New York City Fiscal Crisis: What happened and what is to be done? *American Economic Review*, *66*, 415–429.

Horowitz, J. B., & Spector, L. (2005). Is there a difference between private and public education on college performance? *Economics of Education Review*, *24*, 189–195.

Kornblut, A. E. (2005). Bush urges rigorous high school testing. *The New York Times*, January 13, 26.

Ladd, H. F., & Walsh, R. P. (2002). Implementing value-added measures of school performance: Getting the incentives right. *Economics of Education Review*, *21*, 1–18.

Lee, V. E., & Smith, J. B. (1997). High school size: Which works best and for whom? *Educational Evaluation and Policy Analysis*, *19*, 205–227.

Marchant , G. J., & Paulson, S. E. (2005). The Relationship of High School Graduation Exams to Graduation Rates and SAT Scores. Education Policy Analysis Archives, 13. Retrieved August 24, 2005 from http://epaa.asu.edu/epaa/v13n6/

Rothstein, J. M. (2004). College performance predictions and the SAT. *Journal of Econometrics*, *121*, 297–317.

Rubenstein, R., Schwartz, A. E., & Stiefel, L. (1998). Conceptual and Empirical Issues in the Measurement of School Efficiency. *Proceedings of the 91st annual conference on taxation* (pp. 267–274). Washington, DC: National Tax Association.

Rumberger, R. W., & Palardy, G. J. (2005). Test scores, dropout rates, and transfer rates as alternative indicators of high school performance. *American Educational Research Journal*, *42*, 3–42.

Stiefel, L., Bel Hadj Amor, H., & Schwartz, A. E. (2005). Best Schools, worst schools, and school efficiency: A reconciliation and assessment of alternative classification systems. In: W. J. Fowler (Ed.), *Developments in school finance, 2004* (pp. 81–101). Washington, DC: U.S. Department of Education, Office of Educational Research and Improvement, National Center for Education Statistics.

Stiefel, L., Rubenstein, R., & Schwartz, A. E. (1999). Using adjusted performance measures for evaluating resource use. *Public Budgeting and Finance*, *19*, 67–87.

Stiefel, L., Rubenstein, R., & Schwartz, A. E. (2003). Better than raw: A guide to measuring organizational performance with adjusted performance measures. *Public Administration Review*, *63*, 607–615.

Stiefel, L., Schwartz, A. E., Bel Hadj Amor, H., & Kim, D. Y. (2005). Adjusted measures of school performance: A cross-state perspective. In: L. Stiefel, A. E. Schwartz, R. Rubenstein & J. Zabel (Eds), *Measuring school performance and efficiency: Implications for practice and research, 2005 Yearbook of American Education Finance Association* (pp. 17–36). Larchmont, NY: Eye on Education.

Warren, J. R., & Edwards, M. R. (2003). The impact of high stakes graduation tests on high school diploma acquisition. Paper prepared for presentation at the 4th annual undergraduate research symposium at the University of Washington, May 2001.

APPENDIX: REGRESSION RESULTS

Models of high school performance (likelihood of graduating and English Regents' scores), controlling for student characteristics and prior performance, as reported in Table 3, are similar overall. The relationship with age varies: while the English Regents' score decreases consistently as age increases, the likelihood of graduation decreases as students age to 20, then increases.[18] Asians are more likely to graduate than other students, but their English Regents' scores are lower than those of the other students. The English Regents' are not affected by poverty, and poor students are less likely to graduate than the rest of the students. Immigrant status, the time of entry into the system, and ELL status interact differently in the way they affect the outcomes. One common finding is that ELL students tend to be worse off, especially if they entered the system before 9th grade.

The student-level models with school fixed effects, controlling for student characteristics and prior performance, and estimated using a sample restricted to CUNY enrollees (Table 5) show that females score higher than males on the English Regents', yet they have lower verbal SAT scores than males have, in spite of which they achieve higher GPAs than males do. Age only affects the SAT score, which decreases as students age between 14 and 22, then increases for students between the ages of 22 and 24. Not surprisingly, White students do better than all the other students, and Black students do worse than White, Hispanic, and Asian students. Asians outperform Hispanics on the GPA and Regents', but Hispanics do better on the SAT. Native Americans have the lowest GPAs, but their Regents' and SATs are no different from those of Whites. Interestingly, for the most part, the performance of poor students is on a level with that of non-poor students, except that students who received a reduced-price lunch in the 8th grade have lower GPAs than the rest of the students. While this may suggest that the poor have overcome their academic disadvantage by high school, it may instead reflect the fact that the free lunch data do not fully capture poverty, and caution should be used in interpreting these coefficients.

Native-born students have lower GPAs than foreign-born students, and those among them who are not English language learners do worse than the rest (−0.134 versus −0.02). Time of entry into the system does not affect a student's GPAs. This may be due to enough time passing before college entrance, since time of entry into the system does affect high school outcomes – Regents' scores and SATs.

There is an even more complex relationship between the Regents' and verbal SAT scores, and whether students are native-born, ELL, and their time of entry into the system. The reference group is foreign-born students who enter the system after the 9th grade and are not ELL. One group only outperforms these students, and they are the native-born students who also entered the system after the 9th grade and are not ELL. One other group has a comparable performance to the reference group, and these are foreign-born students who are not ELL but entered the system before the 9th grade. All the other subgroups of students do worse than the reference group on these measures, with foreign-born ELL students doing particularly poorly. Interestingly, students who speak English at home do better on the SATs but worse on their college GPA. Their Regents' scores are not affected.

Students who received part-time special education services in the 8th grade do worse on the Regents' and SATs, but their GPA is unaffected, suggesting that this handicap has been overcome by the time these students reach college, perhaps thanks to the additional services they received in middle school.

The relationships between the outcomes and most 8th grade test scores are non-linear, suggesting that outcomes increase then decrease with 8th grade scores depending on the levels of those scores. The one simpler relationship suggests that GPA increases consistently as 8th grade math scores increase. The GPA is unaffected by 8th grade LAB scores, while Regents' and SAT scores decrease as LAB scores increase.[19]

EFFICIENCY AND PERFORMANCE IN TEXAS PUBLIC SCHOOLS

Timothy J. Gronberg, Dennis W. Jansen and George S. Naufal

ABSTRACT

Do high ratings based upon traditional performance measures go hand in hand with efficiency? This paper addresses this question using stochastic production frontier methods. We utilize a six-year panel of test score, school input, and school student characteristics data for a sample of 3,000 campuses in Texas. We generate estimates of school-specific efficiency based upon the estimates of the one-sided school specific error term in a stochastic production frontier model. School rankings on the basis of estimated efficiency are not well correlated with school rankings on the basis of traditional measures of school performance.

INTRODUCTION

The efficiency of public schools is a topic closely tied to a host of public policy issues and intertwined with attempts to measure or quantify the performance of public schools. Performance of public schools is often measured in public policy circles by student performance on standardized tests, with student performance judged relative to an absolute standard. Meanwhile,

Improving School Accountability: Check-Ups or Choice
Advances in Applied Microeconomics, Volume 14, 81–101

ISSN: 0278-0984/doi:10.1016/S0278-0984(06)14004-3

school efficiency is often judged based on expenditures per pupil, and usually by comparison of expenditure per pupil to some indicators of performance. Student performance and resource efficiency are, obviously, not independent features of a school, but they are not redundant either. In designing a system of school accountability, indicators of both student outcomes and efficient utilization of resources should be included.

Judging school test performance or school efficiency is particularly challenging, since student and home inputs into the production of academic outputs are reasonably modeled as being exogenous to the school producer. Many economists would argue that a value-added approach to measuring performance, or some related method for judging school performance is required. These approaches include controls for differences in student and home inputs and endowments, and perhaps peer characteristics in an attempt to parse out the impact of the publicly provided school inputs. Further, economists would suggest measuring efficiency relative to the value-added performance measure, so that resource management is evaluated relative to the exogenous factors of the production environment.

There are several approaches to this topic, but here we will look at efficiency from a school production function perspective and using data from Texas. We consider several alternative specifications and derive measures of school efficiency for each. We compare these measures of efficiency and discuss the correlation of efficiency measures from different production function specifications and estimations. We also explore the relationship among common indicators of student performance and our estimated indicators of production efficiency.

SCHOOL PRODUCTION FUNCTIONS

Standard Non-Frontier Approach

The school production function maps inputs into a school output. We denote school output as $Y_{s,g,t}$ = performance of school s, grade g, year t. Inputs consist of student inputs, family inputs, and school inputs. Student inputs are $S_{s,g,t}$ = student characteristics at school s, grade g, year t, family inputs are $F_{s,g,t}$ = family characteristics at school s, grade g, year t, and school inputs are denoted as $X_{s,g,t}$.

Drawing upon the analysis of Todd and Wolpin (2003), the school production function can be written in general form as

$$Y_{s,g,t} = f(S_{s,g}(t),\ F_{s,g}(t),\ X_{s,g}(t)) \tag{1}$$

where $S_{s,g}(t)$, $F_{s,g}(t)$, and $X_{s,g}(t)$ represent the complete input histories up to time t of student, family, and school inputs, respectively.

We have data on student achievement by school, grade, and year. This panel data set can be used to estimate specific forms of Eq. (1). In particular, we will estimate a log-linear form of (1) that allows a different production relationship for each grade level. This is

$$\begin{aligned} Y_{s,g,t} = \beta_{0,g} + \beta_{1,g} Y_{s,g-1,t-1} + \beta_{2,g} S_{s,g,t} + \beta_{3,g} F_{s,g,t} \\ + \beta_{4,g} X_{s,g,t} + T_{g,t} + C_{g,s} + \varepsilon_{s,g,t} \end{aligned} \tag{2}$$

where Y, S, F, and X are all measured as log transforms of the raw data. In this value-added specification, $Y_{s,g,t}$ or student performance on test scores for school s, grade g, year t, is the dependent variable. Explanatory variables include the lagged test score $Y_{s,g-1,t-1}$, where the lag is over both year and grade. The lagged test score is included here as a sufficient statistic summarizing the effect of the unobserved input histories. The difference between $Y_{s,g,t}$ and $Y_{s,g-1,t-1}$ would reflect the change in performance at a given school of a given cohort of students as they advance a grade with the change in year. Other explanatory variables include contemporaneous student and family characteristics, school characteristics, and both year and campus fixed effects, represented by $T_{g,t}$ and $C_{g,s}$, respectively.

A version of this basic formulation has been used by Schwartz and Zabel (2005) to generate efficiency rankings of elementary schools in New York City. Student performance in grade g at year t depends in part on student performance in grade $g-1$ at year $t-1$. The campus fixed effect $C_{g,s}$ measures the difference between student performance and the predicted performance based on all the other explanatory variables, and as such can be thought of as a measure of school efficiency. In fact, it is a measure of the impact of everything else that is left out of the regression as well as any campus-specific efficiency.

We follow Schwartz and Zabel in allowing coefficients to differ across grades, thereby allowing grade-specific production functions. We include a time effect that allows changes in productivity over years and by grade.

An important special case of the above model has $\beta_{1,g} = 1$. This is commonly referred to as a gain model. Using the coefficient restriction, we can rewrite (2) as

$$\begin{aligned} Y_{s,g,t} - Y_{s,g-1,t-1} = \beta_{0,g} + \beta_{2,g} S_{s,g,t} + \beta_{3,g} F_{s,g,t} + \beta_{4,g} X_{s,g,t} \\ + T_{g,t} + C_{g,s} + \varepsilon_{s,g,t} \end{aligned} \tag{3}$$

To estimate Eq. (2), we consider several issues. First, Eq. (2) has a lagged dependent variable, and OLS estimation of (2) could lead to inconsistent coefficient estimates due to potential correlation between $Y_{s,g-1,t-1}$ and $C_{g,s}$. The problem of inconsistency associated with lagged dependent variables as regressors in a dynamic panel model are well known (Anderson & Hsiao, 1981). The model in Eq. (2) is, however, not a classical dynamic panel model. The lagged dependent variable is both time lagged and grade lagged. The equation for production in the previous grade in the previous year is

$$\begin{aligned} Y_{s,g-1,t-1} = \beta_{0,g-1} + \beta_{1,g-1} Y_{s,g-2,t-2} + \beta_{2,g-1} S_{g-1,t-1} \\ + \beta_{3,g-1} F_{s,g-1,t-1} + \beta_4 X_{s,g-1,t-1} + T_{g-1,t-1} \\ + C_{s,g-1} + \varepsilon_{s,g-1,t-1} \end{aligned} \tag{4}$$

Thus $Y_{s,g-1,t-1}$ is correlated with $C_{s,g-1}$, but is not necessarily correlated with $C_{s,g}$.

Schwartz and Zabel (2005) attack the estimation problem by conventional dynamic panel methods. Under their approach, we first transform the model to eliminate the fixed effect by time-differencing as follows:

$$\begin{aligned} Y_{s,g,t} - Y_{s,g,t-1} = \beta_{1,g}(Y_{s,g-1,t-1} - Y_{s,g-1,t-2}) + \beta_{2,g}(S_{s,g,t} - S_{s,g,t-1}) \\ + \beta_{3,g}(F_{s,g,t} - F_{s,g,t-1}) + \beta_{4,g}(X_{s,g,t} - X_{s,g,t-1}) \\ + (T_{g,t} - T_{g,t-1}) + (\varepsilon_{s,g,t} - \varepsilon_{s,g,t-1}) \end{aligned} \tag{5a}$$

or

$$\begin{aligned} \Delta_t Y_{s,g,t} = \beta_{1,g} \Delta_t Y_{s,g-1,t-1} + \beta_{2,g} \Delta_t S_{s,g,t} \\ + \beta_{3,g} \Delta_t F_{s,g,t} + \beta_{4,g} \Delta_t X_{s,g,t} + \Delta_t T_{g,t} + \Delta_t \varepsilon_{s,g,t} \end{aligned} \tag{5b}$$

The differencing procedure holds grade fixed, and thus the grade-specific fixed effect is differenced-out. Estimation still requires an instrument for $\Delta_t Y_{s,g-1,t-1}$, because $\Delta_t \varepsilon_{s,g,t}$. and $\Delta_t Y_{s,g-1,t-1}$ are likely to be correlated. The first term contains $\varepsilon_{s,g,t-1}$ and the second contains $\varepsilon_{s,g-1,t-1}$. A common campus-specific effect in year $t-1$ that affects grades g and $g-1$ will generate this correlation and the need for an instrument. Fortunately, we can apply the well-known Arellano and Bond (1991) estimator which is based upon the Anderson and Hsiao (1981) proposal of $Y_{s,g-2,t-2}$ and $\Delta_t Y_{s,g-2,t-2}$ as instruments in this situation. Both are uncorrelated with $\Delta_t \varepsilon_{s,g,t}$, assuming that the errors are serially uncorrelated, and are correlated with $\Delta_t Y_{s,g-1,t-1}$. If additional lags of the dependent variable are available, then there can be further efficiency gains by including them in the estimation as well.

As noted by Schwartz and Zabel, there is another potential bias issue involved in estimating the difference model. If there is measurement error in the test score, then $Y_{s,g-1,t-1}$ is correlated with the error term $\varepsilon_{s,g,t}$, and then

$Y_{s,g-2,t-2}$ will be correlated with $\varepsilon_{s,g-1,t-1}$. In this case, a strategy of using $\Delta_t Y_{s,g-2,t-2}$ and $Y_{s,g-2,t-2}$ as instruments is not available, because both will be correlated with $\Delta_t \varepsilon_{s,g,t}$. In this case, we would want to use $\Delta_t Y_{s,g-1,t-3}$ and $Y_{s,g-1,t-3}$ as instruments. Note, however, that this means we are using three years of lags just to form the instruments for our regression, imposing severe degrees of freedom constraints.

Under this estimation strategy, the campus fixed effects, which are the objects of primary interest in an efficiency evaluation, have been differenced-out. The estimated fixed effect for each school is obtained by taking the mean difference between the predicted and actual value of the dependent variable for a given campus over the length of the panel.

Stochastic Frontier Approach

The standard approach above generates a set of estimated campus fixed effects, and we can interpret these as estimates of the relative efficiency of the schools in the sample. Efficiency in this case is measured relative to the average school efficiency. A well-established alternative strategy for evaluating technical efficiency is to utilize production frontier methods. We adopt a stochastic frontier approach as the key point of departure in our analysis. As presented in Khumbakar and Lovell (2000), the stochastic production frontier model can be written as

$$Y_i = f(x_i;\ \beta) \cdot \exp\{v_i\} \cdot TE_i \tag{6}$$

where $f(x_i;\ \beta) \cdot \exp\{v_i\}$ is the stochastic production frontier. The production frontier $f(x_i;\ \beta)$ is, itself, taken to be deterministic. The second term, $\exp\{v_i\}$, adds producer-specific exogenous random shocks that impact the ability of the firm to reach the production frontier. The final term represents technical efficiency, and is thus measured as the ratio of observed output to the maximum feasible output attainable in an environment captured by $\exp\{v_i\}$. If we specify the deterministic production frontier as in Eq. (1), and if we assume further a specific log-linear functional form as in Eq. (2), the stochastic education production frontier model becomes

$$\begin{aligned} Y_{s,g,t} = \beta_{0,g} + \beta_{1,g} Y_{s,g-1,t-1} + \beta_{2,g} S_{s,g,t} + \beta_{3,g} F_{s,g,t} \\ + \beta_{4,g} X_{s,g,t} + T_{g,t} + C_{g,s} + v_{s,g,t} - u_{s,g} \end{aligned} \tag{7}$$

where $v_{s,g,t}$ represents random statistical noise and the one-sided error $u_{s,g} \geq 0$ represents technical inefficiency.

We consider two different approaches to modeling the error structure in (7). The simplest approach is to treat $u_{s,g}$ as a bounded fixed effect. We address potential consistency concerns by instrumenting for $Y_{s,g-1,t-1}$ with two-period and higher lagged regressors. We then estimate the model in (7) using the predicted values from the instrumental variable estimation. We utilize two different estimators: least squares, with $u_{s,g}$ treated as a dummy variable, and maximum likelihood, with $u_{s,g}$ assumed to be distributed as non-negative half normal. The second approach is to treat $u_{s,g}$ as a random effect. A potential problem with the fixed effects model is the confounding of time-invariant technical efficiency with other time-invariant production factors. This concern would extend to both excluded time-invariant factors and included factors, which are nearly time invariant. The two-step generalized least-squares (GLS) estimator of the random effects model allows for the presence of such time-invariant factors. This advantage comes at the cost of assuming that the $u_{s,g}$ are uncorrelated with the regressors, an assumption which is not required under the fixed effects approach. The random effect model takes the form

$$\begin{aligned} Y_{s,g,t} &= [\beta_{0,g} - E(u_{s,g})] + \beta_{1,g} Y_{s,g-1,t-1} + \beta_{2,g} S_{s,g,t} + \beta_{3,g} F_{s,g,t} \\ &\quad + \beta_{4,g} X_{s,g,t} + T_{g,t} + C_{g,s} + v_{s,g,t} - [u_{s,g} - E(u_{s,g})] \\ &= \beta^{*}_{0,g} + \beta_{1,g} Y_{s,g-1,t-1} + \beta_{2,g} S_{s,g,t} + \beta_{3,g} F_{s,g,t} + \beta_{4,g} X_{s,g,t} \\ &\quad + T_{g,t} + C_{s,g} + v_{s,g,t} - u^{*}_{s,g} \end{aligned}$$

For both the fixed effect and random effect approaches, the estimates of technical efficiency, TE, are obtained by first normalizing the producer-specific effect estimates, $u_{s,g}$, relative to the maximum values under each model. These normalized estimates of the one-sided errors are then used to generate producer-specific estimates of technical efficiency by calculating

$$TE_{s,g} = \exp\{-\hat{u}_{s,g}\}$$

DATA

We obtained math and reading scores for students attending traditional public schools in Texas between the 1996 and 2002 academic years. These data were provided by the Texas Education Agency. The scores are the Texas Learning Index (TLI) adjusted values to the raw scores on the statewide TAAS tests. The TAAS tests were administered to all Texas public school students in grades 3 through 8 and grade 10.[1] The TAAS tests are criterion-referenced tests designed to assess basic grade-level proficiency in math and reading. The TAAS tests were replaced by the TAKS tests in 2003, and the change in testing regime determined the endpoint of our data series. The TLI is a statistic derived from raw TAAS scores that allows comparisons across years and grades. A TLI score of 70 or above is considered a passing score. The pass rate on the TAAS tests has been an important component of the school scorecard for assessment purposes since the introduction of the statewide testing system in 1994.

Unlike many of the previous studies of school performance, we will use the campus rather than the district as the unit of observation. This study uses a balanced panel of 2,266 elementary schools serving third, fourth, and fifth grades during 1994–1995 through 2001–2002. We limit the sample to non-charter schools and to those schools with at least 100 students enrolled. We also dropped all schools that do not have both reading and math scores for that period. This data set was assembled from three different sources. We use data on test scores from the student-level data. School characteristics and resources were extracted from the Texas Education Agency (TEA) campus-level data and from the teachers- and administrators-level data. We also use the student-level data for the student characteristics.

School characteristics include school enrollment, expenditures, teacher–pupil ratio, and percentages of certified teachers, with masters and with more than two years of experience in the district. Student characteristics include variables on grade-specific student background on gender, race, immigrant status, free lunch eligibility, and test scores.

SCHOOL AND STUDENT CHARACTERISTICS

We present summary statistics on a number of school characteristics for academic year 2002 in Table 1. There is a striking degree of heterogeneity across campuses in Texas. While the average campus enrolls 550 students, the largest campus is almost three times that size, and the smallest campus enrolls only 106. Spending on instruction – teachers and staff – averages \$3,564, but varies widely between a low of \$1,297 and a high of \$7,475. The teacher–pupil ratio also displays considerable variation, with a low of 0.04 and a high of 0.14. The student-weighted mean value of 0.06 implies an average fifth-grade classroom of 17 students.

Student demographics also display significant heterogeneity across fifth-grade campuses. Although the average fifth grade is roughly 60% economically disadvantaged, there are campuses with zero poor students (as measured by reported reduced or free lunch eligibility) and other campuses with all poor students. The percentage of students identified as special

Table 1. Descriptive Statistics Academic Year 2001–2002: Averages are Student-Weighted Means.

Variable	Observations	Mean	Minimum	Maximum
Test scores (TLI scores)				
Grade 3				
Reading	2,266	82.6	58.3	92.7
Math	2,266	80.8	55.9	90.9
Grade 4				
Reading	2,266	87.0	69.2	96.2
Math	2,266	83.1	69.3	90.0
Grade 5				
Reading	2,266	88.7	68.8	98.5
Math	2,266	85.9	73.9	91.5
School characteristics and resources				
Total enrollment	2,266	549.70	106	1550
Operating expenditures per pupil in U.S. dollars	2,266	$4,632.5	$2,033	$10,965
Instructional expenditures per pupil in U.S. dollars	2,266	$3489.1	$1,297	$7,475
Teacher–pupil ratio	2,266	0.06	0.04	0.14
Percent certified teachers	2,266	88.04	54.00	100.00
Percent teachers with more than five years of experience	2,266	64.16	13.00	100.00
Percent teachers with more than two years in the district	2,266	57.11	9.43	97.14
Percent teachers with master's degree or higher	2,266	18.99	0.00	70.73
Student characteristics grade 5				
Percent special education students	2,266	7.00	0.00	61.11
Percent students having reading scores	2,266	94.16	61.11	100.00
Percent students having math test scores	2,266	95.12	66.25	100.00
Percent female students	2,266	50.15	18.18	78.57
Percent students eligible for reduced-price or free lunch	2,266	58.08	0.00	100.00
Percent Black students	2,266	14.91	0.00	100.00
Percent Hispanic students	2,266	47.48	0.00	100.00
Percent mobile students	2,266	2.04	0.00	84.78

education varies widely, with a minimum of zero and a maximum of 61%. Racial diversity is also prevalent. As is often the case, the average figures of 15% and 45% for Black students and Hispanic students, respectively, is misleading. Most campuses are much more racially homogeneous, with some campuses having no Blacks and/or no Hispanics, and others composed of 100% Black or Hispanic students.

RESULTS

We first estimate the standard non-frontier model. We provide results for a simple OLS estimation of Eq. (2), which, following Schwartz and Zabel, we refer to as the FE model, results using the instrumental variables panel estimator (DIFF), and results for a GAIN model specification. Our results here provide a benchmark comparison to the results for New York City schools found in Schwartz and Zabel (2005) using our Texas school data.[2] We then take the same data to estimate a stochastic frontier model of elementary school production.

Non-Frontier Model

Our focus is upon the campus fixed effects estimates, which form the basis for the efficiency rankings for schools under the non-frontier methodology. We do, however, provide a look at a few key coefficient estimates in Table 2.

The insignificant coefficients on the two aggregate input variables are consistent with a number of studies in the large education production function literature (a classic summary of the early contributions to that literature is found in Hanushek (1986)). The coefficient on the lagged test score is significantly different from zero for both the FE and DIFF estimators. The FE and DIFF alternatives yield a similar test score lag structure for fourth grade, but significantly different lag structures for fifth grade. For all four of the estimates, the GAIN specification restriction of a coefficient of one on the lagged score is rejected. Schwartz and Zabel (2005) also find insignificant marginal effects for the teacher–pupil ratio and non-instructional spending, and they also reject the GAIN model.

What is the relationship among the fixed effect estimates – here interpreted as efficiency estimates – for our three estimation methods? We provide simple correlation evidence in Table 3. Within a grade, the efficiency measures are not highly correlated. Perhaps the most surprising feature of these findings is the very weak correlation between fixed effect and difference

Table 2. Selected Coefficient Estimates for Non-Frontier Education Production Function.

	Grade 4			Grade 5		
	FE	DIFF	GAIN	FE	DIFF	GAIN
Log-lagged test score	0.426*** (0.004)	0.409*** (0.052)	—	0.448*** (0.004)	0.142* (0.084)	—
Log-teacher-pupil ratio	0.189 (0.217)	0.298 (0.316)	−0.073 (0.263)	0.293 (0.197)	0.127 (0.281)	0.122 (0.235)
Log-non-teacher operating expenditure	0.239 (0.217)	0.332 (0.316)	−0.028 (0.263)	0.341* (0.197)	0.123 (0.280)	0.159 (0.235)
Number of observations	15,400	8,145	15,400	15,400	8,145	15,400
R^2	0.512	0.041	0.041	0.563	0.050	0.047

Notes:

(1) Dependent variables for the FE, DIFF, and GAIN equations are deviations from means of level, difference, and gain test scores, all in logarithmic form.

(2) Regressions also include total enrollment; year dummies; the percentage of students who are enrolled in full-time special education programs; the percentages of teachers certified, with master's degrees and higher, with more than five years of teaching experience, and working more than two years in their current district; and the percentage of grade-level students who are female, free or reduced-price lunch eligible, Black, Hispanic, and recent immigrants. All variables are expressed as deviation from means.

(3) Log-lagged test scores in the DIFF equations are instrumented by the third log-lags test scores.

(4) Standard errors are reported in parentheses.

*Significance at the 10% level;

***Significance at the 1% level.

Table 3. Pearson Correlation Coefficients between School-Efficiency Measures ($N = 2{,}266$).

	Grade 4 FE	Grade 5 FE	Grade 4 DIFF	Grade 5 DIFF	Grade 4 GAIN	Grade 5 GAIN
Grade 4 FE	1.00					
Grade 5 FE	0.46	1.00				
Grade 4 DIFF	−0.43	−0.05	1.00			
Grade 5 DIFF	0.01	−0.48	0.10	1.00		
Grade 4 GAIN	0.31	0.11	−0.07	0.01	1.00	
Grade 5 GAIN	0.13	0.24	0.21	−0.01	0.24	1.00

Table 4. Pearson Correlation Coefficient between School-Efficiency Measure and Average of Reading and Math Test Score ($N = 2{,}266$).

	Level		Difference		Gain	
	Grade 4	Grade 5	Grade 4	Grade5	Grade 4	Grade 5
FE	−0.20	−0.29	0.83	0.86	0.24	0.26
DIFF	−0.16	−0.10	−0.20	−0.29	−0.03	−0.12
GAIN	−0.10	−0.12	0.04	0.02	0.12	0.02

Note: Correlations are based on school-efficiency measures generated from the FE, DIFF, or GAIN model and seven-year average level, difference, or gain test score.

model efficiency estimates. Since the FE and DIFF models are, fundamentally, alternative approaches to estimating the same structural model, this lack of correlation is unanticipated. This lack of correlation also runs counter to the very strong correlation between the efficiency measures based upon these two approaches for the New York sample employed by Schwartz and Zabel. We suspect that our results reflect the potentially weak instrumenting in our DIFF model, as our first stage regression R^2 measures are low (around 0.10).

We also find low correlations between grade 4 and grade 5 efficiency estimates, particularly for the DIFF and GAIN cases. This result indicates that grade-specific production function estimation may be important, in that efficiency estimates vary so much across grades at the same school.

As noted in the introduction, measures of student performance and measures of school efficiency represent two alternative dimensions of potential school accountability. A natural question arises as to the relationship between the two types of accountability measures. We look at the evidence from our Texas sample in Table 4. The general message here is that common test-score measures of performance and our estimated measures of efficiency are not at all correlated. The one exception is that the FE efficiency measures are highly correlated with the DIFF test-score outcomes measures. Our results contrast with those of Schwartz and Zabel, who found the highest correlation between their FE measures and test-score levels in their New York sample.

Stochastic Frontier Model

We estimate the stochastic frontier model as represented in Eq. (7). A selected set of coefficient estimates is reported in Table 5. The estimated input effects are fairly consistent in magnitude across the three estimation

Table 5. Selected Coefficient Estimates for Frontier Educators Productivity Function.

	Grade 4			Grade 5		
	FE: OLS	FE: MLE	RE	FE: OLS	FE: MLE	RE
Log-lagged test score	0.555***	0.616***	0.641***	0.432***	0.495***	0.536***
	(0.010)	(0.009)	(0.009)	(0.009)	(0.008)	(0.008)
Log-teacher-pupil ratio	−0.030***	−0.008**	−0.013***	−0.012***	−0.005*	−0.007***
	(0.005)	(0.003)	(0.003)	(0.004)	(0.002)	(0.003)
Log-non-teacher operating expenditure	0.001	0.003***	0.003***	0.001	0.005***	0.003***
	(0.002)	(0.001)	(0.001)	(0.001)	(0.001)	(0.001)
Number of observations	10,869	10,869	10,869	10,869	10,869	10,869
R^2	0.46	—	0.52	0.48	—	0.56
Log-likelihood	—	37,316.4	—	—	40,738.3	—

Notes:

(1) Regressions also include total enrollment; year dummies; the percentage of students who are enrolled in full-time special education programs; the percentages of teachers certified, with master's degrees and higher, with more than five years of teaching experience, and working more than two years in their current district; and the percentage of grade-level students who are female, free or reduced-price lunch eligible, Black, Hispanic, and recent immigrants.

(2) Log-lagged test scores are instrumented with log-test scores $t-2$, $g-1$ and log-test scores $t-3$, $g-1$.

(3) Standard errors are reported in parentheses.

*Significance at the 10% level;

**Significance at the 5% level;

***Significance at the 1% level.

approaches. The lagged test score is significant, significantly different from one, and coefficient estimates are not statistically different from one another for all the three models. The teacher–pupil ratio is significant in all the three models. It is also negative, a result which runs counter to standard economic reasoning. Non-instructional operating expenditures are positively and significantly related to score performance in two of the three sets of estimates.

Our major interest is in the efficiency estimates. We provide summary statistics for the distribution of the efficiency estimates across the three models in Table 6. We also display the complete distribution for the fifth-grade sample for each of the three models in Figs. 1–3. The distribution of least-squares fixed effect estimates and the generalized least-squares random effect estimates (both with an instrumented lagged test score) are remarkably

Table 6. Descriptive Statistics for Efficiency Measures.

Efficiency Measures	Observations	Mean	Standard Deviation	Minimum	Maximum
FE OLS: Grade 4	2,266	0.895	0.026	0.785	1.00
FE OLS: Grade 5	2,266	0.896	0.027	0.784	1.00
FE MLE: Grade 4	2,266	0.992	0.003	0.970	0.998
FE MLE: Grade 5	2,266	0.993	0.003	0.966	0.998
RE: Grade 4	2,266	0.903	0.022	0.807	1.00
RE: Grade 5	2,266	0.905	0.022	0.795	1.00

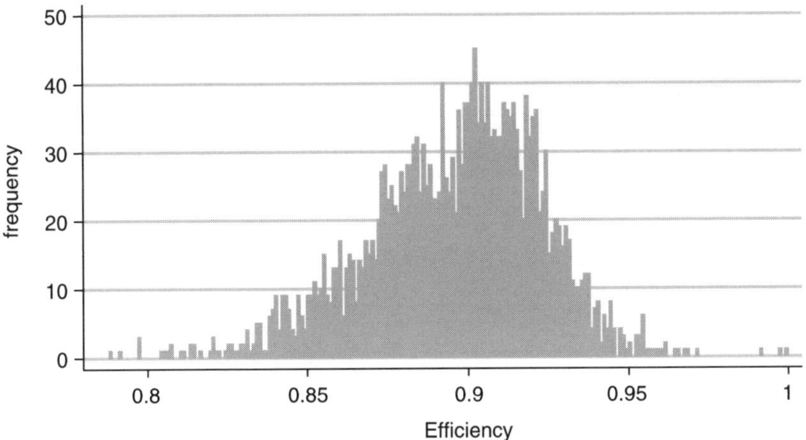

Fig. 1. Efficiency Measures: FE Model.

similar. The estimated mean inefficiency is 10%. This estimate sits between inefficiency estimates for Texas schools found in two papers by Grosskopf, Hayes, Taylor, and Weber (1999, 2001). The low estimated mean inefficiency of 3% from these researchers (Grosskopf et al., 1999) is particularly interesting because their frontier efficiency estimate was based upon a Data Envelopment Approach rather than a stochastic frontier approach. The similarity of the findings from the two disparate modeling strategies warrants future investigation. In their second paper, Grosskopf and her coauthors (Grosskopf et al., 2001) employ a stochastic input distance function estimation approach and find an estimated mean inefficiency of 20%. It should be noted that both these studies estimate efficiency at the district level, whereas our estimates are for the campus level. The potential importance of aggregation on efficiency estimation is yet another topic for future research.

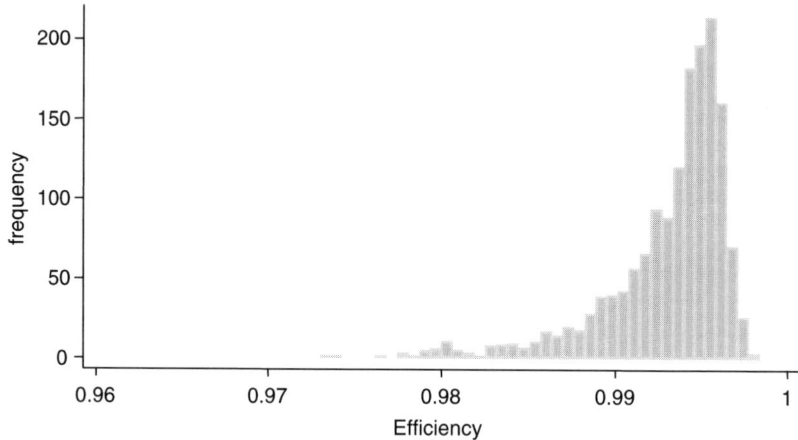

Fig. 2. Efficiency Measures: MLE Model.

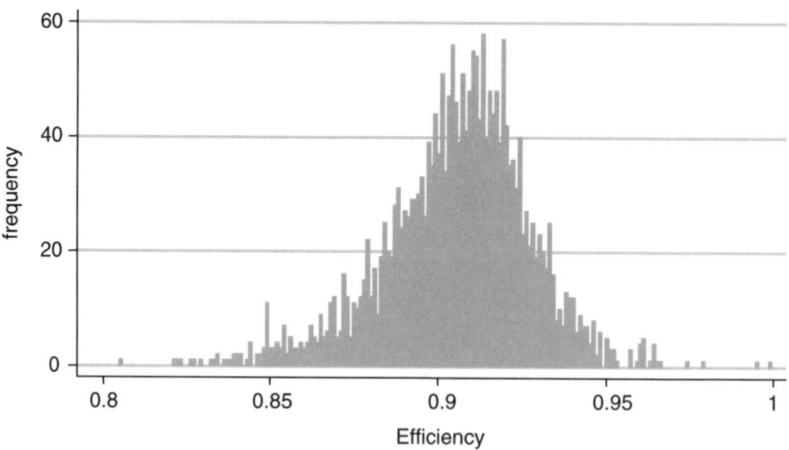

Fig. 3. Efficiency Measures: RE Model.

The maximum-likelihood frontier efficiency estimates seem implausibly high. The half-normal distributional assumption on the one-sided error term does impose an assumption that the modal technical inefficiency is zero, and this can and apparently does lead the model to stack up estimates of the efficiency term at the frontier. It is also possible that the strong assumption of independence in the distribution of the one-sided error and the regressors, an assumption that is required under the maximum-likelihood estimation approach, is not appropriate for these data.

We provide a simple look at the relationship among the estimated efficiency measures from the three alternative models in Table 7. The correlation between the estimated efficiency measures for the two alternative fixed effect models is very high, 0.85 for the fourth grade and 0.84 for the fifth grade. The random effect estimates for the fourth grade are very highly correlated (around 0.90) with the fixed effect fourth-grade values regardless of estimation method, and the fifth-grade random effect estimates are also very highly correlated (around 0.90) with the fixed effect fifth-grade estimates regardless of estimation method. Within each of the three models, the correlation between the fourth- and fifth-grade efficiency estimates is about 0.50. Thus, it seems that the level of inefficiency varies by estimation method, especially the maximum-likelihood fixed effect method, but the correlations indicate an agreement in relative rankings.

Finally, we look at correlations of our Random Effects efficiency measure with the efficiency measures from our DIFF model in Table 2. The correlations are almost zero, indicating that the DIFF model and our efficiency measures reported in Table 7 are not highly correlated. Whatever our DIFF model is estimating as efficiency, it is quite different from what is being measured by any of our measures discussed above.

Do high-score performance and high-efficiency performance go hand in hand? That is the central question we are addressing with our analysis. Our best evidence is reported in the Fig. 4, which graphs TLI scores on the vertical axis against efficiency measured on the horizontal axis. The mean TLI scores on the vertical axis are mean TLI scores over fourth and fifth grades, and over the years of our sample. The efficiency measures are those from the RE model estimated for each school in our sample. In the graph, there is an evident positive relationship between mean TLI scores and our

Table 7. Correlations of Efficiency Measures by Grade and Model.

		Random Effects		Fixed Effects: OLS		Fixed Effects: MLE	
		Grade 4	Grade 5	Grade 4	Grade 5	Grade 4	Grade 5
Random effects	Grade 4	1.00					
	Grade 5	0.505	1.00				
Fixed effects: OLS	Grade 4	0.898	0.512	1.00			
	Grade 5	0.505	0.895	0.691	1.00		
Fixed effects: MLE	Grade 4	0.925	0.500	0.852	0.516	1.00	
	Grade 5	0.478	0.923	0.488	0.836	0.569	1.00

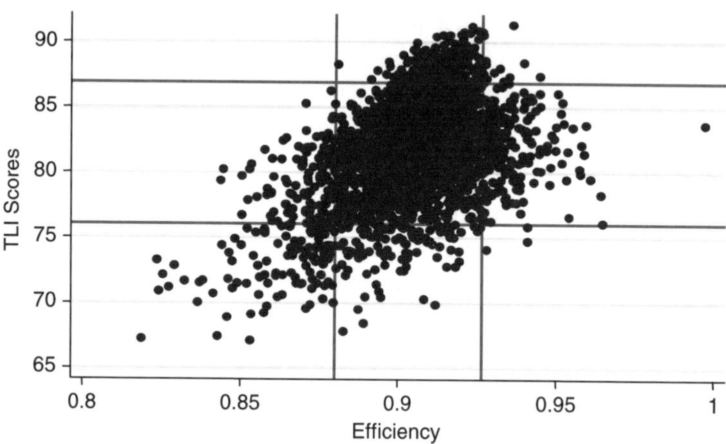

Fig. 4. Mean TLI Scores on Random Effects Efficiency Measures.

efficiency measure. The correlation is 0.45. A simple univariate regression yields an estimated coefficient of 97.20 on the efficiency variable, an estimate that is significant at the 1% level. There is, of course, considerable variation within each efficiency class, and the R^2 is only 0.19.[3]

For future reference, we have calculated the top and bottom deciles of the data graphed in Fig. 4. For mean TLI scores, the top 10% of scores are above 86.86, and the bottom 10% of scores are below 76.05. For our efficiency measure, the top 10% of measures are above 0.927, and the bottom 10% of measures are below 0.880. There are 226 schools in a decile. However, there are only 14 schools that are in both the top decile of mean TLI scores and the top decile of efficiency. There are 111 schools that are in both the bottom decile of mean TLI scores and the bottom decile of efficiency.

Table 8 provides summary statistics to compare certain variables from our entire data set to data from schools in the extreme deciles when ranked by mean TLI scores, by efficiency measures, and when looking at schools that are in both the extreme decile for mean TLI scores and the extreme decile for efficiency measures. The top third of Table 8 allows a comparison of values for the entire set of 2,266 schools with schools in the top and bottom decile of mean TLI scores. Mean spending seems very similar across these three sets of schools. The gain in TLI scores is highest at the bottom decile schools and lowest at the top decile schools, perhaps reflecting the difficulty of improving scores when average scores are already 88% at the top decile schools. Interestingly, the range of TLI gains is much higher at the bottom decile schools, ranging from −0.83 to 7.33 as compared to a range of 0.55 to

Table 8. Summary Statistics by Mean TLI Score and Efficiency Measure.

Variable	All Data (2,266 Observations)	Top Decile by Mean TLI Score	Bottom Decile by Mean TLI Score
TLI scores	81.65	88.19	73.62
	(67.04–91.28)	(86.87–91.28)	(67.04–76.03)
Non-instructional	$953	$939	$1,094
expenditures per pupil	($303–$3,353)	($402–$2,199)	($540–$2,139)
Instructional expenditures per	$3,019	$3,040	$3,035
pupil	($446–$5,592)	($2,121–$5,059)	($2,202–$5,117)
Gain in TLI test scores	3.17	2.53	3.87
	(−1.66–9.06)	(0.55–4.63)	(−0.83–7.33)
Efficiency measures	0.90	0.91	0.88
	(0.81–0.99)	(0.88–0.94)	(0.81–0.94)
Urban	0.84	0.90	0.96
Major urban	0.55	0.65	0.72
Enrollment	561	574	602
	(116–1,412)	(116–1,028)	(156–1,412)

Variable	All Data (2,266 Observations)	Top Decile by Efficiency Score	Bottom Decile by Efficiency Score
TLI scores	81.65	82.18	76.22
	(67.04–91.28)	(74.07–91.28)	(67.04–86.20)
Non-instructional	$953	$1,000	$1,029
expenditures per pupil	($303–$3,353)	($355–$2,024)	($194–$3,353)
Instructional expenditures	$3,019	$3,005	$3,044
per pupil	($446–$5,592)	($2,120–$4,637)	($2,202–$5,592)
Gain in TLI test scores	3.17	4.33	2.57
	(−1.66–9.06)	(1.43–9.06)	(−1.66–6.37)
Efficiency measures	0.90	0.93	0.86
	(0.81–0.99)	(0.92–0.99)	(0.81–0.87)
Urban	0.84	0.91	0.78
Major urban	0.55	0.53	0.54
Enrollment	561	564	544
	(116–1,412)	(127–1,391)	(127–1,332)

Variable	All Data (2,266 Observations)	Top Decile by Mean TLI Scores and by Efficiency Score	Bottom Decile by Mean TLI Scores and by Efficiency Score
TLI scores	81.65	88.32	72.98
	(67.04–91.28)	(86.88–91.28)	(67.04–76.03)
Non-instructional	$953	$913	$1,090
expenditures per pupil	($303–$3,353)	($613–$1,217)	($668–$2,139)

Table 8 (*Continued*)

Variable	All Data (2,266 Observations)	Top Decile by Mean TLI Scores and by Efficiency Score	Bottom Decile by Mean TLI Scores and by Efficiency Score
Instructional expenditures per pupil	$3,019 ($446–$5,592)	$2,881 ($2,315–$3,374)	$2,992 ($2,202–$5,117)
Gain in TLI test scores	3.17 (−1.66–9.06)	3.10 (2.33–4.22)	3.09 (−0.83–6.30)
Efficiency measures	0.90 (0.81–0.99)	0.93 (0.92–0.94)	0.86 (0.81–0.87)
Urban	0.84	0.92	0.95
Major urban	0.55	0.42	0.71
Enrollment	561 (116–1,412)	484 (242–803)	638 (195–1,332)

4.63 at the top decile schools. In terms of other characteristics, top decile schools are a little less likely to be urban or major urban, and tend to have slightly lower enrollment than bottom decile schools. Finally, top decile schools tend to have higher efficiency measures than bottom decile schools.

The middle third of Table 8 allows a comparison of the entire set of 2,266 schools to schools in the top and bottom decile by our estimated efficiency measure. Here, top decile schools by efficiency also tend to have higher mean TLI scores than bottom decile schools. Expenditure averages are similar, although bottom decile schools on average spend slightly more per pupil, as might be expected from the efficiency ranking. But the difference is $29 per pupil in non-instructional spending, roughly 3% of that category, and $39 per pupil in instructional spending, roughly 1.3% of that category. The gain in TLI scores is now higher among top decile schools, and the range among top decile schools is from 1.43 to 9.06. Bottom decile schools had a lower average and a range of −1.66 to 6.37. Finally, top decile schools have the same tendency to be major urban, but a higher tendency to be urban, indicating that rural schools are more heavily represented in the bottom decile of efficiency. There are many possible explanations for why rural schools tend to have lower measured efficiency. These include difficulties that rural schools face due to their relative geographic position, more isolated, and with a less dense student population than urban areas. Consistent with this story is that enrollment is higher, but only slightly higher, among top decile schools.

The bottom third of Table 8 allows a comparison of all schools in our data set with schools in both the top decile as ranked by mean TLI score and the top decile as ranked by efficiency, and schools in both the bottom decile as ranked by mean TLI score and the bottom decile as ranked by efficiency. There are only 14 schools appearing jointly in both extreme top deciles, but 111 schools appearing jointly in both extreme bottom deciles. Obviously, the "top–top" schools have higher TLI scores and higher efficiency measures than the "bottom–bottom" schools. Interestingly, spending if anything tends to be higher at the bottom–bottom schools. TLI gains are on average the same at the two extreme sets of schools, but the range is greater at the bottom–bottom schools, –0.83~6.30, as compared to a range of 2.33–4.22 at the top–top schools. The top–top schools are much less likely to be in major urban districts, 42% versus 71%, while only slightly less likely to be urban. This indicates that top–top schools tend to be in suburbs of major urban areas. Interestingly, bottom–bottom schools are much less likely to be rural than our overall population of schools, 5% versus 16%. Finally, our top–top schools tend to be smaller than are bottom–bottom schools, with a mean enrollment of 484, much below our statewide average of 561 and even further below the mean enrollment of bottom–bottom schools, 638. The range of enrollment is also telling, 242–803 for top–top schools but 195–1,332 for bottom–bottom schools.

The overall picture that emerges from Table 8 is that the mean values of the tabulated descriptive variables tend to be fairly uniform across schools even dividing them up into extreme deciles. There is some tendency for major urban schools to do worse in mean TLI rankings and for rural schools to do worse in efficiency rankings. There may also be a relationship between enrollment and performance.

We can also compare our frontier model measures of school efficiency with a crude measure of average productivity. We simply divide the average test score by operating expenditures per pupil for each school for each year in our sample, and then take the average value over the sample period.[4] The histogram of the relationship between this simple "gross-efficiency" measure and our random effect model estimates of frontier efficiency are displayed in Fig. 5. Absent a couple of outliers, there does not seem to be much of a relationship between the gross-efficiency measure and our technological efficiency measure. The correlation between the two measures is 0.06. The univariate regression of the average score per input dollar on technical efficiency yields a coefficient of 0.098 and the R^2 for the regression is 0.003. It would seem that, whatever technical efficiency is measuring, it is almost unrelated to a measure of efficiency that would seem to appeal strongly to policy makers, test scores per dollar of spending.

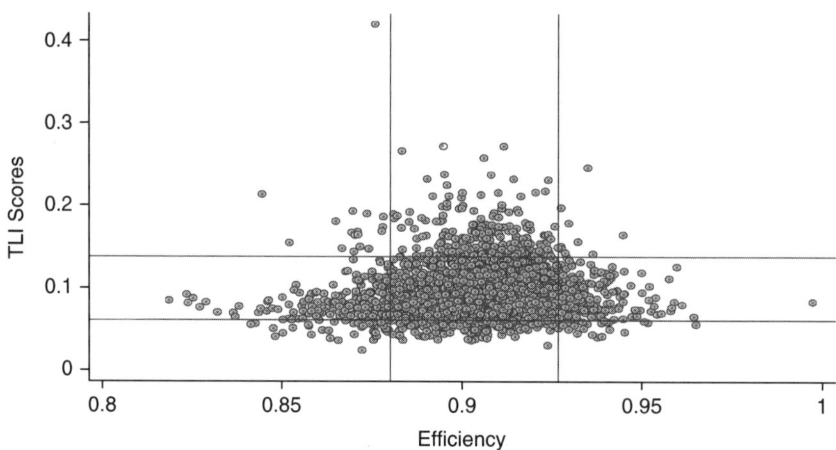

Fig. 5. TLI Scores on Score per Input Dollar Efficiency Measures.

CONCLUSION

We set out to study public school performance and public school technical efficiency. We estimate school production functions to derive alternative efficiency measures based upon different distributional assumptions and different attempts to control for endogeneity of explanatory variables. The efficiency measures are reasonably robust in the sense of finding fairly strong correlations across school rankings derived from the different measures. We do find that school production functions vary by grade even at the same school, and efficiency measures across grades at a given school are only correlated about 50%.

For policy purposes, our findings are in some sense troubling. Our estimated efficiency performance measures for schools are not closely related to the common test-score-based student performance measures. The inclusion of econometric measures of technical efficiency may create a new set of difficult trade-offs in the design of a system of school accountability.

NOTES

1. Exemptions were given for some Special Education students.
2. We estimate a log-linear specification rather than the partially non-linear specification found in Schwartz and Zabel (2005). We do this partly because the

og-linear specification works better with our stochastic frontier framework, which we will introduce later in this paper. In work not reported here, we have estimated a version of their partially non-linear specification with our data, and the results are similar to those we report here.

3. The correlation and regression results convey a very similar message when Mean TLI gains replace Mean TLI levels as the score performance measures.

4. Caroline Hoxby utilizes an analogous measure of productivity for U.S. public schools over time based upon National Assessment of Education Progress scores in the numerator (Hoxby, 2003).

REFERENCES

Anderson, T. W., & Hsiao, C. (1981). Estimation of dynamic models with error components. *Journal of American Statistical Association*, *76*(375), 598–606.

Arellano, M., & Bond, S. (1991). Some tests of specification for panel data: Monte Carlo evidence and application to employment equations. *Review of Economic Studies*, *58*, 277–297.

Grosskopf, S., Hayes, K. J., Taylor, L. L., & Weber, W. L. (1999). Anticipating the consequences of school reform: A new use of DEA. *Management Science*, *45*(4), 608–620.

Grosskopf, S., Hayes, K. J., Taylor, L. L., & Weber, W. L. (2001). On the determinants of school district efficiency: Competition and monitoring. *Journal of Urban Economics*, *49*(3), 425–588.

Hanushek, E. A. (1986). The economics of schooling: Production and efficiency in the public schools. *Journal of Economic Literature*, *XXIV*(3), 1141–1178.

Hoxby, C. M. (2003). School choice and school competition: Evidence from the United States. *Swedish Economic Policy Review*, *10*, 11–67.

Khumbakar, S. C., & Lovell, C. A. K. (2000). *Stochastic frontier analysis*. New York: Cambridge University Press.

Schwartz, A. E., & Zabel, J. (2005). The good, the bad, and the ugly: Measuring school efficiency using school production functions. In: L. Stiefel, A. E. Schwartz, R. Rubenstein & J. Zabel (Eds), *Measuring school performance and efficiency: Implications for practice and research* (pp. 37–56). Yearbook of the American Education Finance Association, Larchmont, NY: Eye on Education, Inc.

Todd, P. E., & Wolpin, K. I. (2003). On the specification and estimation of the production function for cognitive achievement. *Economic Journal*, *113*, F3–F33.

AN EXAMINATION OF STUDENT ACHIEVEMENT IN MICHIGAN CHARTER SCHOOLS

Randall W. Eberts and Kevin M. Hollenbeck

ABSTRACT

This paper examines the effect of charter schools on student achievement in Michigan using a matched student dataset. Proponents of charter schools argue that by applying market pressure to traditional public schools, having the freedom and incentives to apply innovative curricular and instructional ideas, and offering students a choice in the schools they attend, charter schools can raise student achievement. Studies of the effect of charter schools on student achievement have been mixed, however. Methodologies vary widely depending upon the availability of data. Some studies track the same students as they transfer between charter schools and traditional schools; others rely on cross-sectional student or building-level data. We construct a dataset that matches the scores of the same student taking tests in two consecutive years. Estimating a value-added education production function, we find that charter schools are at a disadvantage to traditional public schools by an average of 0.2 standard deviations. These findings depend upon proper matching of students across school types, which in this case is accomplished by using prior test scores as a control variable and as a way to segment the sample. We also find that charter schools run by for-profit companies have an advantage over

Improving School Accountability: Check-Ups or Choice
Advances in Applied Microeconomics, Volume 14, 103–130

ISSN: 0278-0984/doi:10.1016/S0278-0984(06)14005-5

those run by not-for-profits and that charter schools improve the longer they are in operation.

1. INTRODUCTION

Proponents of school reform have argued that school choice can apply sufficient market pressure to schools to bring about improvements in the delivery of education services and ultimately an increase in student achievement. The charter school movement offers students alternatives to attending traditional public schools. Charter schools are encouraged and in many states required to adopt a new instructional or curriculum innovation; they are less encumbered by some regulatory constraints; and their teachers may choose not to be represented by collective bargaining units. In addition, students choosing to attend charter schools may be more motivated to achieve academically and may receive more support at home than those students who have not taken action to select a school that may best fit their needs. Of course, it may be the case that competitive pressures from charter schools result in higher achievement in traditional public schools as well. While reducing or alleviating any academic achievement advantage of charter schools over traditional public schools, their presence may raise achievement of students from both types of schools.[1]

Minnesota passed the first charter school law in 1991, and since then more than 40 states have put such laws in place. Over 3,000 charter schools are in operation nationwide, enrolling over a million students. Arizona, California, Texas, and Michigan have led the movement, accounting for about 50 percent of those schools and over half of the students. Within the dozen years since Michigan enacted charter legislation, it has reached its legislative cap on university-authorized charters. Altogether, the state has 227 charter schools operating nearly 300 buildings with about 87,000 students. With charter schools at the center of school reform, and because of the burgeoning number of schools and students, increasing attention is being paid to the effects of charter schools on student performance. Several studies have examined the effects of charter schools on student test scores, with no clear consensus of the effects. Unfortunately, random assignment has not been a viable option for evaluating charter school performance,[2] so studies of student achievement must artfully construct treatment and comparison groups and must attempt to control for selection bias between attending traditional public schools versus charter schools.

The studies comparing student achievement at charter schools with those at traditional public schools address these issues with various degrees of rigor. In many cases, the extent to which standard procedures to adjust for these issues can be employed depends upon the data available from the various states that have enacted charter laws. Critical to a sound analysis is the availability of student-level data that can be matched over at least two years, standardized tests that are consistent across those years, and sufficient background information on students and preferably on parents, as well as characteristics of other factors, that can be used as an instrument for the choice of schools. Needless to say, not all analyses have had access to such data.

To date, studies of student performance may be categorized along four dimensions: (1) student test scores are aggregated at the school level or at the individual student level; (2) cross-sectional comparisons are made between students in charter schools versus traditional schools or difference-in-difference estimates are derived using tests from consecutive years; (3) school outcomes over consecutive years are tracked (although the student composition of the schools may change) or the same students are tracked over consecutive years, so that leavers and stayers at both public and charter schools can be identified; and (4) students from comparison traditional public schools are selected according to some notion of attendance or market area, which varies from close proximity to the charter school building to all schools within the district that includes the charter school. Studies have shown that the adoption of one or more of these approaches has varying effects on the estimated effects of charters on student achievement.

The purpose of this paper is to estimate the differential effect of student achievement between charter and traditional public schools in Michigan.[3] The analysis is constrained by the availability of student-level data. Individual student test score data are available from 1996, the first year of charter schools in Michigan, through the 2000/2001 school year. Individual student data have not been available since that time. In addition, student identifiers are not supplied with the data so that it is not possible to track the same student from year to year. However, it is possible to match students across two years according to matching criteria based on unique student characteristics. This allows for a difference-in-differences-like estimator, as well as slight variations of that approach. Our analysis focuses on a matched set of students in fourth and fifth grade, which allows us to control for student effects using the same students in both years. We use these findings to gauge bias that may be present in estimates that cannot control for student effects as well. We find little evidence that charter schools have improved student achievement above that achieved in traditional public schools, despite the expectation by some that charter schools can be positive instruments of school reform. In fact, we find statistically significant results showing that charter schools are less effective than traditional charter schools for students within certain ranges of academic ability. Yet, because of data limitations, our analysis stops halfway through the charter school movement in Michigan, and it is possible that five more years of operation of many charter schools may have improved their effectiveness.

2. LITERATURE REVIEW

Charter schools have become the focus of groups that promote school choice and other forms of market-based reform. Therefore, it is not surprising that findings regarding the effectiveness of charter schools vis-à-vis traditional public schools have generated considerable interest and controversy. This brief literature review provides a sample of the different approaches and findings of selected studies and is not intended to be an exhaustive critique.[4]

A study that has generated recent interest and debate, conducted by the American Federation of Teachers (AFT), examined student achievement levels on a multi-state basis. The study used 2003 National Assessment of Educational Progress (NAEP) data to show that test score levels for fourth graders in charter schools were lower than fourth graders in other public schools. The AFT was reported to have found similar results, i.e. lower performance, when the data were disaggregated by race and low-income status. These results are of interest because the NAEP is the only standardized test that is consistent across all states, and its results are used as the Nation's report card. On the other hand, the NAEP is only given to a sample of schools and students, so its results contain sampling error. Furthermore, charter schools are not located in all states, so there may be considerable compositional differences between the charter school and other public school samples.

Hoxby (2004) directly challenges the NAEP results as being suspect on sample size and compositional grounds. She matches virtually all charter schools to their nearest public schools with similar characteristics and reports that on a national basis, the charter schools have higher passing rates on individual states' assessment tests. She shows results for 20 states, and all of them, except Michigan, North Carolina, and Texas, have statistically significant positive effects (higher passing rates) for charter schools.

Greene, Forster, and Winters (2003) paired "untargeted" charter schools with the nearest public school building in 11 states, and found that charter schools had significantly higher year-to-year changes in school-wide average-scale scores on their states' assessments. Somewhat puzzling is the fact that these authors find the most positive results in Texas, a state where other studies have generally found negative results (Hanushek, Kain, & Rivkin, 2002; Hoxby, 2004; Gronberg & Jansen, 2001).

The studies mentioned in the following paragraphs used schools as the unit of analysis. A number of studies have examined individual student-level data. One of the earliest such studies examined Arizona data (Solmon, Paark, & Garcia, 2001) and found that students who persisted in charter schools for two or three consecutive years had higher test score gains than similar students in traditional public schools.[5]

Eberts and Hollenbeck (2002) looked at individual student assessment test-level data for Michigan, and found that fourth graders in charter schools lagged behind fourth graders in traditional public schools in the school districts in which the charter schools were located. Bettinger (2005) finds the same result using Michigan test score data. Interestingly, the same study also finds no evidence that would support the claim that charter schools raise the student achievement in traditional public schools.

The issue with these studies has been the ability to control for student characteristics in order to compare students with similar characteristics and academic abilities across charters and traditional public schools. Eberts and Hollenbeck (2002) use various student characteristics controls and a matched dataset of students taking consecutive year tests, and Bettinger (2005) uses consecutive years of test scores but matched only at the school level. Both studies use a form of difference-in-differences to net out student effects, but Bettinger's study is subject to differences in the student composition of the two types of schools and changes over consecutive years in the composition of the schools. He tries different techniques to address these issues, and finds no statistically significant differences in the performance of charter schools and traditional public schools in Michigan in the early years of charter operation.

Other studies have controlled for differences in student characteristics by following students longitudinally. Booker, Gilpatric, Gronberg, and Jansen (2004), Gronberg and Jansen (2001, 2005), Hanushek et al. (2002), and Bifulco and Ladd (2004) use longitudinal data analytical techniques to estimate the effects of charter schools on test score gains. The first three studies examine charter schools in Texas and the latter analyzes data for North Carolina. The latter two studies yield negative findings for charter schools, whereas the first three find for the most part positive results.

Charter schools are clearly not homogeneous. Two studies have attempted to disaggregate the charter school effect to identify differential aspects of charter schools. Hoxby (2004) shows that the age of the charter school is quite important. Her analysis reveals a strong positive relationship between age of the charter school and its impact on passing rates in the state. Buddin and Zimmer (2005) categorize California charter schools by whether they are conversion schools (existing public schools that converted to become charters) or startup schools and by whether the schools use a classroom or non-classroom approach to instruction. Their evidence shows negative effects of startup versus conversion, and non-classroom approaches versus more traditional classroom approaches.

3. CHARTER SCHOOLS IN MICHIGAN

This paper focuses on student achievement in charter schools in Michigan. Michigan's law was passed in 1993, and currently 227 charter schools now enroll approximately 87,000 students, or about 5.4 percent of Michigan's K-12 student enrollments.[6] According to Michigan law, the primary purposes of charter schools, referred to in the legislation as public school academies (PSAs), are as follows:

- improve pupil achievement;
- stimulate innovative teaching methods;
- create new professional opportunities for teachers;
- achieve school-level accountability for educational performance;
- provide parents and pupils with greater choices among public schools; and
- create competition among public schools to use state funds more effectively, efficiently, and equitably (Horn & Miron, 1999, p. 18).

This set of purposes reflects the intent of the original proponents of charter schools (Hassel, 1999). The state legislation that authorized charter schools established a set of operating rules and practices.

Each school is authorized for a particular mission with identified and explicitly stated goals and purposes unique to that mission. Teachers must be certified just as they are at other public schools. Schools may not screen students, but they may limit the number of students they serve. If more students apply than can be enrolled, a random selection process is used. Charter schools are subject to all laws and regulations that apply to any and all public schools, and charter schools receive the same state foundation grant on a per-pupil basis as do traditional public schools. Charter schools cannot charge tuition but can raise funds through legal foundations and receive grants.

4. METHODOLOGY

Our methodology is based on a simple (stochastic) educational production function (Eq. (1)) that relates student *i*'s learning of subject *k* in school *j* at time *t*, L_{ij}^{kt}, to school-based resources, Z_j^t, observable family and student characteristics, X_i^t, and innate ability in subject *k*, $A^k{}_i$:

$$L_{ij}^{kt} = f\left(Z_j^t,\ X_i^t,\ A_i^k,\ e_t^i\right). \tag{1}$$

The error term, e_{it}, includes measurement error among other things. For heuristic purposes, we assume separability and linearity. In Eq. (2), we have separated out from Z_j a dummy variable C_j that takes on the value of one if *j* is a charter school and zero if it is a traditional public school.

$$L_{ij}^{kt} = \alpha + \beta Z_i^t + \gamma X_i^t + \delta C_j + \eta A_i + \varepsilon_{it}. \tag{2}$$

The charter school dummy variable is intended to capture the effect of any unique mission and innovative curriculum or instructional techniques employed by the charter. When no other building variables are included in the estimating equation, this variable also picks up differences in class size, enrollment, and other measurable factors that may influence student learning as measured by differences in test scores.

Our measure of subject *k* learning is a value-added measure equal to the difference in test scores, Y^k, between the current year and the previous year:

$$L_{ij}^{kt} = Y_{ij}^{kt} - Y_{ij}^{kt-1}. \tag{3}$$

Finally, to get to our estimating equation, we include the test score from the prior year's test as a proxy for ability and thus Y_{ij}^{kt-1} replaces $A^k{}_i$ in Eq. (2), such that[7]

$$L_{ij}^{kt} = \alpha + \beta Z_i^t + \gamma X_i^t + \delta C_j + \eta Y_{ij}^{kt-1} + \varepsilon_{it}. \tag{4}$$

As previously mentioned, we have created a matched sample of fourth- and fifth-grade students by matching the math test score of a student in fourth grade with the science test score the same student received in fifth grade. We converted the total test scores to *z*-scores, so that the change has an interpretation of progress (or lack thereof) with respect to standard deviation units within each year.[8] Thus, we compare the relative position of a student in the cohort of those taking the math test in fourth grade with the relative position of a student in the cohort of those taking the science test in the fifth grade.

An issue with using the value-added approach to estimate educational production functions is the nature of the tests used in the analysis. Eq. (4) is typically interpreted as the difference in student test scores over time between students attending the two types of schools. Ideally, we would prefer tests that measure the gain in achievement over the time period, typically a school year. The tests that best fit this requirement are a pre-test to gain a benchmark of achievement and then a post-test to measure the gains in achievement. These tests are rare, particularly among the state-administered assessment tests. The Michigan Educational Assessment Program (MEAP) test is no exception. Furthermore, the state does not administer MEAP tests in the same subject area in consecutive years. Math and reading are given in fourth grade, and science and writing are administered in fifth. Therefore, the interpretation of the difference in test scores as gains is not entirely appropriate. We would not necessarily expect students to exhibit gains on the two different tests – math in fourth grade and science in fifth grade – from one year to the next, since the tests are not designed as pre- and post-tests. While both tests are partial measures of a student's academic abilities and they are highly correlated, so they capture a common core of competencies, there are other areas of measured competencies that may not overlap.[9]

We have taken a slightly different approach and have assumed that a student's performance on the prior test, in this case math before science and reading before writing, is a good benchmark of the student's performance on the subsequent test. That is, it proxies a student's ability, and as shown later on in this paper math scores are highly correlated with science scores and writing scores are highly collinear with reading scores. Therefore, in estimating Eq. (4) for science, we add the math score (Y^m_{ij}) to the right-hand side of the equation, recognizing that the science test is given in fifth grade and the math test is given the previous year and thus suppressing the time notation

$$L^s_{ij} \approx \left(Y^s_{ij} - Y^m_{ij}\right) = \alpha + \beta C_j + \gamma Y^m_{ij} + \delta X_{ij} + \varepsilon_{it}. \qquad (5)$$

Adding that prior test to the student-specific components of Eq. (4) allows one to subtract out much of the student-related elements that affect differences in student test scores. Therefore, it is a matter of degree to which we can difference out student effects on the observed outcomes of the charter and traditional public schools.[10] We will show the differences in estimates related to the two approaches.[11]

Since our sample contains only those public schools that have a charter school located within their boundaries, we use fixed effects to control for factors in the areas that are common to both types of schools. This approach helps to control for the average difference in students across districts, but it does not control for differences between charter schools and public schools within each district.

5. DATA

To analyze the effectiveness of charter schools relative to their traditional public school counterparts, we examine the difference in student outcomes, as measured by the MEAP.[12] The MEAP tests are convenient measures of the educational outcomes of Michigan students since all public school students, including charter school students, are required to take the tests. The tests are administered to students in specific grade levels. Most relevant for comparing student performance in charter schools versus traditional public schools are the tests administered in the fourth and fifth grades, since most charter schools in the state enroll students in the primary grades. The State makes available the MEAP results each year along with limited demographic data that are self-reported by students when they take the tests. We rely mainly on this dataset together with additional building- and district-level data that are supplied by local districts and made available on the Michigan Department of Education's website. Five years of MEAP scores for individual fourth- and fifth-grade students are available from 1996/1997 through 2000/2001. For this analysis we focus on the 1998/1999 and 1999/2000 school years. We chose these two years because they were the most recent years for which all the data were available and that we could match students, using our matching process. We provide simple statistics regarding the other years to offer perspective.

The MEAP tests are criterion-referenced exams, so the "cut scores" may differ from year to year. However, our analyses are based on levels, not passing rates, and the standards to which the MEAP is aligned did not vary over the five years of our data. Consequently, pooling the data over time is appropriate. We also acknowledge that the MEAP test scores, like any standardized test scores, are "loose" indicators of student achievement. The environmental conditions under which students take the test, test coverage, and student test-taking skills and anxiety all influence the extent to which the scores accurately reflect what students actually know. Furthermore, to the extent that a student's performance on the MEAP is related to the totality of their educational experiences prior to the exam, it is incorrect to attribute fully the test score to the current school of attendance if students have transferred into that school. Many of the charter schools have recently opened, and so the proportion of students who have transferred in is much higher than for traditional public schools.[13] Finally, the MEAP test may not be aligned with the curriculum established by the charter school. Traditional public school administrators and teachers have also echoed this criticism of the MEAP, which underscores the problems of using standardized test measures as evaluation instruments.

Despite these shortcomings, the MEAP test is one of the few ways to compare the performance of all public schools within the state of Michigan. With greater attention given to accountability of schools, the State of Michigan, along with many other states, has stressed the importance of the MEAP scores.[14] Many Michigan school districts are spending considerable time and resources to improve their performance on the MEAP. Furthermore, according to the evaluation, many charter schools use the MEAP as evidence of the success of their program and some charter schools list the MEAP test as their only evidence of student achievement (Horn & Miron, 1999, p. 83).[15]

Our analysis is based on the matched fourth- and fifth-grade sample in which the fourth-grade test scores are extracted from the 1998/1999 school year and the fifth-grade test scores are taken from the 1999/2000 school year. The dataset combines the scores on the fourth-grade math test and the fifth-grade science test for the same student, and the scores on the fourth-grade reading and fifth-grade writing tests. Consequently, we can observe differences in test scores for the same student in two consecutive years. The State of Michigan does not release student identifiers, so we devised an algorithm based on available individual student data in order to make the matches.[16,17] In addition, we included only those traditional public school elementary schools that are located in districts in which a charter school is located. By pairing charter schools with their "host" (meaning geographically co-located) districts, we attempted to create the local "market" for educational services in which both the charter schools and the public school districts compete.[18]

Table 1 provides descriptive statistics for fourth graders attending charter schools and traditional public elementary schools. We use the fourth-grade sample to illustrate the characteristics of charter schools and traditional public schools and the changes in these characteristics over the first four

Table 1. Descriptive Statistics for Selected Student, Building, and District Characteristics, Fourth Grade.

	1996/1997		1997/1998		1998/1999		1999/2000		Matched 1998/1999 and 1999/2000	
	Charter Schools	Traditional (District Match)	Charter Schools	Traditional (District Match)	Charter Schools	Traditional (District Match)	Charter Schools	Traditional (District Match)	Charter Schools	Traditional (District Match)
Number of schools/districts	30	324/25[a]	62	448/42	91	528/52	119	669/63	77	717/69
Number of students	724	12,424	1,611	17,569	2,733	20,874	4,036	27,141	963	10,124
Female (%)	48.3	50.6	50.0	51.3	49.8	50.5	50.7	50.7	51.6	51.0
Non-White (%)	58.3	61.5	58.4	50.0	62.9	51.7	63.8	48.1	59.0	43.6
Free lunch eligibility, bldg.[b] (%)	52.4	59.3	52.3	59.4	59.5	61.0	49.9	54.1	55.0	54.9
Non-White enrollment, bldg.[b] (%)	45.7	68.3	43.9	68.0	54.7	59.3	55.5	54.1	56.6	52.8
Average enrollment, bldg.	324	488	312	493	323	447	324	439	270	400
Average pupil/teacher ratio, bldg.	20.5	24.6	20.5	24.7	20.9	24.5	20.5	24.0	18.6	21.7
Average teacher salary, dist.[b]	$35,650	$47,892	$35,650	$48,175	$34,546	$48,654	$34,895	$48,953	$32,081	$46,897
Avg. expenditure/pupil, dist.	$6,934	$7,874	$6,982	$7,899	$6,490	$7,679	$6,398	$7,648	$5,951	$7,215
Mean math score	506.7	522.7	522.5	535.4	517.3	532.2	516.5	536.3	521.1	535.7
Mean reading score	304.0	310.9	309.8	316.1	307.8	314.9	303.6	314.1	309.4	317.1

[a]For this statistic we refer to the number of schools in the number of districts in which a charter is located.

[b]The means of student-level variables are computed at the student level, and building-level characteristics are computed at the building level.

years of charter school operation. Except for a few observations that have been deleted because of missing values for key variables, the number of students included in the table is exactly equal to those who took the MEAP test in the districts included in the analyses. The test is mandatory in Michigan, with only a few waivers at the elementary level, so the number of test takers is a good proxy for the relative number of students in traditional public and charter elementary schools. Whereas on a statewide basis charter schools enroll about 5.4 percent of all students, the table shows that charters account for about 13 percent of fourth-grade test takers in the districts in which charter schools are located in the 1999/2000 school year.

According to Table 1, charter schools have smaller enrollments and smaller class sizes than public schools, although the differences have narrowed over time as charter schools gained enrollment. In fourth grade for the 1999/2000 school year, the average building enrollment for charters was 324, which is about three-quarters of the average building enrollment in the traditional public schools. The earliest years of data show average student/teacher ratios for charter schools are around 20.5 and remain constant throughout the four years of data. The traditional public schools' average student/teacher ratios have also remained nearly constant at around 24. The ethnicity and poverty status of students in the two types of schools was quite different in the earliest years of data, but have become more similar since then. The percentage of students eligible for free or reduced price lunches at the building level was nearly 7 points lower for charter schools in the first year but the gap narrowed slightly by 1999/2000. In the first year of data, charter schools had a much lower percentage of non-White students than traditional public schools, nearly 23 points lower. However, within four years they were on par with public schools at roughly 54 percent. There has been some concern about trends in the characteristics of charter school students toward majority ethnicity and non-poor economic status.[19] But our data do not suggest any such trend for the two types of schools within the same market area, and in fact, the free lunch eligibility percentage and the non-White building enrollment percentage are quite comparable to the traditional schools in the districts where the charter schools are located.

Average teacher salaries are much lower in charter schools. In fact, they are approximately one-third lower than for teachers in traditional public schools in all four years. Similarly, average expenditures per pupil are lower in charter schools, by about 10–15 percent. These data, along with the much larger gaps in teacher salaries, suggest that charter schools spend a much larger share of their per pupil expenditures on non-instructional items (see Good & Braden, 2000).

The average test scores for math and reading of students in charter schools are approximately two to three percent lower than the scores for students in traditional public schools. (These gaps translate into differences that are approximately 0.3–0.4 standard deviations and are highly statistically significant.) For example, in the last year of data, the average math score is around 536 for fourth graders in traditional public schools and about 517 for fourth graders in charter schools. The last column of Table 1 displays the sample statistics for the matched dataset. Charter school students represent nearly nine percent of the students in the matched sample, which is similar to the percentage of fifth graders in 1999/2000 (which is not shown). The student characteristics and the building and district characteristics in the matched sample are similar to those found in the larger samples for school years 1998/1999 and 1999/2000. In addition, student characteristics are quite similar between those attending charter schools and those attending traditional public schools, with one exception. The percentage of non-White students is much higher for charter schools than traditional public schools when averaging across individual student records, but quite similar when averaging across buildings. This difference in student- and building-level means results basically from two large charter schools that are predominantly non-White. Therefore, the matched dataset appears to be representative of the larger datasets from which it was extracted.

6. ESTIMATION RESULTS

One of the key issues in providing accurate estimates of the effectiveness of charter schools vis-à-vis traditional public schools is the ability to control for differences in student characteristics between the two types of schools. Without adequate controls, the estimates may be biased. We start with the simple specification of the learning equation (Eq. (5)), without including the prior test score ($Y^{m}{}_{ij}$) but including the few student-level characteristics available from the dataset. We then proceed to show the importance of including additional controls (e.g., entering $Y^{m}{}_{ij}$) in order to create a better match between students in charter schools with those in traditional public schools.

We estimate Eq. (5) for both the difference in fifth-grade science scores and fourth-grade math scores and the difference in fifth-grade writing and fourth-grade reading scores. The equation is estimated with district fixed effects and includes student-level characteristics of gender, non-White, and age at the start of the school year.[20] The results for the science and math combination of tests are shown in column A of Table 2. Two of the student characteristic variables are statistically significant – non-White and free and reduced price lunch.[21] The variable of primary interest, the charter school dummy variable, is negative but not statistically significant. This result suggests that there is no statistically significant difference between charter schools and traditional public schools in the difference in science test scores in fifth grade and math test scores in the previous year. The writing and reading test score combination yields similar results in that the charter variable coefficient is not statistically significant, as shown in column E of Table 2. As mentioned in the model specification section, estimates of charter school effects may be biased if significant differences exist in the student composition of the two types of schools and these characteristics are correlated with student achievement. The first clue that there may be substantial differences in student composition was displayed in Table 1, which showed that the percentage of non-White students is substantially higher in the charter schools than traditional ones. The non-White variable is highly negatively correlated with math test scores and reading test scores, so schools with higher concentrations of non-White students have lower initial test scores.[22]

The difference in student composition can be further seen by looking at the distribution of math and reading test scores between the two types of schools. We focus on these two tests because they serve as the prior year proxy for student academic ability. Table 3 displays the distribution. For the z-scores of the math test, it is clear that test scores of students in charter schools are lower than those in traditional public schools throughout the entire distribution, in which the difference averages about half a standard deviation. The same difference between school types exists for z-scores of the reading test, but due to the way that test is scored, only the lower half of the distribution exhibited major differences, with magnitudes similar to the math test.[23]

To examine the effect of including the prior test score as a proxy for student academic ability, we estimate Eq. (5). The results are included in columns B and F of Table 2. As shown in column B, the coefficient on the prior test score is negative and statistically significant, and the magnitude of the coefficient of the charter dummy variable becomes more negative and is statistically significant. The same increase in statistical significance and in the magnitude of the charter coefficient is found for the writing/reading test combination, as shown in column F of Table 2. These results suggest that more accurately matching students with similar academic abilities has a substantial effect on the estimates of charter school performance.

Table 2. Estimates of the Effect of Charter Schools and Other Variables on Test Score Changes.

	Difference in Fifth-Grade Science Test and Fourth-Grade Math (Eq. (4))				Difference in Fifth-Grade Writing and Fourth-Grade Reading			
	A	B	C	D	E	F	G	H
Prior test		−0.433	−0.435	−0.433		−0.73	−0.73	−0.73
		(−57.24)	(−56.39)	(57.25)		(−80.64)	(78.82)	(−80.63)
Charter: All types	−0.015	−0.215	−0.632		0.01	−0.242	−0.397	
	(−0.52)	(−8.28)	(−8.76)		(0.24)	(7.57)	(−4.48)	
Charter: For-profits				−0.182				−0.244
				(−6.07)				(−6.63)
Charter: Not-for-profits				−0.306				−0.235
				(−6.44)				(−4.02)
Female	0.0012	−0.04	−0.046	−0.41	0.137	0.283	0.28	0.283
	(0.08)	(−2.91)	(−16.56)	(−2.94)	(6.38)	(16.48)	(16.06)	(16.48)
Non-White	−0.118	−0.316	−0.314	−0.316	0.169	−0.086	−0.069	−0.086
	(−5.66)	(−17.01)	(−16.56)	(−17.05)	(5.97)	(−3.77)	(−2.98)	(−3.77)
Percent of free lunch	−0.162	−0.451	−0.528	−0.448	−0.166	−0.63	−0.693	−0.63
	(−3.18)	(−10.04)	(−10.53)	(−9.98)	(−2.40)	(−11.39)	(−11.24)	(−11.39)
Age	−5.99E-06	0.00016	0.0002	0.0002	−0.0001	0.0003	0.0003	0.0003
	(−0.06)	(1.78)	(2.04)	(−1.75)	(−0.66)	(2.45)	(2.17)	(2.45)
Age^2	3.09E-07	−5.51E-07	−5.99E-07	−5.49E-07	5.27E-07	−8.27E-07	−8.19E-07	−8.27E-07
	(1.50)	(−3.04)	(−3.20)	(−3.03)	(2.04)	(−3.70)	(−3.55)	(−3.70)

Table 2. (*Continued*)

	Difference in Fifth-Grade Science Test and Fourth-Grade Math (Eq. (4))				Difference in Fifth-Grade Writing and Fourth-Grade Reading			
	A	B	C	D	E	F	G	H
Average teacher Salary (/$1,000)			−0.027 (−3.00)				−0.006 (−0.87)	
Expenditures/pupil (/$1,000)			−0.011 (−0.48)				−0.082 (−2.88)	
Building enrollment (/1,000)			−0.135 (−0.81)				−0.074 (−0.49)	
Pupil/teacher ratio			−0.109 (−0.62)				−0.182 (−1.23)	
Constant	0.117 (4.18)	0.399 (15.92)	2.198 (3.13)	0.399 (15.90)	−0.081 (−2.11)	0.215 (7.04)	1.69 (3.24)	0.215 (7.04)
Fixed district effects	$F = 13.72$	$F = 17.59$	$F = 17.34$	$F = 17.66$	$F = 6.38$	$F = 9.60$	$F = 8.58$	$F = 9.56$
Adj. R^2	0.05	0.27	0.28	0.27	0.03	0.39	0.39	0.39

Notes: *T*-statistics in parentheses.
The standard errors of building-level variables are adjusted for possible within-district correlation.
Estimated on the matched sample of fourth- and fifth-grade students in 1998/1999 and 1999/2000 school years.

Table 3. Distribution of Test Scores.

Math				Science		
Percentiles	School Type		Difference	School Type		Difference
	Traditional	Charter		Traditional	Charter	
10%	−1.2159	−1.7170	0.5011	−1.2154	−1.6773	0.4619
25%	−0.6145	−1.1157	0.5012	−0.6612	−1.0615	0.4003
50%	0.0203	−0.5143	0.5346	0.0470	−0.4765	0.5235
75%	0.7280	0.2208	0.5072	0.7552	0.3241	0.4311
90%	1.2900	0.8222	0.4678	1.3090	1.0324	0.2766

Reading				Writing		
Percentiles	School Type		Difference	School Type		Difference
	Traditional	Charter		Traditional	Charter	
10%	−1.2599	−1.7734	0.5135	−1.0026	−1.0026	0.0000
25%	−0.7036	−0.9176	0.2140	−1.0026	−1.0026	0.0000
50%	0.1523	−0.1901	0.3423	−0.0275	−0.0275	0.0000
75%	0.7514	0.7514	0.0000	0.9475	0.9475	0.0000
90%	1.4361	1.4361	0.0000	0.9475	0.9475	0.0000

Notes: Tests are measured as *z*-scores with respect to their respective grade cohorts.
Math and reading tests are administered in fourth grade and science and writing are administered in fifth grade.
Matched sample of fourth- and fifth-grade students in 1998/1999 and 1999/2000 school years.

The charter dummy variable captures all aspects of the differences in charter schools and traditional public schools. The two school types differ not only by the approach each takes in delivering educational services, but also by the resources each has available to students. Included in the dataset are a few measures of school-based resources, including class size, building enrollment, expenditures per student, and average teacher salary, which have been shown in other studies to affect student achievement. By including these variables in the equation, we can net out these effects from the effects of other factors, which range from the use of innovative curriculum to the motivation of students. Columns C and G of Table 2 show the results of adding these school-based resources. For both combinations of test scores, adding variables measuring school-based resources increases the negative effect of charter schools on test scores relative to traditional public schools.

These results suggest that charter schools have an advantage over traditional public schools with respect to observable school-based resources, presumably because of lower class size and smaller building enrollments. However, once these factors are controlled for, it appears that the effect of factors, unobserved in this dataset, puts charter schools at even greater disadvantage vis-à-vis public schools.

The importance of including the prior test score in the equation is made clearer by understanding the relationship between the prior test score and the difference in the science and math scores and the writing and reading scores. First consider the science/math combination. The coefficient on the math variable is negative and highly statistically significant. This negative relationship suggests that students with lower prior test scores have greater changes in the difference between the two tests. Thus, if more charter school students are found in the lower end of the math score distribution, as is the case, then students in charter schools will have greater increases in the difference in test scores compared with traditional public school students who have a greater tendency to be in the higher range of the math score distribution. Without matching students of similar prior academic abilities, as proxied by the math score, the charter school effects at the two ends of the distribution in essence cancel each other out, yielding the results from estimating Eq. (5) without the prior test score as an explanatory variable. The writing/reading combination yields similar results.

6.1. Estimation within the Distribution of Prior Test Scores

To see which segments of the distributions of math test scores and reading test scores are driving the results, we divide the distribution into quartiles and then re-estimate Eq. (5), but without the math test score or reading test score as explanatory variables. The results are displayed in panels A and B in Table 4. The region of the math score distribution that exhibits the largest difference between the two school types is in the first quartile. The estimated coefficient is −0.343 and is statistically significant. The coefficient is negative and statistically significant for the next two quartiles, but positive and not statistically significant for the highest quartile. The values of the coefficients consistently decline in magnitude throughout the first three quartiles and then turn positive in the fourth quartile. Therefore, the major difference between the effectiveness of charter schools and traditional public schools lies in the lower three quarters of the math score distribution. For students in this range, our results suggest that traditional public schools are more effective than charter schools by between 0.34 and 0.15 standard deviations.

Table 4. Estimates of the Effect of Charter Schools on Test Score Changes within Ranges of Prior Tests and for For-Profit and Not-for-Profit Organizational Types.

		Range of prior math scores (by quartiles)			
		<−0.682	−0.682 to 0.020	0.020 to 0.622	>0.622
A. Difference in z-Scores between Fifth-Grade Science and Fourth-Grade Math Tests					
Charter school		−0.343	−0.216	−0.155	0.006
		(−7.07)	(−4.22)	(−2.69)	(0.09)
Adj. R^2		0.10	0.11	0.11	0.11
		Range of prior reading scores (by quartiles)			
		<−0.704	−0.704 to 0.152	0.152 to 0.751	>0.751
B. Difference in z-Scores between Fifth-Grade Writing and Fourth-Grade Reading Tests					
Charter school		−0.208	−0.224	−0.16	−0.386
		(−3.01)	(−4.46)	(−2.10)	(−4.22)
Adj. R^2		0.04	0.08	0.10	0.10
		Range of prior math scores (by quartiles)			
		<−0.682	−0.682 to 0.020	0.020 to 0.622	>0.622
C. Difference in z-Scores between Fifth-Grade Science and Fourth-Grade Math Tests					
Charter school	For-profit	−0.276	−0.233	−0.118	0.034
	Company	(−5.08)	(−3.82)	(−1.74)	(0.44)
Charter school	Not-for-profit	−0.539	−0.179	−0.24	−0.1
	Organization	(−6.25)	(−2.03)	(−2.31)	(−0.67)
Adj. R^2		0.10	0.11	0.11	0.09
		Range of prior reading scores (by quartiles)			
		<−0.704	−0.704 to 0.152	0.152 to 0.751	>0.751
D. Difference in z-Scores between Fifth-Grade Writing and Fourth-Grade Reading Tests					
Charter school	For-profit	−0.128	−0.239	−0.197	−0.383
	Company	(−1.63)	(−4.17)	(−2.21)	(−3.53)
Charter school	Not-for-profit	−0.42	−0.179	−0.068	−0.394
	Organization	(−3.49)	(−1.89)	(−0.49)	(−2.36)
Adj. R^2		0.04	0.08	0.10	0.10

Notes: All equations include student-level data and fixed effects. *T*-values in parentheses. Estimated on the matched sample of fourth- and fifth-grade students in 1998/1999 and 1999/2000 school years.

The charter effect for the entire lower half of the distribution is −0.236 and is statistically significant, but the coefficient is statistically insignificant when the entire upper half of the distribution is considered together.

The writing/reading test combination yields more robust results across the distribution of the reading test scores. The effects of charter schools are negative and statistically significant for all four quartiles. The magnitude of the effects is different from that displayed for science and math test scores. Instead of a steady decline in the negative effect of charters, the estimates are about the same in the lower half and then spike up in the fourth quartile, suggesting that traditional public schools are considerably more effective than charter schools for students in the top quartile of prior test scores.

The negative coefficients on the charter variable may be interpreted as the direct impacts of charter schools, but they do not necessarily address the indirect impacts. That is, the competition or "threat" posed by charter schools may increase the test scores in traditional public schools, which of course would be a positive impact on education. In an earlier paper (Eberts & Hollenbeck, 2001), we reported the results of tests for such an indirect effect. Specifically, we used three years of MEAP test score data and estimated the same models on all traditional public school buildings in all districts in Michigan, and included a dummy variable for presence of a charter school in the district. The results of the analysis showed that fifth-grade students in traditional public schools of districts that "host" a charter school scored about one and one-half percent higher on the writing test than students from other districts, controlling for student, building, and district characteristics and about 0.15 percent higher on the science test. But fourth-grade students did not score higher on the math or reading tests. Results from other studies are also mixed. Bettinger (2005) found little support for a positive influence of charter school competition on traditional public schools in Michigan. On the other hand, Hoxby (2001) finds strong support for a positive competitive effect of charter schools on the test scores of students in nearby traditional public schools.

6.2. Estimation by Management Type

We also estimate the effect of the two types of management arrangements – for-profit or not-for-profit – on the performance of charter schools relative to traditional public schools. Some proponents of charter schools argue that they offer two dimensions of competition that can improve educational effectiveness. The first is the choice of schools to attend, and the second is the competition for investment capital for those charters operated by for-profit organizations. In Michigan, the majority of charter schools are managed by for-profit businesses – 66 percent. The results, however, are mixed, as shown in columns D and H in Table 2. In these two equations, the single charter school variable is replaced with two variables, one indicating whether or not the charter is managed by a for-profit company and the other indicating whether or not the charter is managed by not-for-profit organization. The two variables are mutually exclusive and together represent the entire group of charter schools that are in the previous analysis. For the science/math test score combination, charter schools operated by for-profit companies have less of a negative effect on test scores vis-à-vis traditional public schools than those operated by not-for-profit organizations. The difference is nearly double, and both coefficients are statistically significant. For the writing/reading test combination, there is virtually no difference in effects of the two management arrangements on test scores.

In addition, we estimated the effects of the two management arrangements with each of the quartiles of the distribution of the prior test scores. Panels C and D in Table 4 show that the results differ by the test score combinations. For the science/math test combination, students in charters operated by not-for-profit organizations experience a lower test score change relative to traditional public schools than those in charters operated by for-profit companies. These results hold for students with math scores in the first and third quartiles. Differences in the second quartile are much more similar, and estimates in the fourth quartile are statistically insignificant. For the writing/reading test score combination, for-profit charter schools have an advantage over a not-for-profit ones only in the first quartile. For the other quartiles, the differences are insignificant or in favor of those run by not-for-profit organizations.

Examining the school characteristics of the two types of management organizations offers few clues in explaining the difference. As shown in Table 5, not-for-profit schools have smaller class size, but by just slightly over a half student per teacher. Not-for-profit charters have also been in operation longer than for-profits by about 300 days. Not-for-profit schools spend about $500 more per pupil than for-profit schools, and with slightly lower salaries more resources may be going toward instructional activities. In addition, not-for-profit charter schools have smaller enrollment than for-profits, which may contribute to a more conducive educational environment. Obviously, differences exist but it is unclear which of these differences affect the performance relative to the two test score combinations. Controlling for these school-based resources by entering these variables into the equation (results not shown) does not change the relative effects, except that

Table 5. Characteristics of For-Profit and Not-for-Profit Charter Schools.

	Averages by Student Management Type		Averages by School Management Type	
	Not-for-profit	For-profit	Not-for-profit	For-profit
Enrollment	228.2	437.5	175	319.5
Average salaries	31,560	32,324	31,376	32,826
Expenditure/pupil	6,049	5,847	6,283	5,781
Pupil/teacher ratio	18.3	19.7	18.1	18.8
Days in operation	1,067	798	1,122	843
Percent of female	49	53	46	52
Percent of non-White	68	56	67	52
Percent of free lunch	55	50	58	53
Percent of students in sample in type of charter	27	73		
Percent of schools in charter sample			34	66
Percent of schools in entire sample	5.4	10.6		

Note: Matched sample of fourth- and fifth-grade students in 1998/1999 and 1999/2000 school years.

charter schools operated by not-for-profit organizations have a slight disadvantage over for-profit schools with respect to the writing/reading test score combination.

6.3. Effect of Length of Time in Operation

Charter schools have been in operation for a relatively short time, so one possible explanation for the lower test score changes of their students may be the inexperience of charter school staff and the inefficiencies of starting up a new venture. One could also argue that students have not been enrolled long enough in charter schools to make a difference in their performance. We include five dummy variables, each representing the number of years the charter school has been operating. As shown in Table 6, the longer a charter school has been in operation, the more effective it is relative to the public schools. The coefficient on the charter school variable falls in magnitude from −0.372 and statistically significant for charters that have been open for two years to −0.036 and statistically insignificant for those schools in operation for four years. For the writing/reading combination, the coefficients

Table 6. The Effect of Length of Operation on Charter School Performance.

	Change in Science and Math Scores	Change in Writing and Reading Scores
One year = 1	−0.127	−0.313
	(−2.76)	(−5.51)
Two years = 1	−0.372	−0.197
	(−7.18)	(−3.05)
Three years = 1	−0.303	−0.257
	(6.45)	(−4.44)
Four years = 1	−0.036	−0.153
	(−0.61)	(−2.08)
Five years = 1	−0.13	−0.273
	(−0.80)	(−1.36)
Prior test score	−0.433	−0.73
	(−57.16)	(−80.65)
Female	−0.41	0.283
	(−2.93)	(16.48)
Non-White	−0.316	−0.085
	(−17.04)	(−3.74)
Percent of free lunch	−0.432	−0.636
	(−9.55)	(−11.41)
Age of student	0.0002	0.0003
	(1.79)	(2.49)
Age of student squared	−5.53E-07	−8.35E-07
	(−3.05)	(−3.74)
Constant	0.39	0.22
	(15.46)	(7.07)
Fixed district effects	$F = 17.70$	$F = 9.37$
Adj. R^2	0.27	0.38

Notes: Years of operation are dummy variables.
T-statistics in parentheses.
Estimated on the matched sample of fourth- and fifth-grade students in 1998/1999 and 1999/2000 school years.

on the days in operation are statistically significant for all lengths of time except for five years. The magnitude of the results for the writing/reading combination does not change as much over length of time in operation as does the science/math combination. Yet, there is some evidence to suggest that charter schools that have been in operation longer close the gap between their performance and that of students from traditional public schools.

7. SUMMARY AND CONCLUSIONS

The analysis of individual student test scores suggests that charter schools, during their early years of operation in Michigan, did not improve student achievement relative to traditional public schools. In fact, for students with initial math test scores and reading test scores below the mean of their cohort, those in charter schools have lower increases in test scores across consecutive years than students in traditional public schools. We also examined the relative performance of charters operated by for-profit companies and those operated by not-for-profit organizations. We found mixed results, in that for the science/math test combination, for-profits outperformed not-for-profits, and for the writing/reading test combination, little difference was found. Results also show that the length of time charters are in operation improves their performance, and by the fourth year of operations there is no difference in the science/math test score combination and by the fifth year there is no difference in the writing/reading test combination.

These estimates can be biased in either direction due to selection bias and other factors. We have tried to control as much as possible for differences in student composition across the various types of schools and management styles and found that taking into the account the prior test score, whether by including it directly in the regression or using it to partition the dataset, makes a difference in the signs and statistical significance of the coefficients of the variables related to charter schools and student characteristics. Without the variable or partitioning, the coefficient on the charter dummy variable is not statistically significant. Examining the test score changes reveals a strong negative relationship with the prior test score and the change in matched test scores. Since charter schools have a disproportionately larger share of students with lower prior test scores than traditional public schools, charter schools are associated with higher test score gains. When students are matched by their academic abilities, proxied by the prior test score, this bias is reduced and estimates suggest that traditional public schools have an advantage over charter schools.

Another potential bias is the effect of competition from charter schools on the traditional public schools within their "market area" schools in the district. Furthermore, the active choice by parents to send their children to charter schools would suggest that these students have home support for education, which would suggest a bias in favor of higher gains in test scores by charter schools. Consequently, one could argue that our estimates of the differential between test scores of traditional public schools and charters may be smaller than they actually are, since we have not controlled for this selection bias.

The results presented here on the effect of charter school attendance on student achievement are not conclusive. Test scores are imperfect indicators of achievement. While we examine test scores of individual students, we are able to control for student and teacher characteristics in only a limited way and some of our explanatory variables are based on aggregate building- and district-level information. Were it possible to design a controlled experiment, or find an appropriate natural experiment so that we could rigorously control for selection bias, we could have more confidence in the estimated gaps. Nevertheless, our analyses suggest that despite the fact that charter schools have the ability to introduce competition and new innovations in the provision of education, the evidence so far suggests that they will need to make up considerable ground as they become more established in order to overtake the test score gains of students at traditional public schools.

NOTES

1. See Hoxby (2004) for an analysis of the effects of charter school competition on public schools. Bettinger (2005), in contrast to Hoxby, finds no evidence of a positive impact on public schools.

2. Hoxby and Rockoff (2005) report the results of the first random assignment evaluation of charter schools. Students applying to three charter schools in Chicago drew a lottery number to determine admission. Those who "won" the lottery became the treatment group, and those who lost were included in the control group. They found that students in charter schools outperformed a comparable group of lotteried-out students who remained in traditional public schools by 5–6 percentile points in math and about 5 percentile points in reading. Undoubtedly, a random assignment evaluation based on a sufficiently large sample is ideal for examining the relative effects of charter schools vis-à-vis traditional public schools. These are the first results from a random assignment design. Unfortunately, the sample is small and the possibility of using random assignment evaluation in other locations is quite limited.

3. This paper is an extension of the authors' earlier (2002) working paper. It differs by focusing on the matched student dataset and providing a more in-depth examination of differences in changes in test scores over consecutive years between charters and traditional public schools.

4. Gill, Timpane, Ross, and Brewer (2001) provide an exhaustive review of school improvement initiatives that rely on choice mechanisms such as vouchers or charter schools.

5. Hollenbeck and Nelson (2001) raise a number of methodological questions about this study.

6. We use the term traditional public schools to denote buildings administered by local districts, and not chartered.

7. We tried another way to control for prior learning and academic ability. We regressed the prior test score on student characteristics and used the residual as the proxy for ability. This approach netted out the influence of student characteristics on the proxy for ability. We found, however, that the results using the actual test score and the residual were virtually identical, presumably because the student characteristics explained little of the variation in test scores, so we included the prior test score as the variable measuring ability.

8. It should be noted that similar results from the regression analysis are obtained when the differences in the total score are used.

9. There are also issues regarding intervening circumstances in which students with the same abilities may score differently on the tests. These circumstances may include test anxiety, illness, family issues, and other factors that could affect test taking and could lead to regression to the mean with regard to differences between science and math tests scores.

10. Several studies, including Hanushek et al. (2002) and Gronberg and Jansen (2001) have used student-specific effects as a way of dealing with this issue.

11. Eq. (5) is the same as Bettinger's (2005) lagged specification, except that he used only the same schools as his match and not the same students in the schools as we do. As he describes, this leaves open the possibility of changes in the student composition of the schools, which he documents.

12. The evaluation conducted by Horn and Miron (1999) did not examine differences in student test scores between PSAs and regular public schools using regression analysis and controlling for additional factors.

13. Hanushek et al. (2002) report the negative effects of student transfers on student achievement.

14. Some states, notably South Carolina and Kentucky, use statewide tests, along with other factors, to allocate state resources to schools. Michigan does not, but the State does award postsecondary scholarships to students based on their middle school and high school MEAP tests.

15. Researchers and evaluators use other measures of student outcomes, such as dropout rates (e.g., Hoxby, 1996). However, since most charter schools include only K-8 grades, dropout rates are not meaningful and are not recorded.

16. The procedures that we followed for matching students from fourth to fifth grade were as follows: (1) all observations with missing values for ethnicity, gender, and date of birth were deleted; (2) remaining observations were matched by district, building, ethnicity, gender, and date of birth; and (3) all observations with multiple matches were deleted. This procedure yielded a match rate of about 24 percent. Many of the non-matches were presumably due to students moving to different schools.

17. The (zero-order) correlations between the fourth-grade reading test score and the fifth-grade writing test score and between the fourth-grade math test score and the fifth-grade science test score were on the order of 0.76.

18. We also used the intermediate school district as the market area for charter schools, but found little difference in our results. The same was true for Bettinger (2005). He defined the market area as fixed distant around a charter school. He used various distances, including 5-, 1-, and 40-mile radii, and found that the results regarding the effectiveness of charter schools relative to traditional public schools are similar, except that the differences are smaller in value.

19. In their evaluation, Horn and Miron (1999) report that although many charter schools formed during the first few years targeted minority students, the trend in more recent years has been the opposite. The percentage of White students has risen from 35 percent in 1995 to about 60 percent in 1999.

20. The student's age is measured in days relative to the date of September 1, 1989. A person born on this date would turn nine years of age as the fourth-grade school year began. Those born before this date would be older when they entered the fourth grade. It is expected that, up to a certain date, older students would do better on tests than younger students. We entered age as a quadratic variable to take into account that students who have been held back for an extended period of time, presumably due to learning problems, will not perform as well on tests.

21. Since the dependent variable is the change in test scores, it is not obvious what the expected sign for the student characteristics should be. For levels, one might expect the coefficients on non-White and free and reduced price lunch to be negative but for differences, particularly since these tests are not designed as pre- and post-tests, the expected signs are ambiguous.

22. The correlation coefficient between the z-score of math tests and the non-White variable is -0.274, and the regression coefficient of the z-score of the math test regressed on the non-White variable and district fixed effects is -0.539 with a t-statistic of -23.86. The regression result suggests that a non-White student scores half a standard deviation lower on the math test than a White student. For the z-score reading tests, the results are similar: a correlation coefficient of -0.211 and a regression coefficient of -0.428 with a t-statistic of -18.42.

23. The writing test scores have only 7 unique values and the reading test scores have 21 unique values when compared to more than 80 unique values for the math test scores and 50 unique values for the science test scores.

ACKNOWLEDGMENTS

The authors greatly appreciate the detailed and insightful comments of Joe Stone on earlier analyses of charter schools and of Timothy Bartik for instructive insights on this paper. The authors also thank Kristine Heffel and Phyllis Molhoek for their valuable assistance in preparing this paper.

REFERENCES

Bettinger, E. P. (2005). The effect of charter schools on charter students and public schools. *Economics of Education Review*, *24*(2), 133–147.

Bifulco, R., & Ladd, H. F. (2004). *The impacts of charter schools on student achievement: Evidence from North Carolina*. Terry Sanford Institute of Public Policy, Duke Working Papers Series SAN04-01, Durham, NC.

Booker, K., Gilpatric, S., Gronberg, T. J., & Jansen, D. W. (2004). *Charter school performance in Texas.* Private Enterprise Research Center Working Paper, Texas A&M University.

Buddin, R., & Zimmer, R. (2005). A closer look at charter school student achievement. *Journal of Policy Analysis and Management, 24*(2), 351–372.

Eberts, R. W., & Hollenbeck, K. M. (2001). *An examination of student achievement in Michigan charter schools.* W. E. Upjohn Institute Staff Working Paper no. 01–68, Kalamazoo, MI.

Eberts, R. W., & Hollenbeck, K. M. (2002). *Impact of charter school attendance on student achievement in Michigan.* W. E. Upjohn Institute Working Paper no. 02-80. Kalamazoo, MI.

Gill, B. P., Timpane, P. M., Ross, K. E., & Brewer, D. J. (2001). *Rhetoric versus reality: What we know and what we need to know about vouchers and charter schools.* Santa Monica, CA: RAND.

Good, T. L., & Braden, J. S. (with contributions by D. W. Drury). (2000). *Charting a new course: Fact and fiction about charter schools.* Alexandria, VA: National School Boards Association.

Greene, J. P., Forster, G., & Winters, M. A. (2003). *Apples to apples: An evaluation of charter schools serving general student populations.* Manhattan Institute for Policy Research. Education Working Paper no. 1. New York, NY.

Gronberg, T. J., & Jansen, D. W. (2001). *Navigating newly chartered waters.* Austin, TX: Texas Public Policy Foundation.

Gronberg, T. J., & Jansen, D. W. (2005). *Texas charter schools: An assessment in 2005.* Texas Public Policy Foundation.

Hanushek, E. A., Kain, J. F., & Rivkin, S. G. (2002). The impact of charter schools on academic achievement. Paper prepared for Smith Richardson Foundation and the Packard Humanities Institute.

Hassel, B. C. (1999). *The charter school challenge: Avoiding the pitfalls, fulfilling the promise.* Washington, DC: Brookings Institution Press.

Horn, J., & Miron, G. (1999). *Evaluation of the Michigan Public School academy initiative.* Western Michigan University, Kalamazoo, MI: The Evaluation Center.

Hoxby, C. M. (1996). How teachers' unions affect public education production. *Quarterly Journal of Economics, 111*, 671–718.

Hoxby, C. M. (2001). How school choice affects the achievement of public school students. Paper prepared for Koret Task Force meeting, Hoover Institution, Stanford, CA, September 20–21.

Hoxby, C. M. (2004). Achievement in charter schools and regular public schools in the United States: Understanding the differences. Paper prepared for the National Institute for Child Health and Human Development.

Hoxby, C. M., & Rockoff, J. E. (2005). Findings from the city of big shoulders. *Education Next, 4*(Fall), 52–59.

Michigan Department of Education. (2000). Director of Michigan Public School academics. Unpublished document dated October 13.

Hollenbeck, K. M., & Nelson, C. (2001). *Does charter school attendance improve test scores?* W. E. Upjohn Institute Staff Working Paper no. 01–70. Kalamazoo, MI.

Solmon, L., Paark, K., & Garcia, D. (2001). *Does charter school attendance improve test scores? The Arizona results.* Phoenix, AZ: The Goldwater Institute's Center for Market-Based Education.

DOES SCHOOL CHOICE INCREASE SCHOOL QUALITY? EVIDENCE FROM NORTH CAROLINA CHARTER SCHOOLS

George M. Holmes, Jeff DeSimone and Nicholas G. Rupp

ABSTRACT

Federal "No Child Left Behind" legislation, which enables students of low-performing schools to exercise public school choice, exemplifies a widespread belief that competing for students will spur public schools to higher achievement. We investigate how the introduction of school choice in North Carolina, via a dramatic increase in the number of charter schools, affects student performance on statewide end-of-year testing at traditional public schools. We find test score gains from competition that are robust to a variety of specifications. Charter school competition causes an approximately one percent increase in the score, which constitutes about one quarter of the average yearly growth.

Improving School Accountability: Check-Ups or Choice
Advances in Applied Microeconomics, Volume 14, 131–155

ISSN: 0278-0984/doi:10.1016/S0278-0984(06)14006-7

1. INTRODUCTION

School choice has become one of the most contentious public policy debates in the United States. Voters in Michigan and California rejected statewide voucher programs in 2000. Federal "No Child Left Behind" legislation implemented in Fall 2002 mandates limited school choice. One of the underlying assumptions motivating school choice is that introducing competition into education will increase school quality as schools face market pressures to attract students and their associated public funding.[1]

However, not only do we know little about the effect of school choice on the students who switch schools, we know even less about the effect on students who do not exercise the option to switch schools. In this paper, we explore the latter effect by examining the link between increased competition for students and the quality of schools facing competition. If the introduction of school choice, and the subsequent competition for students, encourages schools to improve quality, then the argument supporting the expansion of school choice is strengthened.

The expansion of North Carolina's charter school system provides a natural experiment for exploring this hypothesis. In the 1996–1997 school year, North Carolina had no charter schools. Just three years later nearly 100 were operating. This expansion of charter schools, which provides parents with more schooling options, is expected to spur improvement in the traditional public schools, which have long dominated public and secondary education. We examine the expansion of the charter school system, both temporally and geographically, in order to estimate the effect of school choice on the performance of public schools.

Charter schools are public schools that are founded by community leaders and parents.[2] Charter schools receive public funds but are allowed greater curricular flexibility than traditional public schools.[3] Across the United States, the charter school system has expanded rapidly. According to the National Center for Education Statistics, approximately 2,000 charter schools operated in 2000–2001 (U.S. Department of Education, 2002). The enrollment mechanism varies by state, but typically students can leave a traditional school and enroll in a charter school for no monetary cost.

Charter schools cannot discriminate against students, either by ability, socioeconomic status, or exceptional student status. Charter schools, however, can subtly dissuade potential high-cost students from enrolling. Fiske and Ladd (2000) found that public schools commonly encouraged a donation to the school upon enrollment, and this donation was increased with perceived quality. Their study focuses on New Zealand schools; it is possible that similar mechanisms operate with charter schools in the United States, although this has not been documented. Of course, charters could effectively discriminate in other ways. The physical setup of the school could deter enrollment by students with certain physical limitations; a curriculum heavy in advanced work would discourage students of marginal ability.

Two justifications are commonly offered in support of charter schools. The first is that increased curricular flexibility allows charter schools to adapt their curricula to particular needs of their student populations. Although most charters focus on traditional subjects, some specialize in the arts while others specialize in vocational education. Therefore, potential benefits conveyed by charter schools likely accrue primarily to students attending the charter school as opposed to those remaining in traditional schools.[4]

The second justification is that the infusion of competition into the public education system provides an incentive for traditional schools to increase quality. This follows the standard economic argument that competition forces firms to increase quality and/or lower price. For instance, when a charter school opens, the traditional school no longer has a monopoly on public education in a feeder district and faces the prospect of losing students to a new competitor. To the extent that the school's agent (ostensibly a principal) experiences disutility from a decline in enrollment, this might lead to an increase in the traditional school's quality in order to retain students. Such disutility might result from a decline in stature of the school in the community, lessened prospects for career advancement, a loss of personnel and budget provided by the funding agency, or a decrease in job satisfaction. Depending on the form of the public education cost function, a decrease in enrollment might also increase average costs and lower the quality of instruction for remaining students.

This second effect is particularly interesting from a policy perspective. The idea that empowered parents can "vote with their feet" (Tiebout, 1956) is the primary tenet behind other current experiments in school choice. For example, while some parents desire vouchers in order to switch their children from the assigned traditional public school to a private school, others are likely interested in vouchers so they can credibly threaten to remove children from a traditional school unless improvements are made. By exploring the degree to which the availability of charter schools affects the quality of competing traditional schools, we add to the debate on school choice.

Current evidence that links school choice and quality is limited, but typically finds some quality gains to choice. Hoxby (2000a) looks at choice within Metropolitan Stastistical Area's (MSA), finding some benefits to competition. Blair and Staley (1995) report that test performance in a school district is correlated with performance in neighboring districts, though their results may be partially explained by spatial correlation. Borland and Howsen (1992) find weak evidence that lower school district concentration leads to higher achievement. Rouse (1998) finds that the Milwaukee voucher program increased student achievement. Hoxby (2002) examines the effects of vouchers in Milwaukee and charter schools in Michigan and Arizona and finds productivity and achievement gains from increased choice. Cullen, Levitt, and Jacob (2000) use Chicago Public School data to analyze the effect of choice on the students who change schools, obtaining mixed results. Greene and Forster (2002) report gains to competition as measured by an index of the distance between traditional schools and charters. Finally, Holmes (2003) finds small gains from charter school expansion in North Carolina using student-level data. In contrast, Bettinger (2005) finds no gains to competition from Michigan charter schools, and Bifulco and Ladd (2004) reach a similar conclusion using student-level data from North Carolina. In addition, Cardon (2003) theoretically addresses the issue using a model of quality choice with capacity constraints, finding that an equilibrium exists in which charter schools offer a higher quality that competing public schools will not match.

We contribute to the school choice literature by exploiting an expansion of the North Carolina charter school system in combination with extensive school achievement data. Our hypothesis is that the expansion of the charter school system has encouraged traditional schools to increase achievement by offering greater school choice to North Carolina parents. Our results generally support this hypothesis. In particular, we find that the closer a charter school is to a traditional school (and hence the greater the competition facing the traditional school), the greater the achievement gains. These results persist across a wide set of models. The gain is not inconsequential, since the average achievement increase due to charter school competition (one percent) is about one-fourth of the average yearly increase.[5]

The remainder of the paper is organized as follows. Section 2 develops a theoretical model and Section 3 presents the econometric model. Sections 4 and 5 discuss the data and the estimation results. Section 6 summarizes the main findings, addresses limitations, and offers suggestions for future research.

2. CONCEPTUAL MODEL

Consider an agent (e.g. a school principal) who manages the sole traditional public school in the feeder district. Parents can choose for their children to attend either the traditional school or a competing charter school that has a price of attendance p, which includes non-monetary costs such as travel time.[6] Assume that the utility function of the agent,

$$U(M, e) \tag{1}$$

has two components, effort exerted by the agent (e) and membership of the school (M). M is a demand function defined as

$$M(q(e), p) \tag{2}$$

where q is the quality of the traditional school.

We assume that U is increasing in M, decreasing in e (holding M constant) and concave in each. Since M is a demand function, it is increasing in both the price of a substitute good (p) and quality (q). The agent can increase the quality of the school by exerting more effort, perhaps through more staff meetings, greater vigilance over instruction quality, or implementation of after-school programs, although the second derivative of $q(e)$ is negative.

The agent chooses e to maximize

$$U(e, M(q(e), p)) \tag{3}$$

The first-order condition is

$$U_e + U_M M_q q_e = 0 \tag{4}$$

where subscripts denote partial derivatives. Eq. (4) indicates that at the optimal effort level the marginal disutility from effort equals the marginal utility stemming from the increased membership that results from the positive impact of additional effort on school quality.

We examine the impact of increased charter school availability on traditional school test scores, or in terms of the model, the effect of decreases in p on q. Since $(\partial q/\partial e) > 0$, the sign of $\partial q/\partial p$ is the same as the sign of $\partial e/\partial p$. Using the implicit function theorem, it can be shown that a sufficient condition for $(\partial e/\partial p) < 0$ is

$$\frac{\partial^2 U}{\partial e \partial M} < 0 \tag{5}$$

That is, a decrease in cost of charter school attendance increases the quality of the competing traditional school if the marginal disutility of effort is increasing in membership or, symmetrically, the marginal utility of membership is decreasing in effort. This implies that as enrollment in the traditional school increases, the agent has less incentive to exert substantial effort. Alternatively, at high levels of effort, increases in membership provide little benefit. Although Eq. (5) does not hold with certainty, the practical implications seem intuitively probable.

We define the traditional school's competitor as the nearest charter school and examine whether the distance to the competitor influences the performance of the traditional school.[7] Since charter schools charge no tuition, a major component of the price of attending the competitor is travel cost, in terms of lost wages, depreciation of the transport vehicle, and lost leisure time. Travel cost increases as distance from the traditional school increases, holding other factors constant. This is especially important in North Carolina since charter schools are not required to provide transportation. Thus, we use the distance to the nearest charter school as a proxy for travel cost – and the price of attendance p – to examine whether charter school competition increases traditional school quality.

Private schools and neighboring traditional school districts also compete with traditional schools. We ignore these two additional sources of competition because the cost of switching to either is substantially higher than that of switching to a charter school. Unlike traditional and charter schools, tuition at private schools is considerable. In addition to travel cost, students that change schools also incur a switching cost. This difficult-to-quantify cost involves the psychological and emotional distress from attending a new school. We should note, however, that the switching cost of moving from a traditional school to a charter school is less than switching between neighboring traditional school districts since the latter typically requires the family to move its residence. Thus, threats to transfer to a nearby charter school are more credible than threats to transfer to a neighboring traditional or private school.

3. ECONOMETRIC MODEL

The primary effect of interest is that of a change in the price of charter school attendance, as represented by distance to the nearest charter school, on the quality of the traditional school. Our measure of quality is the achievement of the students in the traditional school as represented by end-of-year test scores. We therefore estimate the following school-level test score production function:

$$\text{SCORE}_{it} = \theta\text{SCORE}_{it-1} + \gamma\text{DISTANCE}_{it} + \beta X_{it} + \mu_i + \varepsilon_{it} \qquad (6)$$

The lagged test score accounts for underlying student quality and its inclusion as an explanatory variable in a flexible way to implement the "value-added" test score production specification that is commonly used in the literature. We also include observed time-varying characteristics of the school X_{it} that potentially influence achievement. Error components μ_i, which is time invariant, and ε_{it}, which is transitory, are unobserved. The parameter of interest is γ, the effect of price on quality.

We estimate two types of models. First, we estimate cross-sectional models by year. Because the lagged SCORE term and the μ_i term (a school-specific time-invariant component) are correlated, OLS estimation will be inconsistent. We therefore estimate the cross-sectional models by standard instrumental variables (IV) technique.

Our data, however, are longitudinal, and cross-sectional models yield inefficient estimates by disregarding potentially important information. To account for the panel nature of the data and to test for robustness, we estimate panel models using the Arellano–Bond (1991) procedure for dynamic panel models, an IV method that accounts for the inclusion of the lagged dependent variable in a longitudinal framework.

4. DATA

The data for this study come primarily from three sources. School test performance data are provided by the North Carolina Department of Public Instruction (NCDPI). Beginning in 1996–1997, NCDPI has tested students at the end of each school year as part of its "ABC's of Public Education" program. These end-of-year tests are taken statewide by all students in grades 3 through 12. Tests vary by grade. We analyze outcomes of math, reading, and writing tests taken by students in grades 3 through 8. The measure we use is the school-level "performance composite", which NCDPI computes as the percentage of tests taken that meet a NCDPI-defined achievement standard. The performance composite is a combination of the math, reading, and writing scores, so that the performance composite reflects NCDPI's estimate of the percent of students with satisfactory achievement. Since the performance composite is widely reported and disseminated by the media, traditional schools have added market pressure to improve test performance. Although parents would likely suspect which schools are "good" and "bad" in the absence of test results, publication of the NCDPI scores provides parents with quantitative information on which they can form their judgments if they choose.

The use of test scores to measure school quality is potentially contentious. Researchers have used various alternative measures of school quality, such as labor market outcomes (e.g. Card & Krueger, 1992) and further educational attainment (e.g. Krueger, 1999; Betts, 2001) of attendees. Hanushek (1979) argues that test scores proxy school quality relatively well in earlier grades. Hence, this paper examines achievement only in elementary and middle schools. Only charter schools that offer at least one grade between 3 and 8 (inclusive) are included as potential competitors.

Our price variable is the distance from the traditional school to the nearest charter school. To generate this measure, we map the latitude and longitude of traditional schools and charter schools throughout the state, identify the closest charter school to each traditional school, and compute the aerial distance between the two.[8] The distance measure could not be computed for schools with addresses that we were unable to map (about 100 schools, or seven percent of the sample). These schools, which are disproportionately rural, listed addresses with rural routes or streets that could not be located and thus are excluded from the analysis.

The third major data source is the National Center for Education Statistics' Common Core of Data (CCD). The CCD contains measures of the student population, including racial and ethnic composition, the percentage qualifying for free lunch, and the total enrollment of the school. These files also contain information on personnel counts, allowing us to use the ratio of pupils to full-time equivalent instruction personnel to proxy for class size. Although Hanushek, Rivkin, and Taylor (1996) find that the use of school-level measures may lead to biased estimators, neither the CCD nor NCDPI provide class size measures. One additional factor that might affect test performance is the degree of urbanization. Thus, we calculate the county's population density and include it as a regressor.

To balance our panel, we exclude schools with missing test performance measures for any year during our sample period, which spans from 1996–1997 to 1999–2000. This assumes that the sample attrition process is random. Schools with missing test performance data include those that did not report ABC results in a year (due to insufficient student testing or some other technical reason), began operating after 1996–1997, or ceased operations before 1999–2000. We also drop schools located in three North Carolina Outer Banks counties with substantial water boundaries, making the straight-line distance a poor proxy for actual travel time to and from these localities.

5. RESULTS

We begin by describing the growth of *all* charter schools in North Carolina. Table 1 shows that the charter school system (including schools not in our

Table 1. Charter Schools in North Carolina.

Year	Total Public Enrollment	Charter School Enrollment	Percent of Public Students in Charter (%)	Charter Schools in Operation
1997–1998	1,208,368	4,456	0.37	28
1998–1999	1,229,929	8,183	0.67	52
1999–2000	1,249,922	12,128	0.97	74
2000–2001	1,268,406	14,899	1.17	91

Source: North Carolina Department of Public Instruction.

Table 2. Means of Distance Measures for North Carolina Schools.

Measure	1997–1998	1998–1999	1999–2000
Continuous			
Distance (km)	32.036	27.322	21.426
Log (distance)	3.180	2.970	2.698
Indicators			
Within 5 km	0.093	0.142	0.193
Within 10 km	0.178	0.265	0.350
Within 15 km	0.272	0.366	0.480
Within 20 km	0.353	0.454	0.590
Within 25 km	0.425	0.539	0.694
Within County	0.329	0.464	0.570

Note: For the distance indicators, "mean" refers to the proportion of traditional schools within the given distance of the nearest charter.

study sample that do not enroll any students in grades 3 through 8) has grown substantially during the sample period. In 1996–1997, there were no charter schools. The following year, there were 28 charter schools in operation that included at least some of the grades 3 through 8. By 1999–2000, there were 74 such charter schools. Despite the rapid growth in the charter school system, charter school attendees comprise just over one percent of North Carolina public school enrollment in 2000–2001.

Table 2 presents various measures of distance to the nearest charter school for the sample years. As the number of charter schools nearly tripled, the average distance to the closest charter school has fallen by about one-third, from 32 km in 1997–1998 to 21 km in 1999–2000. As an alternative to distance (or the log of distance in some regressions), we calculate five indicator variables that equal one if and only if the traditional school is within a given number of kilometers (5, 10, 15, 20, and 25 km) of the nearest charter. For example, the distance to the nearest charter school is less than 5 km for about nine percent of traditional schools in 1997–1998, but twice as many traditional schools are within 5 km of the nearest charter school in 1999–2000. We also calculate an indicator for whether a charter school is operating in the same county as the traditional school, the mean of which also increases over time.

The influence of a nearby charter school on traditional school performance depends, in part, on the credibility of students' threats to switch to the charter. Threats are more credible as the distance between the schools decreases. In order to frame the distances over which charter schools might affect traditional school enrollment, we examine separate data on approximately 2,000 North Carolina students in grades 3 through 8 who switch from a traditional school to a charter school. The median distance between the two schools for these switchers is about 6 km, with a 95th percentile of around 22 km. Although these data represent actual rather than potential migration patterns, these statistics suggest that effects of charter schools located beyond 25 km from a traditional school should be small.[9]

Fig. 1 maps North Carolina counties and their charter school status during the three sample years. It is evident that counties in metropolitan statistical areas are more likely to contain a charter school. There is also considerable variation over time with many new charter schools opening each year. Fig. 2 tabulates distance from the traditional school to the nearest charter by whether any charter was operating in the same county as the traditional school in 1999. For example, 90 percent of schools in counties with a charter school are located within 20 km of the charter.

Table 3 summarizes the mean performance composite among traditional schools and changes from the previous year. The mean performance composite increased over time from roughly 67 in 1996–1997 to 75 in 1999–2000. The yearly increase fell over time, though, from around four in 1997–1998 to just over one in 1999–2000.

Table 4 presents sample summary statistics. In the typical traditional school, approximately 3 percent of students are Hispanic, 32 percent are African-American, and 38 percent are eligible for free lunch. On average schools have 15 students per faculty member, an enrollment of 566 students, and a performance composite of about 72.

5.1. Cross-Section Regressions

We begin by exploring cross-section regression models. The cross-section models estimate the effect of five different distance measures. Two of these

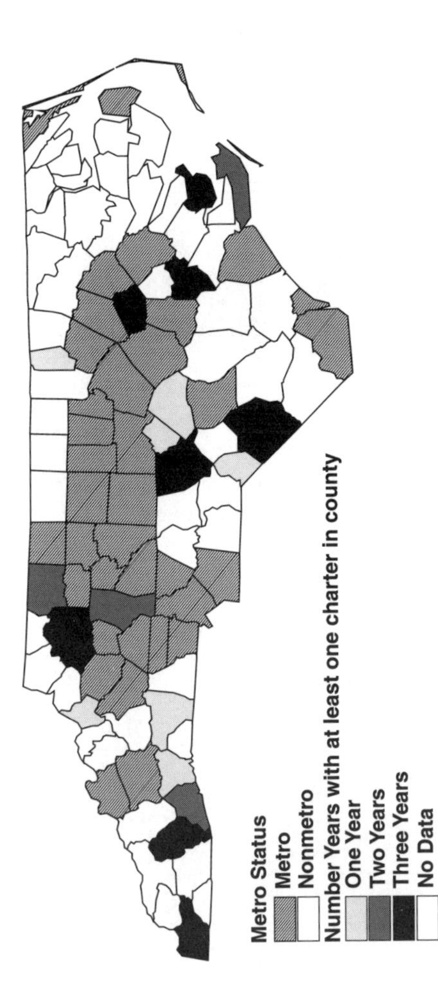

Fig. 1. North Carolina Charter Schools: 1997–2000 Years Refer to Academic School Years: 1997–1998, 1998–1999, and 1999–2000.

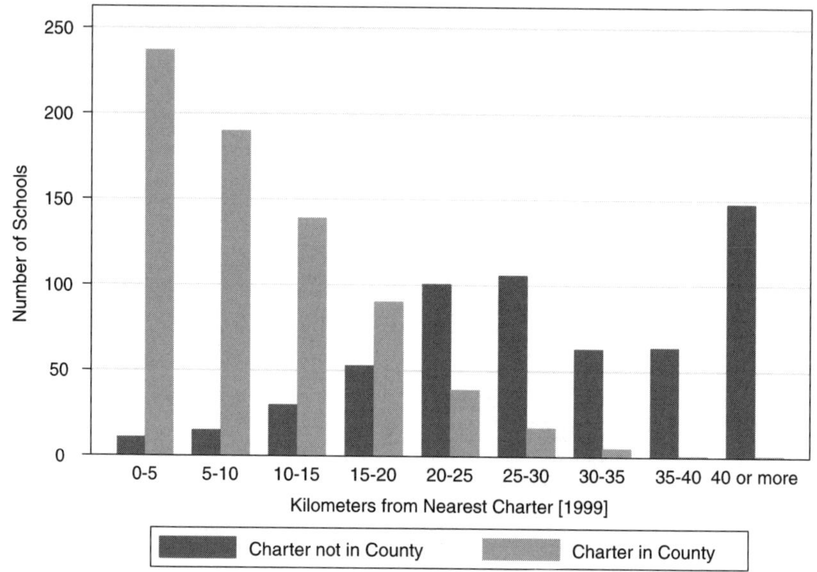

Fig. 2. Distribution of Distance from Nearest Charter for Schools with and without Charters in the Same County.

Table 3. Achievement of Traditional Schools in North Carolina for End-of-Year Testing.

Year	Performance Composite		Increase from Previous Year	
	Mean	S.D.	Mean	S.D.
1996–1997	66.93	11.34		
1997–1998	71.11	10.37	4.18	5.43
1998–1999	73.69	9.88	2.58	4.76
1999–2000	74.80	9.94	1.12	4.52

Source: North Carolina Department of Public Instruction (NCDPI). $N = 1307$ in each year.
Note: The performance composite is the percentage of tests taken that meet an NCDPI-defined achievement standard, based on a combination of math, reading, and writing scores, and thus reflects NCDPI's estimate of the percent of students with satisfactory achievement.

are parametric: the number of kilometers to the nearest charter school and the log of this measure. We also explore three binary indicators. Two of these indicate whether the traditional school is within 10 or 20 km, respectively, of the nearest charter school. The third is an indicator for whether a

Table 4. Summary Statistics for North Carolina Traditional Schools in the Study Sample, 1996–2000.

Variable	Mean	S.D.
Proportion of students Hispanic	0.033	0.042
Proportion of students free lunch eligible	0.382	0.194
Proportion of students African-American	0.319	0.247
Student–faculty ratio	15.216	2.438
County population density	1.080	0.955
Enrollment of school	566.564	229.276
Performance composite	71.632	10.828
Log (performance composite)	4.273	0.163

Note: Study sample consist of 1307 schools. Multiple years of data exist for each school.

charter school is located in the county that year. Since our hypothesis predicts that traditional school quality will decrease as the distance to the nearest charter increases, the predicted coefficients are negative for parametric measures and positive for the indicators.

Beyond the potential inconsistency from using the lagged dependent variable as a regressor, this specification has two possible limitations. First, the lagged performance composite score that proxies for student ability is measured with error, because the score is an imperfect measure of underlying student quality. To account for this problem, we use the twice-lagged score as an instrument for the once-lagged score. Second, Bettinger (2005) found that charter school placement, and thus distance from the traditional school to the nearest charter school, may be a function of traditional school quality. For example, charters may locate in areas with above-average student quality in order to "skim" the high-performing students and appear to be particularly effective. In this situation, a cross-section regression would indicate a beneficial effect of charter school competition because the average traditional school facing competition has higher quality students than the average school not facing competition. Alternatively, charters may originate in locales in which parents are dissatisfied with the performance of the traditional school. If students in these areas have below-average achievement, competition would appear detrimental to traditional school performance because the average school facing competition has lower quality students than the average school not facing competition.

We specify an IV model to address the possibility that charter schools are endogenously placed. Since North Carolina charter schools are heterogeneous in focus and history, including some schools that converted from traditional public or private administration, no single model explains how charter schools are instituted in North Carolina, and therefore there is no "ideal" instrument for charter school placement. Instead, we use three county-level factors that plausibly influence charter school location as instruments for the distance measure: the average performance composite in the county, the proportion of African-American students and the total number of students. The F-test of joint significance of these variables in the (log) distance regressions yields an F-statistic of 34, with a p-value of 0.0001, meaning that our instruments have sufficient power to explain variations in distance. Moreover, although these instruments could in principle directly influence student achievement, in all specifications they jointly pass tests of overidentification at the 5 percent significance level. Thus, our instruments can credibly be used to test for the exogeneity of charter school placement. In fact, for all distance variable specifications, Hausman tests of exogeneity are insignificant (i.e. the IV estimates are not significantly different from ordinary least squares estimates), implying that the distance measure can be treated as exogenous.[10] For example, one specification generated a Hausman of 0.21 $\sim\chi^2(1)$, a p-value of 0.65. Therefore, our cross-sectional and panel IV analysis assumes that charter school placement, and thus distance to the nearest charter school, is exogenous. We continue to instrument for the lagged performance score, however.

Table 5 summarizes the cross-section regression results. A separate regression is estimated for each of the three sample years and for each of the five distance measures, resulting in 15 separate models. Eight of the fifteen distance estimates are significantly different from zero and all have the expected sign. In the first and third year, all three distance indicators are significant. In 1997–1998, the magnitude of the charter effect is invariant to whether the charter is within 10 or 20 km, while in 1999–2000, the magnitude is twice as large for the shorter distance. This pattern, as well as the larger coefficient for "charter in county" in 1997–1998, is consistent with the dramatic growth of the charter system during these two years: in 1999–2000 more traditional schools were likely to have charters within the county and charters within 20 km. In these two years, the only parametric measure that is significant is the log of distance in 1999–2000. The results for 1998–1999 are the opposite, since distance is significant but the indicators are not.[11]

The relevant policy question, however, is what happens to the quality of traditional schools after the onset of charter school competition. We explore this question, most appropriately addressed from a longitudinal perspective, in the next section.

Table 5. Cross-Sectional IV Models.

Year	1997–1998	1998–1999	1999–2000
Distance in km	-4×10^{-5}	-2×10^{-4}*	-1×10^{-4}
	(8×10^{-5})	(8×10^{-5})	(8×10^{-5})
Log (distance)	−0.003	−0.002	−0.007**
	(0.002)	(0.002)	(0.002)
Charter within 10 km	0.012*	−0.002	0.018**
	(0.006)	(0.005)	(0.004)
Charter within 20 km	0.012*	0.004	0.010**
	(0.005)	(0.004)	(0.004)
Charter in county	0.013**	0.003	0.008*
	(0.005)	(0.004)	(0.004)
Observations	1,286	1,307	1,307

Note: Dependent variable: Log (performance composite); standard errors are in parentheses; Each cell contains the parameter estimate on the distance measure from a regression using data only from the indicated year with the corresponding distance variable as the only included distance measure. Thus, the table reports an estimate for $3 \times 5 = 15$ regressions.
Other included regressors include the percent of the students that are African-American, Hispanic, and free lunch eligible, the county population density, school enrollment, and the natural log of the lagged performance score (instrumented by the natural log of the twice-lagged score); The sample size in 1997–1998 is less than 1,307 due to missing data for the twice-lagged score.
*Significant at 5%;
**Significant at 1%.

5.2. IV Panel Models

Table 6 presents results from the Arellano-Bond (1991) panel IV models. Again, we instrument the once-lagged score with the twice-lagged score to account for measurement error. Model (1) uses the natural log of the kilometers from the nearest charter school to account for the degree of competition. The estimated elasticity of Model (1) is 0.003, which is statistically insignificant. This elasticity might seem small at first blush, but recall that it is conditional on the previous year performance composite. The average performance composite gain in 1999–2000, for example, is 1.1 points (1.7 percent), so halving the distance to the nearest charter would bring about an increase of just less than 10 percent of the average achievement gain.

Models (2) through (6) control for charter school competition using indicators for whether a charter school was operating within a given distance. In all of these models, charter school competition raises the performance composite of the traditional school. The effect is significant at standard

Table 6. Arellano–Bond IV Models.

	(1)	(2)	(3)	(4)	(5)	(6)	(7)
Log (distance)	−0.003 (0.003)						
Charter within 5 km		0.011 (0.006)					
Charter within 10 km			0.010* (0.005)				
Charter within 15 km				0.010* (0.005)			
Charter within 20 km					0.010* (0.004)		
Charter within 25 km						0.010* (0.004)	
Charter in County							0.008 (0.004)
Log (lagged performance composite)	0.415** (0.028)	0.633** (0.022)	0.634** (0.022)	0.637** (0.022)	0.638** (0.022)	0.638** (0.022)	0.635** (0.022)
Percent of students Hispanic	−.246* (0.100)	−.316** (0.106)	−.314** (0.106)	−.315** (0.106)	−.311** (0.106)	−.310** (0.106)	−.310** (0.106)
Percent of students free lunch eligible	0.066** (0.026)	0.119** (0.027)	0.118** (0.027)	0.119** (0.027)	0.120** (0.027)	0.119** (0.027)	0.118** (0.027)
Percent of students African-American	−0.359** (0.046)	−0.381** (0.052)	−0.381** (0.052)	−0.379** (0.052)	−0.380** (0.052)	−0.380** (0.052)	−0.378** (0.052)
Student–faculty ratio	−0.002 (0.001)	−0.002 (0.001)	−0.002 (0.001)	−0.002 (0.001)	−0.002 (0.001)	−0.002 (0.001)	−0.002 (0.001)
Constant	0.007** (0.002)	−0.035** (0.003)	−0.035** (0.003)	−0.035** (0.003)	−0.035** (0.003)	−.035** (0.003)	−0.035** (0.003)

Note: Standard errors are in parentheses. Dependent variable: Natural log of performance composite. $N = 1{,}307$ in all regressions. Models also include year indicators. Each regression contains four years of data except for the first column, which contains only three years because distance is infinite in 1996–1997.

*Significant at 5%;

**Significant at 1%.

significance levels for all indicators except within 5 km, and is nearly significant for that indicator.

In all five cases, charter school competition increases traditional school performance by about one percent. This represents more than one-half of the average achievement gain of 1.7 percent in 1999–2000. Although the estimated charter school effect from a cross-sectional perspective seems rather small, from an intertemporal perspective – which, after all, is how policy is implemented – the increase is nontrivial. Viewed alternatively, if we use the estimated increase in performance composite of one percent and the performance of the average school not located within 10 km of a charter school in 1999–2000 (75 percent), introducing charter school competition would increase the proportion of students "passing" from 75 percent to 75.75 percent, thus reducing the percent not achieving the standard from 25 to 24.25, a three percent decrease. As the average scores increase, further increases will be harder and harder to achieve; the effects we find here demonstrate an increase in average scores that may not be large but are nontrivial increases nonetheless.

The magnitudes of these effects are roughly two to five times as large as that of decreasing the student/faculty ratio by 1. Introducing school choice seems like a promising alternative to lowering class size, which has received substantially more public policy attention, and is likely more cost-effective in the context of charter schools. Since state funding follows the student, an increase in the charter school system implies no increase in spending.[12] For instance, in 2002, the North Carolina Governor's Office proposed a $26 million increase in the state budget to reduce average class size by roughly 1.8 students. Ignoring statistical significance, this would increase scores by approximately 0.36 percent, about one-third of the increase attributable to the opening of a neighboring charter school.

We estimate a large positive significant effect of charter school competition despite the fact that one aspect of our research design likely biases this estimate downward. Our measure of charter competition, whether a charter is within a certain distance from the traditional school, assumes that all charter schools provide competition for traditional schools. But a substantial percentage of charter schools (both nationwide and in North Carolina) target below-average achieving student populations. For example, charter schools designed for dropout recovery, adjudicated youth, or at-risk students presumably do not pose a competitive threat to traditional schools, which may not have many such students and in any case would see their mean achievement scores increase if such students were lost to nearby charters. Thus, our competition variables, i.e. distance indicators, are biased upward (more competitors are considered to be within certain distances than is actually the case), which biases the estimated effect of competition downward. Belfield and Levin (2002), in a review of the literature, find that a one standard deviation increase in private school enrollment leads to less than a 0.1 standard deviation change in achievement. Our estimated effect is about 0.02 of a standard deviation.

Model (7) uses an indicator for whether a charter school is operating in the same county as the traditional school. The point estimate on this parameter is again positive and similar in magnitude to the other indicators, although it is marginally insignificant.

5.3. Is Selection Driving These Results?

One possible alternative explanation for improved traditional school achievement when a charter school opens nearby is migration from the traditional school to the charter by lower performing students. Simple tests, however, suggest that, if anything, the *opposite* phenomenon occurs in our sample: students switching from traditional to charter schools are *above*-average performers.

We can explore this issue using student-level data: although we lack comprehensive individual student tracking data necessary to follow all students longitudinally, we have once-lagged test scores for all students contributing current scores from a school. Thus, we calculate a once-lagged score specific to each school, grade, and test subject (math and reading) as the average score the previous year in that subject for all students enrolled in that grade and school this year. For example, we obtain the average 1998–1999 math score for all students in school s, grade 4, in 1999–2000. If low-performing students leave school s for a charter school that opened nearby in 1999–2000, then the average score in 1998–1999 for the students attending this traditional school in 1999–2000 should be higher than the corresponding score for an otherwise identical school not facing new charter school competition.

Note that this approach uses pre-intervention data – the scores from 1998–1999 for those students attending school s in 1999–2000. In the absence of systematic selection, the 1998–1999 scores for students attending the school in 1999–2000 should be similar to the 1997–1998 scores for students attending the school in 1998–1999. The difference from the data discussed in this paper is that those measures are school averages for a given year (e.g. the percent of students attending the school in 1998–1999 who passed the test in 1998–1999), although the data used here is the previous year score for those students attending in the current year (e.g. the percent of students attending the school in 1999–2000 who attended the same school in 1998–1999 and passed the test in 1998–1999). These data allow the separation of competition effects from selection effects.

This can be tested using within-school variation by estimating Eq. (7), where subscripts denote school (s), cohort (c), and time (t). As described above, LAGSCORE represents the once-lagged performance composite and COMPETE is a dummy for whether a charter school is located within 10 km. Unobserved effects include time effects (τ_t), school-cohort effects ($\mu_{s,c}$), and idiosyncratic school-time-cohort effects ($\varepsilon_{c,s,t}$). Parameter γ thus measures whether the change in the lagged score differs by whether the school faced charter school competition. If lower scoring students switch from traditional schools to competing charter schools, and the result is an increase in the observed achievement, then γ will be positive:

$$\text{LAGSCORE}_{s,c,t} = \theta + \tau_t + \gamma\text{COMPETE}_{s,c,t} + \mu_{s,c} + \varepsilon_{s,c,t} \tag{7}$$

Table 7 reports the estimates of Eq. (7) for all six cohorts that we can follow longitudinally. Of the 12 cohort–subject pairs beginning with grade 3 in 1997–1998 and ending with grade 8 in 1998–1999 for both subjects (reading and math), only three experience a significant change in lagged test score, all of which are *lower* after the introduction of a charter school. This provides evidence that *above*-average students are more likely to exit traditional schools for charters than below-average students.

Table 7. Relationship between Charter Competition and Average Performance Composites.

Cohort	Year	Math	Reading
7th grade	1997–1998	0.1289	−0.167
8th grade	1998–1999	(0.357)	(0.214)
6th grade	1997–1998	−0.2111	−0.1381
7th grade	1998–1999	(0.233)	(0.140)
8th grade	1999–2000		
5th grade	1997–1998	0.1592	0.0059
6th grade	1998–1999	(0.407)	(0.240)
7th grade	1999–2000		
4th grade	1997–1998	−0.3846	−0.0717
5th grade	1998–1999	(0.168)	(0.121)
6th grade	1999–2000		
3rd grade	1997–1998	−0.7604**	−0.4347**
4th grade	1998–1999	(0.168)	(0.121)
5th grade	1999–2000		
3rd grade	1998–1999	−0.4649	−0.4611*
4th grade	1999–2000	(0.271)	(0.207)

Note: Standard errors are in parentheses. Each cell contains the parameter estimate on "a charter within 10 km" indicator in a fixed-effect average score regression that also includes year indicators. The samples are cohorts of students over time. For example, the top panel follows those students in 7th grade in 1997–1998 to 8th grade 1998–1999, the cohort is not observed the following year, because students are not observed after 8th grade. The second row "6th grade 1997–1998" contains data for the three years 1997–1998 (6th grade), 1998–1999 (7th grade), and 1999–2000 (8th grade).

*Significant at 5%;

**Significant at 1%.

Finally, for those students that we are able to identify, we examine the performance of students who switched from a traditional school to a charter.[13] We find that approximately 75 percent of those who switched had a higher score than the average score in the traditional school the year before they left. This is direct evidence that charter-induced growth in traditional school performance is not a manifestation of an exodus of low-scoring students.

In sum, traditional schools experience net gains in performance despite a decrease in average student quality (in some cohorts), suggesting that our estimated effects of charter school competition provide a lower bound for the true effect.

5.4. Comparison with Previous Results for North Carolina Charter Schools

Our findings differ from those of two previous studies that examine the same hypothesis for North Carolina charter schools. Bifulco and Ladd (2004) fail to find an effect of charter schools on traditional school student achievement, while Holmes (2003) estimates gains for traditional school students that are smaller than the ones estimated here. There are several possible reasons for this disagreement.

Most importantly, both Bifulco and Ladd (2004) and Holmes (2003) use student-level data, while we use school-level data. Our conceptual model specifies a response at the school rather than student level: principals are motivated by the school performance composite rather than student-level achievement. One manner in which principals can alter the performance composite is to target students who score just below the passing cutoff, since roughly three percent of students in any given year fail by only one point. If a principal can, for example, entice one-third of these students to gain one point, the performance composite will increase by one percentage point, while the average student-level gain is only 0.01 percentile. Indeed, results in Holmes (2003) suggest greater gains near the level III threshold.

In addition, Bifulco and Ladd (2004) include multiple-distance indicators jointly, which reduces statistical power relative to our specification of only one distance measure in each model, and student fixed effects, which subsume one-quarter of their degrees of freedom. Moreover, Bifulco and Ladd (2004) normalize the dependent variable by the standard deviation, which could bias estimated gains downward: if some of the sample experiences a gain from competition, the estimated standard deviation will increase. Thus, though our approach is not necessarily superior to those of Bifulco and Ladd (2004) or Holmes (2003), it differs in many respects that could explain the disagreement between results from the three studies.

6. CONCLUSION

Using North Carolina data on charter school location and achievement test results, we explore the effect of school choice on school quality. We find traditional school achievement gains to charter school competition across a wide set of models. Overall, the results imply an approximate one percent increase in achievement when a traditional school faces competition from a charter school. This increase represents approximately one-quarter of the mean standard deviation of observed gains, suggesting a considerable return to school choice.

Our results conflict with Bettinger's (2005) finding that charter school competition has no effect on traditional schools, but this difference may be due to different pre-charter competitive environments in North Carolina and Michigan. North Carolina has 117 independent traditional school districts while Michigan has over 500. North Carolina school districts correspond roughly to counties, so residents have less ability to exert Tiebout choice over their school districts. Michigan parents, in contrast, have a much larger number of school districts within a small distance of their residences.[14]

A caveat is that we make two sets of simplifying assumptions regarding school choice. First, we ignore all non-charter school intra-system choices. For example, almost 70 percent of North Carolina school districts offer some form of school choice (North Carolina Office of Lieutenant Governor, 2000). Combined with private and alternative schools, and home-schooling, residents of most North Carolina counties have some form of school choice, such as intra-district transfers, magnet schools, and year-round schools. Ignoring these alternatives leads to an overestimate of the distance to the nearest competitor. The direction of any resulting bias is not clear. However, if one interprets our results as estimates of the effect of charter school choice, rather than school choice in general, then this problem is irrelevant.

Second, we make some important assumptions about transferring into a charter school. Inter-district transfers are allowed in the model. It is assumed that there are open seats in the charter so that a threat to leave the traditional school is credible. We also assume that the size of the charter has no effect on the impact of competition, though it is possible that this impact will increase with size of the charter.

Finally, our use of school-level outcomes (rather than student-level) may potentially lead to biased findings. In principle, student-level outcomes are preferred for many reasons, including both statistical (such as the findings of Hanushek et al. (1996) on aggregation bias) and conceptually, since students are the policy targets of interest. The second-best use of schools, however, is fairly common in the literature.

Nevertheless, this paper adds to the literature on school competition using a simple model that incorporates cost and quality and heretofore unanalyzed data. The results suggest important gains in traditional school achievement due to the introduction and growth of charter school choice.

NOTES

1. For example, see Friedman (1962) for a discussion.

2. For more on charter schools, see Geske, Davis, and Hingle (1997).

3. We define "traditional school" as the public school that is managed by the local education agency, in contrast with the "charter school". The term "traditional" is not meant to suggest that charter schools necessarily adopt an atypical curriculum.

4. There may be peer effects on students remaining in traditional schools as charter-bound students disenroll (e.g. Hoxby, 2000b), but these effects are likely small relative to the benefits received by charter school enrollees. Furthermore, such peer effects may be negative depending on the type of students disenrolling.

5. A potential criticism of our results is that achievement scores among North Carolina charter school students are lower than those of students in nearby traditional schools (Hoxby, 2004), even holding constant student characteristics (Bifulco & Ladd, 2004), which suggests that the competitive threat of charter schools is minimal. However, it is unclear that parents would know this in advance, particularly in the early years of North Carolina charter school expansion that we study. Furthermore, Hoxby (2004) emphasizes that North Carolina is the only state in which charter students' proficiency is significantly lower for both reading and math. She also reports that nationally, the average charter student is more likely to be proficient in both reading and mathematics compared to the average student in the nearest traditional school with a similar racial composition, and that charter students' proficiency advantage tends to be higher in states where charter schools are well established.

6. For linguistic convenience we adopt the convention that the parents choose the school that their children attend. This is reasonable given that our data consist of third through eighth graders.

7. Our use of distance as the relevant cost component follows originally from Hotelling (1949), who proposed that travel cost, which is a function of distance, is an important determinant of the demand for recreational goods. Smith and Kaoru (1990) perform a meta-analysis on the effects of travel cost in the recreational economics literature. In the education literature, distance has been extensively used as a determinant for school attendance. For example, in a study of school choice in Pakistan, Alderman, Orazem, and Paterno (2001) find that changes of only one kilometer in distance to the nearest school have a substantial effect on the probability of attending that school. Collins and Snell (2000) find, in UK data, that students living farther from a school were less likely to attend it. Goldring and Hausman (1999) find that distance was an important consideration for Saint Louis' parents.

8. Bettinger (2005) uses the number of charter schools within a given radius as a measure of charter school competition.

9. We also spoke with a North Carolina charter school administrator who indicates that his school draws students primarily from four nearby schools located approximately 2, 5, 6, and 9 km away.

10. Bettinger (2005) used distance to the nearest public university for which the governor (a charter school proponent) appoints the board as an instrument for charter school competition, motivated by the fact that in Michigan universities issue the charters for charter schools. Since school systems issue the charters in North Carolina, there is little theoretical justification for using a similar instrument in our regressions. We estimated IV models analogous to those of Bettinger (2005). Although distance to the nearest public university passed instrument validity tests, Hausman tests failed to reject its exogeneity in the test score equation.

11. Schools may experience large shifts in enrollment if nearby schools open or close. To test for robustness, we run the IV models on the subsample of schools with yearly changes of enrollment of less than five percent. The results are, in general, more statistically and practically significant.

12. Technically, the state may even save money from charter school expansion, since, for example, the state provides no capital funding for charter schools.

13. Identifying students who switch involves finding unique matches on test scores, race, gender, and birth date. We search for unique matches only within a county for those students who do not match within a school between years. We can identify 2,140 students who switch from a traditional school to a charter school.

14. For example, Kent County (Michigan) and Wake County (North Carolina) have similar populations and land areas, but while Wake County has one (traditional) school district, Kent County has 19.

ACKNOWLEDGMENTS

Holmes's research was supported by the East Carolina University College of Arts and Sciences Research Award for Spring 2001. The views expressed herein are those of the authors and not necessarily those of East Carolina University or the College of Arts and Sciences. Helpful comments were given by Eric Bettinger and participants at the 2001 Midwest Economics Association Meetings. Shuang Chen provided research assistance. The usual caveat applies.

REFERENCES

Alderman, H., Orazem, P. F., & Paterno, E. M. (2001). School quality, school cost, and the public/private school choices of low-income households in Pakistan. *Journal of Human Resources*, *36*(2), 304–326.

Arellano, M., & Bond, S. (1991). Some tests of specification for panel data: Monte Carlo evidence and an application to employment equations. *Review of Economic Studies*, *58*, 277–297.

Belfield, C. R., & Levin, H. M. (2002). The effects of competition between schools on educational outcomes: A review for the United States. *Review of Educational Research*, *72*(2), 279–341.

Bettinger, E. P. (2005). The effect of charter schools on charter students and public schools. *Economics of Education Review*, *24*(2), 133–147.

Betts, J. R. (2001). The impact of school resources on women's earnings and educational attainment: Findings from the National Longitudinal Survey of Young Women. *Journal of Labor Economics*, *19*(3), 635–657.

Bifulco, R., & Ladd, H. F. (2004). *The impacts of charter schools on student achievement: Evidence from North Carolina*. Sanford Institute Working Paper.

Blair, J. P., & Staley, S. (1995). Quality competition and public schools: Further evidence. *Economics of Education Review*, *14*(2), 193–198.

Borland, M. V., & Howsen, R. M. (1992). Student achievement and the degree of market concentration in education. *Economics of Education Review*, *11*(1), 31–39.

Card, D., & Krueger, A. (1992). School quality and black-white relative earnings: A direct assessment. *Journal of Political Economy*, *100*, 1–40.

Cardon, J. H. (2003). Strategic quality choice and charter schools. *Journal of Public Economics*, *87*(3–4), 729–737.

Collins, A., & Snell, M. C. (2000). Parental preferences and choice of school. *Applied Economics*, *32*(7), 803–813.

Cullen, J. B., Levitt, S., & Jacob, B. (2000). *The impact of school choice on student outcomes: An analysis of the Chicago Public Schools*. NBER Working Paper no. 7888.

Fiske, E. B., & Ladd, H. F. (2000). *When schools compete: A cautionary tale*. Washington, DC: Brookings Institution Press.

Friedman, M. (1962). *Capitalism and freedom*. University of Chicago Press.

Geske, T. G., Davis, D. R., & Hingle, P. L. (1997). Charter schools: A viable public school choice option. *Economics of Education Review*, *16*(1), 15–23.

Goldring, E. B., & Hausman, C. S. (1999). Reasons for parental choice of urban schools. *Journal of Educational Policy*, *14*(5), 469–490.

Greene, J. P., & Forster, G. (2002). *Rising to the challenge: The effect of school choice on public schools in Milwaukee and San Antonio*. Mimeo, The Manhattan Institute.

Hanushek, E. A. (1979). Conceptual and empirical issues in the estimation of educational production functions. *Journal of Human Resources*, *14*(3), 351–388.

Hanushek, E. A., Rivkin, S. G., & Taylor, L. L. (1996). Aggregation and the estimated effects of schools resources. *Review of Economics and Statistics*, *78*(4), 611–627.

Holmes, G. M. (2003). *Do charter schools increase student achievement at traditional public schools*? Unpublished manuscript, East Carolina University.

Hotelling, H. (1949). Letter to National Park Service. In: *An econometric study of the monetary evaluation of recreation in the National Parks*. Washington, DC: U.S. Department of Interior, NPS and Recreational Planning Division.

Hoxby, C. M. (2000a). Does competition among public schools benefit students and taxpayers. *American Economic Review*, *90*(5), 1209–1238.

Hoxby, C. M. (2000b). *Peer effects in the classroom: Learning from gender and race variation*. NBER Working Paper no. 7867.

Hoxby, C. M. (2002). *School choice and school productivity (or could school choice be a tide that lifts all boats?)*. NBER Working Paper no. 8873.

Hoxby, C. M. (2004). *A straightforward comparison of charter schools and regular public schools in the United States*. Working Paper, Harvard University.

Krueger, A. (1999). Experimental estimates of education production functions. *Quarterly Journal of Economics*, *114*(2), 497–532.

North Carolina Office of the Lieutenant Governor. (2000). *The status of school choice in North Carolina*. Unpublished memorandum, Raleigh, NC.

Rouse, C. E. (1998). Private school vouchers and student achievement: An evaluation of the Milwaukee parental choice program. *Quarterly Journal of Economics*, *113*(2), 553–602.

Smith, V. K., & Kaoru, Y. (1990). What have we learned since Hotelling's letter? A meta-analysis. *Economics Letters*, *32*, 267–272.

Tiebout, C. M. (1956). A pure theory of local expenditures. *The Journal of Political Economy*, *64*(5), 416–424.

U.S. Department of Education. (2002). Overview of public elementary and secondary schools and districts: School year 2000–01. In: L. M. Hoffman (Ed.), *NCES 2002–356*. Washington, DC: National Center for Education statistics.

COMPETITION AND ACCESSIBILITY IN SCHOOL MARKETS: EMPIRICAL ANALYSIS USING BOUNDARY DISCONTINUITIES

Stephen Gibbons and Olmo Silva

ABSTRACT

Advocates of market-based reforms in the public sector argue that competition between providers drives up performance. But in the context of schooling, the concern is that any improvements in efficiency may come at the cost of increased stratification of schools along lines of pupil ability and attainments. In this chapter, we discuss our empirical work on competition and parental choice in English primary schools and present a methodology for identifying competition effects that exploits discontinuities in market access close to education district boundaries.

1. INTRODUCTION

Government education policies in England, as in the US, have increasingly favoured competition among schools. Supporters of market-based reforms

Improving School Accountability: Check-Ups or Choice
Advances in Applied Microeconomics, Volume 14, 157–184

ISSN: 0278-0984/doi:10.1016/S0278-0984(06)14007-9

argue that autonomy and competition among education providers are effective tools with which to lift student achievements. These gains are assumed to come from market discipline incentives and better matching of pupil needs to school provision. Yet, critics of these ideas point to increased demographic stratification of schools as the most likely outcome, with high-ability children of highly motivated, high-income, parents securing admission to the best schools.

Despite a growing literature on the topic, evidence on the effects of quasi-markets in education remains rather mixed. One reason for this is that it is difficult to find truly exogenous variation in the competitiveness of school markets with which to identify the effects of competition on pupil attainments and stratification. In this chapter, we discuss evidence from primary-phase schooling in England, which, we argue, succeeds in isolating very localised variation in school accessibility close to attendance district boundaries. The chapter highlights the potential for the use of data with detailed geographical information in the identification of market effects, and in empirical analysis more generally.

The starting point for the empirical methods and results we present is a large and detailed pupil census that includes precise information on pupil and school addresses. This allows us to: (i) use the de facto pupil travel-to-school patterns to construct choice indices from the number of alternative schools available to a pupil at their place of residence; and (ii) construct measures of competition faced by a school based on the number of choices available to the pupils it enrols. We argue that these are meaningful measures of choice and competition, which offer a conceptually attractive alternative to more traditional indices. Indeed, the same idea could be extended to analyse competition in any markets, when data is available on the location of service providers (such as health care facilities, retail outlets, entertainment centres) and the location of potential consumers. The drawback of our suggested indices is that they are potentially endogenous to the quality of service provided – particularly in the case of schooling, where it is well known that families engage in Tiebout-type residential sorting to secure access to schools of their choice. We suggest that this problem can be overcome when market areas have clearly defined boundaries – as is often the case in public sector services – because these introduce discontinuities in market access from which the effects of choice and competition can be identified.

The short summary of our empirical work on English schools is that competition – measured as the number of alternative school choices that pupils attending a school have – has no effect on the performance of schools; although there are significant correlations between school competition and mean pupil attainments, these relationships are not *causal*. On the other hand, school competition seems to exacerbate polarisation of schools by student attainment; while not statistically significant, our estimates hint at fairly large impact of school-market competitiveness on stratification. As such, our results cast additional doubt on there being any real performance benefits from policy to promote competition in schooling markets; they also suggest that there is some cost in terms of increased stratification to be expected from quasi-market reforms.

The remainder of this chapter is organised as follows. In Section 2, we discuss some of the key empirical literature on competition in school markets. In Section 3, we outline our methodology, discuss the merits of our indices in comparison with alternatives and show how our approach to identification relates to some other works exploiting geographical discontinuities. Section 4 explains why our methods are appropriate in the context of English primary schools, summarises our previous work on competition and pupil achievement and presents new results on the effects of competition on school stratification. Concluding remarks follow in Section 5.

2. THEORETICAL ISSUES AND GENERAL EMPIRICAL APPROACH

2.1. Background and Literature

While heterogeneous in their details, public school admissions systems can be broadly organised around two 'ideal' models of school provision: (a) *neighbourhood*-based systems; and (b) *choice*-based systems. In *neighbourhood*-based models, admission is determined purely by where a pupil lives, typically with rigidly defined catchment zones. *Choice*-based systems, instead, are intended to give parents a wider choice set that is not limited to neighbouring schools.

Traditionally, public schooling systems have been neighbourhood based, but this tends to tie school quality to the socioeconomic status of local areas and has become – in many public and policy makers' imaginations at least – linked to poor standards. Since attempts to find appropriate ways to raise standards using resource-based interventions have met with mixed success (Hanushek, 2003), attention has turned to interventions that change the incentives for school leaders and teachers; among these, market-oriented reforms of public education have found growing support. At the most basic level, this involves changing the school admissions system to increase parental choice and adjusting the system of funding to reward schools that attract pupils and penalise those that do not. This creates direct market incentive mechanisms, with popular schools gaining pupils and additional funding, and unpopular schools failing to do so, and eventually closing. Additional benefits may come in the form of allocative efficiency gains, if pupils can find schools that are better matched to their educational needs and preferences.

Despite policy enthusiasm for these reforms, evidence of their performance-related benefits remains very mixed. Much of this comes from a wide range of studies analyzing the US experience. Some of these explore the effects of implicit variation in the level of choice available in different school markets on pupil achievements (e.g. some of the work reviewed in Belfield & Levin, 2003; Hoxby, 2000; Rothstein, 2004). A second approach evaluates the effects of the competition threat imposed on state schools by private institutions (see Hoxby, 1994, 2004). Finally, another body of research evaluates the impact of policy changes introducing greater competition into geographically localised educational markets (Cullen, Jacob, & Levitt, 2003; Hoxby & Rockoff, 2004; Hoxby, 2003). These studies are mixed in their findings, and Belfield and Levin (2003) suggest 'the gains from competition are modest in scope with respect to realistic changes in levels of competition' and that many results are statistically insignificant.

Evidence for Britain is more limited, but similarly mixed. On the one hand, Levacic (2004) finds that secondary school head-teachers' self-reports of perceived competition are linked to school performance indicators. Similarly, Bradley, Crouchley, Millington, and Taylor (2000) show a number of 'market'-type effects in secondary education following admissions reforms in the late 1980s – for example, schools that performed better than their neighbours attracted more pupils. On the other, Clark (2004) reports that reforms that handed more power to schools (in late 1980s) only exerted modest efficiency gains through competition effects. Finally, Gibbons, Machin, and Silva (2006) – with results related to those we report later – find little evidence of a positive impact of competition and choice on primary school pupil achievements.

Critics of choice-based reforms point to their potential costs in terms of increased stratification of schools along socioeconomic lines, although the theoretical foundation for this claim is not entirely sound. The idea is that higher socioeconomic status parents benefit more from choice-based interventions, as they are better equipped at making good decisions about school quality and getting what they want from the admissions authorities as well as less constrained by transport costs. However, school choice under a neighbourhood-based school admissions system can be exercised by residential choice, which can just as easily lead to stratification through the housing market. There is, for example, ample evidence that school quality influences local housing prices in neighbourhood-based systems (Black, 1999; Gibbons & Machin, 2003, 2006; Kane, Staiger, & Riegg, 2005), which indirectly suggests stratification by income.

Evidence that looks more directly at the stratification effects of choice availability is more limited, but again mixed in its conclusions. For the US, Hoxby (2000) suggests that the effects of choice on productivity are more likely caused by competitive pressure rather than sorting. To stronger conclusions comes Hoxby (2004): enhanced school choice (mainly voucher systems and charter schools) is *not* associated with more cream skimming and segregation. Yet, findings in Rothstein (2004) and Smith and Meier (1995) provide ground for opposite conclusions: parents value peers more than effective schools; most choice-based policies produce their effects via sorting.

UK-based evidence has also been produced on this issue. On the one hand, Bradley et al. (2000), Bradley and Taylor (2002), Goldstein and Noden (2003), and Burgess, McConnell, Propper, and Wilson (2004), among others, suggest that increased competition and greater parental choice are associated with more polarisation in English *secondary* schools. On the other hand, Gorard, Taylor, and Fitz (2003), summarising the results of a large-scale research programme and assessing the impact of competition on segregation in English *secondary* schools, show that these became *less* socially segregated in the 1990s after the introduction of the market-oriented reforms during the late 1980s. Yet, to the best of our knowledge, no in-depth analysis of the impact of school competition on the polarisation (and performance) of *primary* institutions exists; moreover, our methods are unique in finding credibly exogenous variation in school accessibility, with which to identify the effects of competition on pupil stratification and achievements.

2.2. Defining and Measuring Competition

Our modelling strategy is motivated by the following conceptual points: *choice* availability is a property of residential location and depends on the accessibility of alternative service providers; *competition* is a property of the location of service providers and depends on the number of alternatives available to users of the service.

A starting point for the development of indices that measure choice and competition in public-sector schooling is the assumption that residential locations differ in terms of the accessibility of alternative schools (or service providers in the general market context). This means that choice among schools is more constrained in some places than others, in part because of the transport costs involved, but also because of institutional barriers to access that may apply even if a school is geographically within easy reach. The level of competition that a school faces in the market is in turn dependent on the number of alternative choices that were available to its pupils.

The existing literature that measures the effects of competition in public sector markets has largely inherited techniques from work in industrial organisation and takes one of two approaches. Firstly, competitiveness of a market may be defined in terms of an index of market concentration, such as the Herfindahl index, using the share of pupils in different schools (or the share of pupils in different admissions districts) in some pre-defined school market area. The market area can be an education authority's zone of jurisdiction (Bradley et al., 2000), an entire metropolitan area (Hoxby, 2000) or some other geographical area. A drawback of this approach is that low market concentration cannot really be equated with more choice and greater competition unless all operators in the market are equally accessible to all customers. Geographical restrictions on school admission mean that this criterion is unlikely to be met, unless the notion of choice under consideration includes Tiebout choice that is exercised by residential re-location (as in Hoxby, 2000). This seems however a contradictory way to define competition when the idea of relaxing constraints on choice is usually to offer more alternatives *conditional* on where a person lives.

A second approach is based on the reasoning implicit in spatial competition theories (Hotelling, 1929), where what really matters is the number of providers that can be reached within a given travel cost, time or distance. The simplest way to operationalise this is to define a provider's market area as the area encompassed by a circle of fixed radius, then to consider all people living within this area as potential consumers and all other providers within the circle as competitors. A first drawback of this approach is that the number of providers (and consumers) within a fixed radius is dependent on their areal density, so it becomes difficult to disentangle competition from general urban density effects. Another drawback is that a fixed distance represents very different travel times in urban, suburban and rural environments, so it is hard to see that a fixed radius circular region is meaningful as a market definition in all of these cases. Furthermore, geographical barriers that may obstruct access (rivers, railways, ravines etc.) are easily ignored. More sophisticated analyses try to model market areas on likely journey times. These methods take account of urban–suburban–rural differences and geographical barriers by measuring distances along transport networks, and by adjusting the distance limits of the market area to take account of travel speeds along different classes of road and different types of built environment. A major limitation of this approach is that it requires geographical data on transport networks and is very dependent on the assumptions made about travel mode and travel speeds. For example, a market area defined for schools in terms of car drive times (Burgess et al., 2004) may not be appropriate if school-travel is usually on foot or by bus.

The indices of competition and choice we develop here are grounded in this second approach, but circumvent some of its problems by inferring a school's *catchment area* from the actual travel patterns of its pupils. This allows us to construct an index of choice availability at a residential location based on the number of schools that could easily be reached from that location – ease of access being inferred from the actual travel behaviour of neighbouring pupils. As a first step in developing these indices, we find the spatial coordinate pairs of each school j and each pupil i's home address, and use a geographical information system[1] to compute the straight line distances d^j_{ij} between a pupil's home address and the school he or she attends. We then take the median of distances d^j_{ij} for each school and define this distance $\bar{d}_j$ as the radius of the *catchment area* for school j.[2] Finally, we compute the distances d_{ik} between a pupil's home and the other schools in the local area (within some limiting distance, e.g. 10 km). A school k is then classified as within the feasible set of choices for pupil i if the distance between pupil i and school k is less than the radius of the market area for school k, that is if $d_{ik} \leq \bar{d}_k$. The *choice index* for pupil i is defined as the number of schools that fall in this set of feasible choices. The choice index thus depends on the place of residence and the travel patterns of pupils in neighbouring schools.

The next step is to infer a measure of the competitive pressures faced by each school in our study area, from this choice index. For a given school, the competition it faces depends on the number of feasible alternatives its pupils had available; hence a natural *competition index* is the average number of choices available to pupils in that school. This is easily derived as the mean of the choice indices of the pupils on the school role. The derivation of the competition index is illustrated in Fig. 1, where the triangles represent schools, squares represent pupils and the circles represent their market areas.

2.3. Measuring Performance and Stratification

As outlined above, the debate about the effects of expansion of competition and choice in public services centres on the influence this has on performance and stratification across institutions. The type of competition we have in mind in this chapter is one of spatial competition: state schools compete with

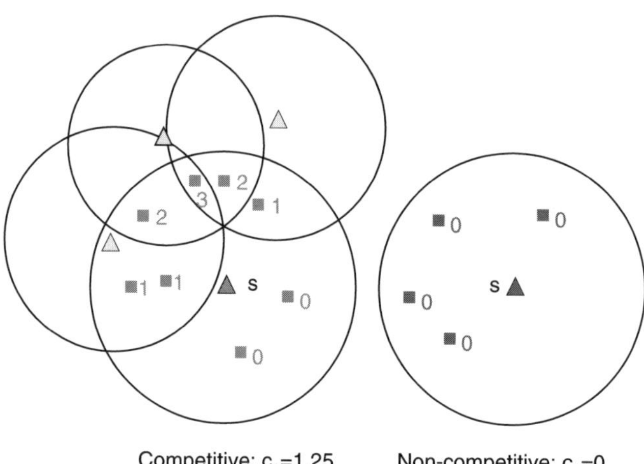

Fig. 1. Schematic Presentation of the Choice and Competition Measures. *Note:* Numbers 0, 1, 2, 3 Indicate the Choice Index that would be Assigned to Pupils Living in Each Area (Assuming they Attend School s) and the Number c_s is the Average of these Choice Indices.

others for pupils in a community in order to maximise their revenues and minimise the costs associated with disruptive and challenging pupils. Since state schools cannot easily change location or vary their price, they can only increase their market share by offering a higher quality product. This is one reason why we might expect schools in more competitive environments to offer their pupils higher educational standards.[3]

In the context of schools, better performance is usually taken to imply higher pupil attainments. Therefore, it has become standard to measure pupil attainments in terms of test scores and to assess the effectiveness of a school in terms of the gain in attainments of pupils enrolled there over a number of years. In the empirical work described below, we follow this approach and consider the gain in pupil attainments between ages 7 and 11 as the main 'output' of primary-phase schooling (i.e. what is called pupil 'value-added').

Stratification, on the other hand, is a more complex issue, since it is not obvious along what demographic or educational lines this should be measured, or how it should be measured. Indeed, whether stratification is considered a problem depends on the interaction between stratification and performance – if, for example, peer group quality influences pupil attainments – or on social preferences over the degree of integration of pupils of different abilities and social backgrounds. In our view, the key concern regarding school stratification is the mix of pupils in terms of their abilities and attainments; therefore, we focus our empirical work on this.

Competition could be causally linked to stratification in abilities and attainments in two ways. Firstly, if schools can choose which pupils they admit, then competition may increase the incentives for schools to try to select pupils who are easier to teach and are likely to boost their performance indicators; some schools may win out over others in this game.[4] More importantly, the degree of competition in a school market is, by our definition, related to the number of choices that pupils and their parents have available to them. Increased stratification will therefore be a by-product of increased competition if expansion of choice leads to greater sorting of pupils across schools along lines of ability or other demographic characteristics that are correlated with ability.

Measurement of stratification also poses some conceptual and empirical problems. It is possible to approach this in two ways, either in terms of the between-group inequality in school means, or within-school inequality in pupil characteristics. Stronger sorting of pupils into schools by some characteristic will be evident in a decrease in the within-school dispersion and an increase in the between-school dispersion. A common way to look for stratification in some characteristic x is to look at a measure of the dispersion x between schools in a market area, using segregation indices such as the *dissimilarity index*, or inequality measures such as the *Gini coefficient* or standard statistical moments.[5]

We adopt a different approach that takes advantage of pupil level micro data, and explicitly model the inequality in x across pupils within a school. We define stratified schools as those characterised by a more homogenous pupil enrolment (e.g. either predominantly *good* or predominantly *bad* pupils), while less-stratified schools are more mixed in terms of student attainment. An advantage of this approach is that it allows us to model the effects of competition on stratification at school level rather than at the level of some predefined market. This method also allows us to compare the effects of competition on within-school pupil inequality with the inequality in attainments within the school's catchment area (as defined in Section 2.2).

We will focus on stratification in attainments of two cohorts at two times in the school career: early on in primary schooling at age 7 – the earliest point at which we can measure pupil attainments; and at age 11 when pupils leave the primary school system and move on to secondary school. The first measure is an indication of stratification in terms of the schools' pupil intake; the second measure is an indication of the stratification that exists as a result of these intake differences, plus any influences over the intervening years up to the time pupils leave primary school. In both the cases, we adopt the Gini coefficient as an index of inequality. We use the Gini coefficient as a measure of *dissimilarity* between pupils in a school (not between schools); this approaches zero when all pupils at a school are similar in terms of their attainments and tends towards one when pupils are more heterogeneous. To state it differently, a school in a highly stratified system will have a small Gini coefficient, while school in a less stratified system will have a high value for the measure.[6]

2.4. Competition and Choice near Administrative Boundaries

We argue that the choice and competition indices defined in Section 2.3 offer an improvement over existing methods, in that they are based on observed pupil travel patterns. This means we can be more confident about inferring which schools are accessible from any residential location, but this in turn brings some disadvantages because pupils' travel patterns are the joint outcome of residential location and school attendance decisions, meaning that the indices are potentially endogenous in models of school quality and stratification.

As a first example of this kind of problem, note that it is well known from the literature on the effect of school quality on housing prices that schools have an influence on local housing demand (op cit.). This has a bearing on our choice and competition measures, because any tendency for residential crowding of similar families around good schools would tend to shrink the travel area of these schools, making them seem less competitive and more segregated. Conversely, if motivated families with high-achieving children are more successful at exercising choice (conditional on residence), then more popular, higher performing and potentially more segregated schools may appear competitive, even though it is parental choice that has spread their geographical intake and increased their polarisation. Moreover, the diversity of pupil attainments within a school must also be tied to diversity in pupil attainments in the neighbouring area, which in turn could be related to fragmentation in terms of housing and environmental characteristics and so to school accessibility. Finally, although school opening and closures are quite rare, it is not implausible that the current spatial distribution of schools is related to the socioeconomic characteristics of an area, and consequently, via housing markets and family background, to its pupil characteristics and polarisation. In particular, we suspect that faith schools may operate in places where economic and educational conditions are more favourable.

So, identification of the causal effects of choice and competition on pupil attainments and stratification poses a serious challenge. To succeed, we require variation in accessibility that may determine school quality and the within-school distribution of pupil attainments (through competition and choice), but is not itself determined by pupil or parental preferences or otherwise related to neighbourhood characteristics. As a starting point, we argue that such variation exists because different residential locations that provide access to a particular school can be very different in terms of the number of *alternative* schools that are available. Importantly, and plausibly, we assume that is the quality of a particular school that is the object of choice and not the range of alternatives available. Nevertheless, we need some specific sources of variation that we can use as instruments for school choice and competition in our school quality and stratification regression models.

One possibility that arises out of earlier literature is to exploit discontinuities in accessibility that occur around geographical barriers such as rivers, roads and railways, which obstruct access to schools in one or more directions; similar ideas have been used in the past in the analysis of school competition (Hoxby, 2000), neighbourhood stratification (Cutler & Glaeser, 1997) and other areas. But these tangible geographical features are unsuitable when we are worried about the interaction between residential choice and school quality, because these features tend to divide up neighbourhoods along socioeconomic strata and are linked to environmental amenities that are in themselves factors in household location decisions. For instance, finding that attainments are lower for pupils living in homes with poor school accessibility close to railway lines could easily be explained by the fact that these pupils come from poorer families living in low-cost housing rather than any causal impact from reduced choice.

Instead, we propose to identify competition effects by variation in accessibility that occurs close to the *boundaries of the administrative authorities* that are responsible for school admissions – namely Local Education Authorities (LEAs) in the English school system. Pupils living close to these boundaries, relative to other pupils in the same education authority, face a restricted choice set because institutional barriers make it harder to access schools on the opposite side of the boundary; this implies that they are more likely to attend their closest school than are pupils living in more central locations, because the average cost to the alternatives is higher.[7]

To see this, consider Fig. 2: this shows a linear district with five schools k, m, n, p, and q spaced at equal intervals. Schools k and q are located at the district boundaries at the left and right ends of the district, respectively. The dashed lines show the cost of reaching each school, from each point i along the linear district. The bold line shows the average cost of reaching schools other than the nearest school, at any point i along the linear district. As can be seen, the average costs of travel to schools other than the nearest is higher

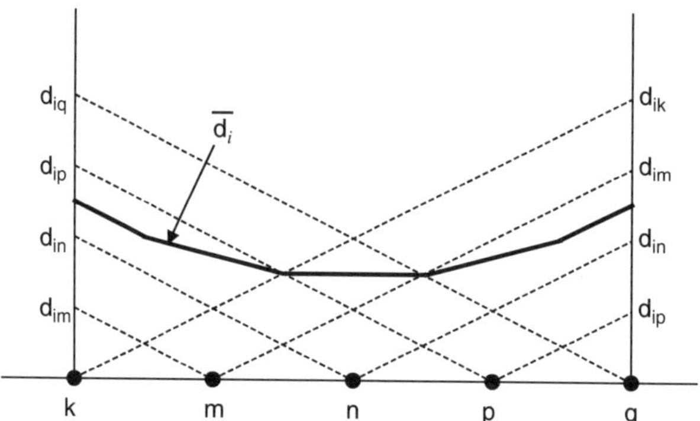

Fig. 2. Illustration of the Instrumentation Strategy. *Note:* Figure Shows a Linear District with Five Schools: *k*, *m*, *n*, *p*, and *q*; d_{ij} is the Distance to Each School; and $\bar{d}_i$ the Average Distance to Schools Other than the Nearest.

for residents near the edge than in the centre. As a result, residents near boundaries will be more likely to attend their local school, and schools nearby LEA boundaries will mainly enrol pupils from local families, who have that school as the nearest choice.

In conclusion, schools in locations close to LEA boundaries face less competition because: (a) the catchment area shrinks in radius and land area, closer to catchment area boundaries; and (b) the catchment area may be partially truncated on one side, which is a restriction that we can impose by excluding the few pupils who do cross LEA boundaries in the calculation of our competition index. This means that we can use distance of a school from a boundary as a predictor of the competition it faces in the local school market. As it turns out, (a) is most important in terms of driving variation in our competition index.

In general, the distance of a place from an administrative boundary will provide a valid instrument for choice availability and the level of market competition at that place if: (a) the administrative boundary increases the costs associated with access to services on the opposite side of the boundary; and (b) the distance from the boundary is otherwise uncorrelated with the outcomes that are being analysed. The extent to which such barriers exist and are impervious depends on the particular institutional context, but we argue below (and demonstrate in our estimates) that LEA boundaries act as real impediments to access in the English primary school system. Moreover, there are no strong reasons for believing that households have any preference about how close they live to boundaries relative to other households in the LEA, or that household characteristics are correlated with this distance, or that teaching quality and other factors that drive school effectiveness are directly linked to it.[8]

A similar strategy might be appropriate in the analysis of competition effects in public health and other services, when access is allocated according to zone of residence and discontinuities in accessibility occur close to administrative boundaries. For example, access to general practitioners or hospital medical services provided by a local health authority may be limited to those living within the health authority's jurisdiction. In these cases, distance to health authority boundaries may provide appropriate instruments for the level of competition measured among neighbouring hospitals, when there is unobserved area heterogeneity which may be correlated with competition and performance measures (a problem that is often only partially addressed, e.g. Propper, Burgess, & Green, 2004; Mobley, 2003).

Closely related thinking lies behind studies which investigate the effects of market access when there are changes in national borders or their permeability. Examples include changes that occurred during German division and re-unification (Redding & Sturm, 2005) or close to the Mexican border as a result of the North American Free Trade Agreement (Hanson, 2003). Our strategy has similarities with these approaches, in that competition, like market access, declines as one moves closer to the boundary on either side. However, because we have observations on both sides of multiple boundaries, we are able to distinguish competition effects from more general monotonic changes that may occur in one direction over the study area. Our approach is, however, distinctly different to the type of empirical analysis that exploits the discontinuities in the *level* of some variable of interest that occurs as one moves from one side of a boundary to the other – for example, the boundary fixed effects strategy used by Black (1999) and Kane et al. (2005) in the analysis of school quality effects on house prices, and by Bayer and McMillan (2005) in the context of school choice.

3. MEASURING THE EFFECTS OF COMPETITION IN PRIMARY SCHOOLS IN THE LONDON METROPOLITAN AREA

3.1. Data and Context

If our proposed methods are to work, we need a setting where there is some freedom of school choice, given where a family lives, but where there are constraints that mean that some places offer greater accessibility to schools than others. We argue here that the primary school system in and around London provides such a context.

The current state-school system in England is a hybrid of a neighbourhood-based and a choice-based system. Since the Education Reform act of 1988, the principle of choice has been extended to a greater or lesser extent in different districts (see e.g. Glennester, 1991); the trend continues in more recent legislation (e.g. school Standards and Framework Act 1998 and the Education Reform Act 2002). Although competition in *secondary* (post-11) education tends to dominate the political landscape, we consider the effects of competition at the *primary* (pre-11) phase. The reasons for this are partly methodological: travel distances have a greater role to play in primary school choice (than for secondary schools), because children of this age are not independent travellers and need to live much closer to the school they attend. This means it is much easier to infer which schools are accessible from a particular residential location. Moreover, admissions arrangements make it much easier for pupils in secondary schools to cross LEA boundaries – which would undermine the identification strategy we described above. At primary level, there are institutional barriers hindering admission of pupils to schools outside their home LEA and only a very small number do so.[9] Aside from this, there are good theoretical reasons for focusing on primary-age attainments, because educational and behavioural development at primary age is critical for lifetime success (Heckman, 2000; Dearden, McGranahan, & Sianesi, 2004).

Although primary school pupils tend to live quite close to their schools, there is still a great deal of scope for parents to choose between alternative schools in the state sector. All primary schools are non-selective, but there is variety in terms of the way schools are governed and admissions organised, and schools differ in terms of aims, ethos and religious character. The basic division is between institutions which are affiliated with a church and 'Community' schools which are not. Roughly, 60% of schools are Community schools, 26% Church of England, 11% Catholic and the remaining 3% affiliated to other churches or charitable organisations. In most cases (75%), the LEA administers school admissions. The LEA also funds the schools, mostly through central government grant, and provides administrative and managerial support. Importantly, for the empirical work we carry out here, the law states that parental choice must be the guiding principle in prioritising admissions (although local differences exist in the way applications are prioritised when schools are over-subscribed). Indeed, there is clear evidence in our data that admissions are not tied to place of residence since neighbouring pupils attend many different schools and only 48% of pupils attend their nearest school.

Our empirical analysis of the primary school system requires micro data on pupil attainments, linked to information on pupil background and residential addresses. This is available through the Department of Education and Skills' (DfES) National Pupil Database (NPD) for 1996–2003, linked to the Pupil Level Annual Census (PLASC) for 2002 and 2003. These are administrative survey datasets that cover the entire school population, and record pupil scores in standard tests at ages 7 and 11 (and higher ages in secondary school). Our focus is on the tests at ages 7 and 11, the start and end dates of what is called Key Stage 2 in the UK National Curriculum. To construct measures of school-mean value-added between ages 7 and 11, we work with standard DfES 'point scores' which provide a summary measure of pupil achievement based on levels of attainment in maths and English tests. The school value-added point score is simply the difference between age-11 and age-7 point scores, averaged at school level. To measure within-school attainment dispersion at age 7, we convert the point scores into percentiles (in the whole sample) and then calculate the within-school Gini coefficient on these percentiles. To measure dispersion at age 11, we use the Gini on the percentiles of the actual test scores in these subjects (which are not available at age 7).

Pupil and school addresses are geo-coded to British National Grid coordinates using Ordnance Survey 'Codepoint' data, which provides grid references for postcode unit (usually street) centroids. Finally, for our instrumental variables strategy, we derive LEA boundaries from the County and District boundaries obtainable from the 'UK Borders' service for Geographical Information Systems data. The sample is then restricted to a geographical zone within a 50 km radius of central London, in order to focus on primarily urban school markets.

3.2. Results

Table 1 summarises the most important variables in the data we analyse, namely competition, performance and segregation measures.[10] All variables are defined at the school level of aggregation. A key question is whether there is in fact much variation in the competition and segregation measure we have constructed. If all schools serve only the local community, or if any school within an LEA is easily accessible from any residence within an LEA, then there is no variation in the level of competition. Similarly, if all schools are populated by similarly heterogeneous pupils, or if all neighbourhoods

Table 1. Competition, Stratification (Gini Coefficient) and Value-Added Summary Statistics.

Variable	Observations	Mean	Standard Deviation	Minimum, Maximum
Competition measures				
Average number of schools accessible to pupils in school	4,707	1.39	1.06	0, 8.31
Stratification measures				
Gini coefficient, pupils in school, age-7	4,707	0.33	0.08	0.06, 0.63
Gini coefficient, pupils in school, age-11	4,703	0.31	0.08	0, 0.60
Gini coefficient, catchment area	4,707	0.34	0.08	0.06, 0.58
Performance measures				
KS2-1 value added	4,707	38.72	3.70	23.16, 55.18

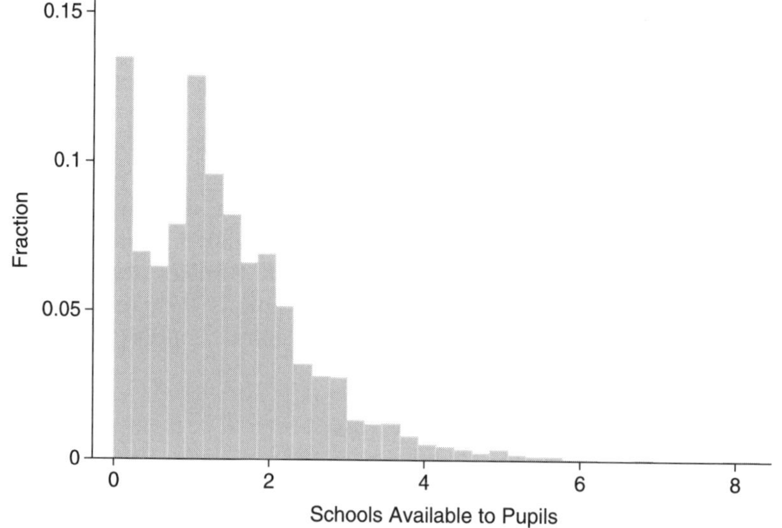

Fig. 3. Distribution of the Competition Index.

are characterised by diversified students, with schools implementing no differential admission policies, then our polarisation measures would display no variation. Table 1 and Figs. 3 and 4 below show that our data display some interesting features.

Fig. 4. Primary School Competition in the Greater London Area. *Note:* Figure Shows Local Averages of the School-Level Competition Index (Inverse Distance Weighted Means of the Nearest Six Schools on a 250 m Raster). Each Shading Class Corresponds to Intervals [0,1], [1,2], … [6,7] from Lighter to Darker.

Looking first at the competition index, the first row of Table 1 tabulates summary statistics, while Fig. 3 graphs the distribution of the competition index for all schools, and Fig. 4 (taken from Gibbons et al., 2006) maps the spatial distribution of school competition in London (part of our study area); all these show that there is substantial variation in the competition indices we have at hand.[11] Around one in four pupils have no school (other than the one they attend) within a short travel distance, but only 1 in 10 schools have all pupils with no local alternatives. Finally, from the map in Fig. 4 we can also deduce that the competition indices are only partly related to urban centrality and density.

The central panel of Table 1 reports summary statistics for our measures of segregation. The Gini coefficient at the school level varies between 0.06 and 0.63 (with a standard deviation of 0.08): this suggests that the most segregated schools are 10 times more homogeneous, in terms of their pupil ability, than the least polarised ones. The Gini index on the catchment areas we construct around schools shows a very similar pattern.

Next, the panels of Fig. 5 present a simple graphical analysis of the raw relationship between the competition a school faces and (a) its performance; and (b) the mix of attainments of its pupils at age 7. These plots are smoothed over the competition index range using running means, with 95% confidence intervals. Both the value-added measure and the dispersion in pupil attainments (Gini) show an increasing pattern: more competition is associated with higher-value-added and less-stratified schools. Yet, as already mentioned, this result could simply be the result of unobserved neighbourhood factors, residential choice patterns and strategic school location.

To go further, and estimate a causal impact of competition on either performance or stratification, we need to implement the strategy described in Section 2.4, which makes use of variation in competition near LEA boundaries. First, however, we start our analysis with simple ordinary least squares regression estimates, which model the relationships observed in Fig. 5, with some additional control variables.

Columns 1 and 2 of Table 2 present the first set of these regression results based on ordinary least squares (OLS) estimates of a regression of age-7 to age-11 pupil achievement progression (value added). Column 1 has no controls; Column 2, instead, includes a set of controls for school and neighbourhood characteristics (listed in Table A1). In both the cases, the coefficient on our competition index is strongly significant and the sign suggests that schools facing more competitive markets have a performance advantage. The order of magnitude is fairly small, though, with one

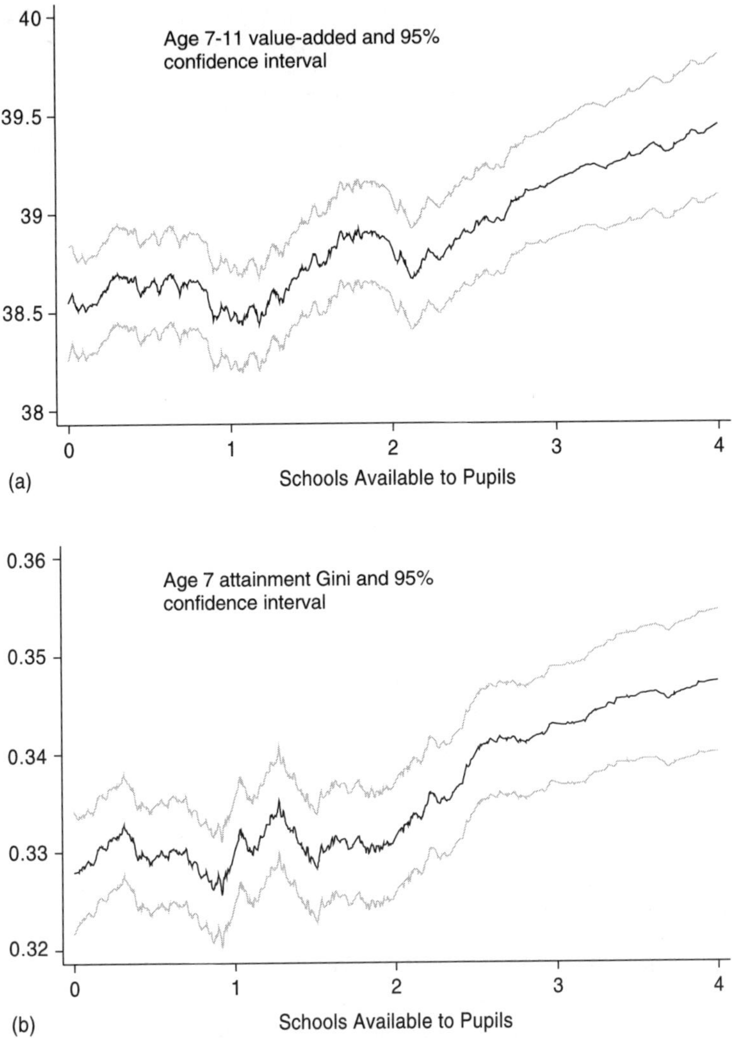

Fig. 5. (a) Association between Competition and School Performance (b) Association between Competition and Within-School Dispersion in Attainment (Gini).

standard deviations increase in our competition index – roughly one alternative school available to its pupils – associated with 5% of a standard deviation increase in performance.[12] In Columns 3 and 4, we introduce our instrumental variables methodology, using the (logarithm of) distance to

Table 2. Primary School Competition and School Performance 2001/2002–2002/2003.

	Age-7 to Age-11 Value-Added Points, Pupils Age 11 in 2001/2002–2002/2003			
	(1)	(2)	(3)	(4)
	OLS	OLS	IV	IV
Competition index: number of schools	***0.222*** (0.064)	***0.197*** (0.073)	−0.261 (0.309)	−0.294 (0.316)
First-stage regression Log of school–LEA boundary distance	—	—	***0.232*** (0.020)	***0.224*** (0.018)
Controls	No	Yes	No	Yes

Note: Regression at the school level. Standard errors clustered on school in parentheses: Values in bold italic significant at 1%. Controls are listed in the appendix (Table A1). Instrument is the log of the distance between school and LEA boundary, controlling for the log average school–LEA boundary. Number of schools, 2,412; number of observations, 4,707.

LEA boundaries as an instrument for school competition.[13] The results of this are striking: with our without additional controls, our point estimates suggest that competition is really linked to marginally lower school performance, though the coefficients are not statistically significant. Examination of the first stage coefficient and standard error, reported in the second row of Table 2, suggests that our instrument is quite powerful. Our interpretation is that exogenous changes in competition do not have a positive effect on school performance, and the OLS results simply pick up unobserved neighbourhood heterogeneity or the fact that pupils with a large number of alternative schools tend to choose the ones that perform best.

Even if competition has weak effects on mean attainments, there may be effects on pupil sorting which lead schools to become more stratified with less competitive schools attracting low-ability pupils and others attracting high-ability pupils. Or perhaps competition breaks the link between residential sorting and school stratification, leading to greater mixing of abilities in competitive schools. We investigate these issues in Table 3, which reports the results of regressions that model the within-school dispersion of age-7 and age-11 attainments using the Gini index. All the figures in the first row are multiplied by 100, so they show the effect of a unit change in our competition index in percentage points.

Table 3. Primary School Competition and School Stratification.

	Gini Index of Within-School Attainments, Pupils in Age 11 in 2001/2002–2002/2003, Scaled 0–100							
	OLS				IV			
	Age-7	Age-11	Age-7	Age-11	Age-7	Age-11	Age-7	Age-11
	(1)	(2)	(3)	(4)	(5)	(6)	(7)	(8)
Competition index: number of schools	***0.423*** (0.137)	−0.040 (0.145)	0.219 (0.133)	−0.199 (0.148)	−0.962 (0.689)	−0.657 (0.674)	−0.367 (0.696)	−0.261 (0.678)
First-stage regression Log of school–LEA boundary distance	—		—		***0.232*** (0.020)	***0.232*** (0.020)	***0.213*** (0.019)	***0.214*** (0.019)
Controls	No	No	Yes	Yes	No	No	Yes	Yes

Note: Regression at the school level. Standard errors in parentheses, clustered on school: values in bold italic significant at 1%. Controls are listed in the appendix (Table A1), excluding: fraction of females, of FSM students and SEN students at school, and postcode-level controls. Instrument is the log of the distance between school and LEA boundary, controlling for the log average school–LEA boundary. Number of schools, 2,412; number of observations, 4,707 (4,703 in age-11 models).

Columns 1 and 2 are simple OLS results without controls. Column 1 indicates that dispersion in attainment at age 7 is higher in schools that are located in what appear to be competitive markets; yet, this is not true for age-11 achievements, where the association is small in magnitude and statistically insignificant. Moving right across the table we first add some basic neighbourhood controls to account for neighbourhood heterogeneity. Now, the evidence for more dispersion of age-7 attainments in competitive schools is much weaker, and the age-11 attainments appear less dispersed in these schools. This suggests, perhaps, that unobserved neighbourhood attributes may be driving the first OLS results. Yet, one might argue that this method is inappropriate, because some of the effects of competition are absorbed by changes in neighbourhood composition. Turning to our IV methodology, however, gives us bigger *negative* point estimates (Columns 5–8), implying lower ability dispersion, or more school stratification, in competitive markets. The effect is similar whether we measure attainment at age 7 or at age 11.

Although none of these IV coefficients is precisely estimated, they all suggest that increased competition may have an economically meaningful impact on stratification by attainment. In fact, an increase of one in the number of alternatives with which a school has to compete (one standard deviation in our index) reduces the Gini of the dispersion of attainments at age 7 by just under one percentage point, i.e. 12.5% of a standard deviation. Then again, this means quite a substantial change if we move over the full range of the data: expanding the number of alternative schools from 0 to 8 would reduce the within-school dispersion Gini from 0.41 to 0.25.

Our results so far suggest that there may be small adverse effects from competition on pupil performance and somewhat larger impacts on school stratification. However, our estimates are imprecisely measured. One possibility is that competition has stronger impacts on neighbourhoods, even if the school stratification effects are quite weak. For example, an expansion of school choice, conditional on place of residence, may lessen residential sorting because it is no longer necessary to live close to a particular school in order to get in. We explore this hypothesis in Table 4, in an identical manner to Table 3 – but this time the Gini index is computed on the attainments of *all* pupils who live in the catchment area of a school, not just those who attend it. We define the catchment area using the area we construct for our *competition measure.* What we might expect to see is that neighbourhoods

Table 4. Primary School Competition and Neighbourhood Stratification, 2001/2002–2002/2003.

	Stratification in Catchment Area							
	OLS				IV			
	Age-7	Age-11	Age-7	Age-11	Age-7	Age-11	Age-7	Age-11
	(1)	(2)	(3)	(4)	(5)	(6)	(7)	(8)
Competition index: number of schools	*0.902*	*0.416*	0.193	−0.171	−0.060	0.552	−0.451	0.075
	(0.104)	(0.103)	(0.104)	(0.103)	(0.511)	(0.510)	(0.537)	(0.543)
First stage regression								
Log of school–LEA boundary distance	—	—	—	—	***0.232***	***0.232***	***0.213***	***0.213***
					(0.020)	(0.020)	(0.018)	(0.018)
Controls	No	No	Yes	Yes	No	No	Yes	Yes

Note: Regression at the school level. Standard errors in parentheses, clustered on school: values in italic significant at 5%; values in bold italic significant at 1%. Controls are listed in the appendix (Table A1). Instrument is the log of the distance between school and LEA boundary, controlling for the log average school–LEA boundary. Number of schools, 2,412; number of observations, 4,707.

around schools that have many competitors are quite diverse, while those neighbourhoods which are served by just one school are more segregated. Looking across the columns of table, we see that this appears to be the case in the basic OLS estimates without controls (Columns 1 and 2). But again, once controls are included in the age-7 models, or we use our LEA-boundary distance IV strategy, the coefficients become negative and insignificant. In fact, the pattern for the age-7 attainment mix in the neighbourhood is much the same as in the school models of Table 3, though weaker. The pattern of results for age-11 attainments is more indicative of greater school competition (more parental choice) leading to reduced residential sorting; but again the estimates are imprecise. Interpretation of the age-11 results is also clouded by the fact that the mix of age-11 attainments in the neighbourhood will depend on the effectiveness of the schools that serve the neighbourhood, and not just residential sorting.

Ultimately, the plausibility of our IV strategy depends on whether the first stages in the instrumented regressions are effective, and whether the underlying assumptions are supported by the data.

Looking at the first-stage coefficients reported in Tables 2 and 3, we see that a 10% increase in the distance from LEA boundary to a school increases the number of schools in the competition index by about 0.023, or about 1.7% relative to the mean (0.023/1.390). This instrument is significant, with *t*-statistics of around 10. This is not an artefact of the fact that we impose the constraint the pupils do not cross LEA boundaries in the construction of our competition index. We can form the index without this restriction and get nearly identical results (see Table A2). In this case, identification comes from the fact that catchment areas shrink near LEA boundaries, because, according to our theoretical reasoning, pupils are more likely to attend their nearest schools given they have fewer schools within feasible travel distance.

Further results from pupil-level regressions show that the instrument works in line with this theoretical reasoning: the probability that a pupil attends their nearest school decreases with distance of their home from the nearest LEA boundary, and the average distance between a pupil's residence and the nearest four schools (other than the one he or she actually attends) decreases. In other words, pupils near admissions district boundaries seem to be more constrained in their choice of school.

Finally, we addressed the question of whether school or residence distance from LEA boundaries has a direct impact on pupil characteristics, and hence possibly on achievements and stratification. Yet again, we found that this is not the case, lending further support to our IV strategy.

To conclude, our evidence using credible and powerful instrumental variables suggests that competition in primary schooling does not drive up school performance; if anything, policy that promotes competition through greater access in schooling markets may come at the cost of increased polarisation in pupil achievements, and marginally *worse* performance.

4. CONCLUDING REMARKS

Government education policies in England as well as in the US and other countries have increasingly expanded the role of parental choice, and competition among public schools, with the aim of improving educational outcomes. Critics of market-oriented reforms have, however, warned that these may come at the cost of increased stratification by pupil ability and attainments.

While a growing body of literature has been produced on the topic, the evidence of the effects of competition on pupil achievements and segregation remains controversial, and a weak foundation for policy conclusions. In fact, most research has been confronted with the difficult challenge of finding credible exogenous variation to identify the effects of competition on pupil outcomes.

In this chapter, we have presented a methodology to identify the impact of school competition and choice on pupil outcomes, using discontinuities in market access generated by proximity to administrative boundaries. This allows isolation of exogenous variation in the competitive pressure faced schools, which can be used to identify the impact of competition on pupil achievements and stratification by attainments.

Using a large pupil census with detailed information on pupil and school addresses, we have constructed a measure of school competition based on the number of alternative schools that pupils enrolled in a school could access. We infer this accessibility from the geographical location of homes, schools and the de facto pupil travel-to-school patterns. This is an intuitive measure of competition, which can be easily extended to the analysis of other markets: competition pressures faced by a service are simply captured by the number of alternatives that its users had within convenient travel distance. A drawback of these indices, shared with most of the alternatives used in the previous analysis, is that they may be endogenous to the quality of the service provided.

Our solution to this problem has exploited discontinuities in market access generated by clearly defined administrative boundaries. In fact, families near school admission district boundaries face a restricted choice compared to others in more central locations, because institutional barriers make it difficult for them to access schools on the other side of the boundaries, and it is costly to travel to alternatives further away towards the centre of the district. As a result, schools in the proximity of boundaries will enrol the vast majority of local students, and face little competition from other providers. We have argued that this methodology can be easily extended to similar contexts in public service provision, such as public health, where access is ruled by zone of residence.

Our findings for English primary schools suggest that competition has no *causal* effect on the performance of schools. Most of the observed positive correlation between the number of competing schools and pupil attainments is driven by unobserved neighbourhood characteristics or endogenous selection of pupils with choice into better quality schools. Yet, we uncovered evidence that school competition may exacerbate stratification of schools by student attainment. Although our results are imprecisely estimated, they hint at a potentially large impact from expansion of competition on polarisation of schools by pupil abilities. All in all, our analysis suggests that further expansion of quasi-market discipline in the public education sector *may* come at some costs, and with few evident benefits.

ACKNOWLEDGMENTS

We would like to thank the Department for Education and Skills for funding this work under the Centre for the Economic of Education work programme, participants at various seminars and Joan Wilson for stimulating discussions on this project. We are responsible for any remaining errors.

NOTES

1. We use the industry-standard ESRI *ArcGIS* software.
2. For the results that follow, we also experimented using the 25th and 75th percentiles of the pupil home–school distance distribution rather than the median. Our conclusions are robust to these experiments.
3. Although there are arguments that would lead in the opposite direction, such as competition leading to more stressful teaching environments or higher pupil turnover (see for example Hanushek, Kain, & Rivkin, 2004).
4. In the English primary school system, this is unlikely to be a major issue since only a small proportion of schools run their own admissions.

5. For an interesting discussion about the properties of segregation and stratification measures, see, Massey and Denton (1988).

6. We have experimented with alternative measures of polarisation, such as the 90th–10th percentile ratio, the 75th–25th percentile ratio, and the coefficient of variation. Our main conclusions were fully confirmed.

7. The underlying assumption is that the probability of family i attending school j is decreasing in the distance to the school d_{ij} due to transport costs.

8. In fact, evidence discussed in Gibbons et al. (2006) suggests that these assumptions are empirically valid.

9. 4.7% overall for Community school pupils in our sample. 85% of residents living right on the LEA boundary attend a school in their home LEA.

10. Descriptive statistics for a set of controls used in our analysis are reported in Table A1.

11. Additional details can be found in Gibbons et al. (2006).

12. These results are similar to those reported using pupil-level regressions in Gibbons et al. (2006), though the school-level results here pick up the effects of both technological efficiency and sorting on school performance.

13. While controlling for the average logarithm of the distance of schools to LEA boundaries in each LEA; this ensures that we are comparing like with like, taking into account the relative size and density of each LEA.

REFERENCES

Bayer, P., & McMillan, R. (2005). *Choice and competition in local education markets.* Working Paper no. 11802. National Bureau of Economic Research.

Belfield, C., & Levin, H. (2003). The effects of competition between schools on educational outcomes: A review for the United States. *Review of Educational Research, 72*, 279–341.

Black, S. (1999). Do better schools matter? Parental evaluation of elementary education. *Quarterly Journal of Economics, 114*, 578–599.

Bradley, S., Crouchley, R., Millington, J., & Taylor, J. (2000). Testing for quasi-market forces in secondary education. *Oxford Bulletin of Economics and Statistics, 62*, 357–390.

Bradley, S., & Taylor, J. (2002). The effect of the quasi-market on the efficiency-equity trade-off in the secondary school sector. *Bulletin of Economic Research, 54*, 295–314.

Burgess, S., McConnell, B., Propper, C., & Wilson, D. (2004). *Sorting and choice in English secondary schools.* Bristol: Centre for Market and Public Organisation W.P. 04/111.

Clark, D. (2004). *Politics, markets and schools: Quasi-experimental evidence on the impact of autonomy and competition from a truly revolutionary UK reform.* Mimeo, Berkeley: University of California.

Cullen, J., Jacob, B., & Levitt, S. (2003). *The effect of school choice on student outcomes: Evidence from randomized lotteries.* Working Paper no. 10113. National Bureau of Economic Research.

Cutler, D., & Glaeser, E. (1997). Are ghettos good or bad? *Quarterly Journal of Economics, 112*, 827–872.

Dearden, L., McGranahan, L., & Sianesi, B. (2004). *The role of credit constraints in educational choices: Evidence from NCDS and BCS70.* London: Centre for the Economics of Education DP0048.

Gibbons, S., & Machin, S. (2003). Valuing English primary schools. *Journal of Urban Economics, 53*, 197–219.

Gibbons, S., & Machin, S. (2006). Paying for primary schools: Supply constraints, school popularity or congestion. *Economic Journal, 116*, C77–C92.

Gibbons, S., Machin, S., & Silva, O. (2006). *Competition, choice and pupil achievement*. London: Centre for Economics of Education DP0056.

Glennester, H. (1991). Quasi-markets for education. *Economic Journal, 101*, 1268–1276.

Goldstein, H., & Noden, P. (2003). Modelling social segregation. *Oxford Review of Education, 29*, 225–237.

Gorard, S., Taylor, C., & Fitz, J. (2003). *Schools, markets and choice policies*. London: Routledge-Farmer.

Hanson, G. (2003). *What has happened to wages in Mexico since Nafta? Implications for hemispheric free trade*. Working Paper no. 9563. National Bureau of Economic Research.

Hanushek, E. (2003). The failure of input-based school policies. *Economic Journal, 113*, F64–F98.

Hanushek, E., Kain, J., & Rivkin, S. (2004). Disruption versus Tiebout improvement: The costs and benefits of switching schools. *Journal of Public Economics, 88*, 1721–1746.

Heckman, J. (2000). Policies to foster human capital. *Research in Economics, 54*, 3–56.

Hotelling, H. (1929). Stability in competition. *Economic Journal, 39*, 41–57.

Hoxby, C. (1994). *Do private school provide competition for public schools?* Working Paper no. 4978. National Bureau of Economic Research.

Hoxby, C. (2000). Does competition among public schools benefit students and taxpayers? *American Economic Review, 90*, 1209–1238.

Hoxby, C. (2003). School choice and school productivity (or, could school choice be a rising tide that lifts all boats?). In: C. Hoxby (Ed.), *The economics of school choice*. Chicago: University of Chicago Press.

Hoxby, C. (2004). School choice and school competition: Evidence from the United States. *Swedish Economic Policy Review, 10*(2).

Hoxby, C., & Rockoff, J. (2004). *The impact of charter schools on student achievement*. HIER Working Paper.

Kane, T., Staiger, D. O., & Riegg, S. K. (2005). *School quality, neighborhoods and housing prices: The impacts of desegregation*. Working Paper no. 11347. National Bureau of Economic Research.

Levacic, R. (2004). Competition and the performance of English secondary schools: Further evidence. *Education Economics, 12*, 177–193.

Massey, D., & Denton, N. (1988). The dimensions of residential sorting. *Social Forces, 67*, 281–315.

Mobley, L. (2003). Estimating hospital market pricing: An equilibrium approach using spatial econometrics. *Regional Science and Urban Economics, 33*, 489–516.

Propper, C., Burgess, S., & Green, K. (2004). Does competition between hospitals improve the quality of care? Hospital death rates and the NHS internal market. *Journal of Public Economics, 88*, 1247–1272.

Redding, S., & Sturm, D. (2005). *The costs of remoteness: Evidence from German division and reunification*. London: Centre for Economic Performance DP0688.

Rothstein, J. (2004). Good principals or good peers? *Parental valuation of school characteristics, Tiebout equilibrium, and the incentive effects of competition among jurisdictions*. Working Paper no. 10666. National Bureau of Economic Research.

Smith, B., & Meier, K. (1995). Public choice: Markets and the demand for quality education. *Political Research Quarterly, 48*, 461–478.

APPENDIX

Table A1. Controls and Summary Statistics.

Variable	Observations	Mean	Standard Deviation	Minimum, Maximum
School-level variables				
Fraction of female in schools	4,707	0.477	0.042	0, 1
Pupil/qualified teacher ratio	4,707	23.25	4.27	11.2, 108.3
Total school size	4,707	324.3	132.02	52, 1,373
Fraction of pupils with SEN	4,707	0.211	0.091	0, 0.65
Fraction of pupils with FSME	4,707	0.210	0.167	0, 0.77
Median travel distance all schools	4,707	755.99	520.51	102, 6,157
Number of pupils in the travel area	4,707	75.59	74.93	2, 1,015
Average school distance from competitors	4,707	217.50	328.37	0, 3,525
Postcode-level variables				
Fraction of lone parents	4,707	0.282	0.127	0, 0.617
Fraction of unemployed	4,707	0.040	0.020	0, 0.104
Fraction with no school qualifications	4,707	0.267	0.075	0, 0.576
Fraction with Black ethnicity	4,707	0.088	0.101	0, 0.557
Fraction with Chinese ethnicity	4,707	0.019	0.015	0, 0.128
Fraction with other Asian ethnicities	4,707	0.090	0.120	0, 0.766
LEA-level controls				
Total LEA expenditure in 2000 (in £1,000)	4,707	2,258.39	1,747.31	493.5, 5,982.7
LEA area (in 1,000,000 m^2)	4,707	719.31	1,100.18	12.4, 3,450.8

Note: SEN, Special Education Needs; FSME, Free School Meals Eligibility.

Table A2. Primary School Competition, School Performance and School Stratification, 2001/2002–2002/2003; Without no-LEA Boundary Crossing Restriction.

	Age-7 to Age-11 Value-Added Points		School Stratification Age-7 (KS1)	
	(1)	(2)	(3)	(4)
	OLS	IV	OLS	IV
Competition index: number of schools	***0.205***	−0.635	−0.150	−0.423
	(0.069)	(0.701)	(0.121)	(1.543)
First-stage regression				
Log of school–LEA boundary distance	—	***0.103***	—	***0.093***
		(0.019)		(0.020)
Controls	Yes	Yes	Yes	Yes

Note: Regression at the school level. Standard errors clustered on school: values in bold italic significant at 1%; and *t*-statistics in parentheses. Controls are listed in the appendix (Table A1). Instrument is the log of the distance between school and LEA boundary, controlling for the log average school–LEA boundary. Number of schools, 2,412; number of observations, 4,707.

THE EFFECT OF SCHOOL CHOICE AND RESIDENTIAL LOCATION ON THE RACIAL SEGREGATION OF STUDENTS

Hamilton Lankford and James Wyckoff

ABSTRACT

The pattern of racial segregation in U.S. elementary and secondary schools has changed significantly over the last 25 years. This chapter examines the relationship between the racial composition of schools and the choices white parents make concerning the schools their children attend. Restricted access files at the Bureau of the Census allow us to identify each household's Census block of residence and, in turn, suburban public school districts and urban public school attendance areas. We find that the racial composition of schools and neighborhoods are very important in the school and location decisions of white families.

1. INTRODUCTION

Issues of racial balance across schools have played an important role in educational policy in America over the last 35 years. Following the 1954 Supreme

Improving School Accountability: Check-Ups or Choice
Advances in Applied Microeconomics, Volume 14, 185–239

ISSN: 0278-0984/doi:10.1016/S0278-0984(06)14008-0

Court desegregation ruling in *Brown v. Topeka Board of Education* and beginning in earnest with the civil rights movement in the mid-1960s, the country embarked on a sustained effort to address issues of segregation in elementary and secondary schools. The separate-but-equal doctrine was dismantled throughout the South and busing was employed in many northern cities. Although the causes of segregation varied, desegregation efforts resulted in substantial reductions in racial segregation within school districts. Segregation in America's schools virtually vanished from the public agenda in the 1980s.

Concerns about racial segregation in America's schools have re-emerged in recent years and generally take two forms:

- Opponents of private school choice proposals (e.g., the use of vouchers) fear that white parents opting for private schools will leave public schools disproportionately nonwhite.
- Several authors have noted that urban public schools are becoming increasingly segregated, with the conjecture that white parents are opting to locate in largely white suburban school districts, leaving less mobile nonwhites in urban schools.

The realization of such changes would have profound implications for educational and social policy. However, the likelihood and exact nature of such effects are unknown, as we know little about the role that school choice and residential location decisions play in determining the racial imbalance in America's schools.

Examining the nature of segregation in New York public schools over the last 30 years helps frame the issues examined in this paper. Upstate New York elementary schools are substantially more segregated in 1995 than they were in 1970. As shown in Table 1, overall segregation, as measured by the Theil inequality coefficient, doubled during this 25-year period. What is even more provocative than the level is the changing pattern of segregation in schools. In 1970, racial segregation in upstate New York metropolitan elementary schools was largely attributable to segregated residential location patterns *within* districts[1] (60.8 percent of this variation occurred within urban public districts). By 1995, whites increasingly were opting out of urban districts and locating in suburban districts. As a result, segregation in schools is increasingly attributable to residential location patterns *between* districts (68.4 percent was between the three sectors). This is a remarkable transformation and raises the question of what factors are relevant in determining both public–private school choice decisions and the residential choices of households.[2]

In this paper, we empirically model the school choice and residential location decisions of white families in eight New York metropolitan areas.

Table 1. Racial Composition and Segregation in New York Elementary Schools,[a] 1970–1995.

	1970	1995
Percent of students who are white		
All schools	93.1	85.5
Private schools	95.5	90.0
Public suburban schools	98.7	96.4
Public urban schools	77.2	53.6
Percent of all white students		
Private schools	19.3	14.1
Public suburban schools	61.0	70.8
Public urban schools	19.7	15.1
Overall Theil coefficient	0.0240	0.0519
Within urban public sector		
Theil coefficient	0.0146	0.0124
Share	60.8	24.0
Within private sector		
Theil coefficient	0.0022	0.0031
Share	9.1	6.0
Within suburban public sector		
Theil coefficient	0.0003	0.0008
Share	1.4	1.6
Between sectors		
Theil coefficient	0.0069	0.0355
Share	28.7	68.4

[a]The statistics are for elementary school in the following eight metropolitan areas: Albany–Schenectady–Troy, Binghamton, Dunkirk–Jamestown, Elmira, Poughkeepsie, Rome–Utica, Rochester and Syracuse.

The paper examines the relationship between the racial composition of schools and the choices parents make concerning the public and private schools their children attend. Controlling for a host of individual, peer, school, and local government characteristics, we find that the racial composition of schools and neighborhoods is very important in school choice and residential location decisions. The remainder of this paper includes five sections. The next section examines the school choice environment and data employed in the empirical analysis. Section 3 sets out the specification and estimation of the nested multinomial logit, random utility model. Estimates of how the school and residential location decisions of white households are affected by the racial composition of schools and neighborhoods are discussed in Section 4. Section 5 provides concluding remarks.

2. BACKGROUND

Conditional on living in a given metropolitan area, each household chooses a particular residential location and a school for each child from the array of alternatives within the metropolitan area. Private school and location decisions are linked to the extent that the attractiveness of particular residential location and private school combinations depend upon student transportation costs. Public school and location decisions are linked as a result of residential location largely determining the public school option.[3]

Most empirical work related to the Tiebout hypothesis has focused on whether local taxes and public amenities are capitalized into property values. In contrast, there has been relatively little empirical work directly quantifying the extent to which local public services and taxes affect the residential location and mobility decisions of households. Nechyba and Strauss (1998) provide a good summary of the literature examining the relationship of community attributes and housing values and the separate literature that examines residential choice. As they suggest, work in these areas are related but the data necessary to explore these decisions jointly is not typically available, leaving researchers to examine one issue or the other. For example, research examining the effect of community-specific attributes typically employs housing hedonics to understand the impact of these variables on house prices. The residential location research, which usually employs discrete choice models, typically includes only the attributes of individuals and the housing stock, and do not account for attributes of the local communities. Nechyba and Strauss (1998) move this literature forward by examining the community choice of individuals employing tax and service levels specific to each community in a discrete choice model. More recently, Bayer, McMillan, and Rueben (2003) use Census micro-data to examine the issues that affect residential segregation.

Two attitudinal surveys provide evidence regarding the link between residential location and school choice. In a survey by the U.S. Department of Education (1983), over 50 percent of parents with children attending public schools reported having considered the quality of public schools when making their residential location decisions; 18 percent reported that public school quality was the most important consideration. In a Harris survey (1976) concerned with factors affecting the residential location decisions of households, public schools was the reason most frequently given by parents with school-age children. These findings, together with the fact that roughly 88 percent of all students attend public schools, underscore the importance of the choice among various public schools inherent in residential location decisions.

Research concerned with public–private school choice has employed either aggregate (e.g., public school district) or student-level data.[4] Estimating the separate effects of students' own characteristics and student-body attributes is difficult using aggregate data, even if the empirical model used is based on an explicit aggregation of a student-level model of choice.[5] For example, sorting out the effect of a students' own race from the effects of the racial composition of schools is problematic. Simultaneity also complicates the use of aggregate data, as school characteristics affect the proportion and attributes of students attending particular schools, which, in turn, are reflected in the school characteristics.

Ideally, an empirical analysis of the determinants of public–private school choice would be based on detailed data characterizing individual students and their families matched with data characterizing the attributes of the schools among which they choose. Publicly available data fall short of this ideal. The difficulty in using data such as the Census of Population PUMS is that it is not possible to identify the exact public school option and its attributes since only the county, or county group, of residence is identified. Data from High School and Beyond and the National Education Longitudinal Survey 1988 identify attributes of individual students as well as a wide variety of characteristics for the school each student attends, but provide no information regarding the other schools in each student's set of alternatives. In general, the problem is that available data characterizing individual students and their families do not include the geographical identifiers needed to merge in data characterizing the attributes of the schools among which they choose. This difficulty helps explain why past studies using student-level data have included only aggregate data, or no information, regarding school characteristics. Without measures of academic quality and other attributes of the schools in the set of alternatives, empirical models of choice are misspecified. In particular, a full set of school attributes must be included if the direct effect of school racial composition is to be estimated with any degree of confidence.

An analysis of school choice needs to account for the choice among public schools inherent in residential location as well as the self-selection of families into communities that results from such location choice. The relevance of public school attributes in location choice will depend upon the likelihood that children in each family will attend the public alternative.[6] Similarly, the relevance of private alternatives in school choice will partially depend upon whether families have optimally chosen public school alternatives through residential location. Analysis of the full range of school choice would require detailed micro-data that include the geographical information needed to identify residential locations and the associated public schools.

3. DATA EMPLOYED

We have constructed a household-level data set for eight metropolitan areas in upstate New York that addresses the data limitations noted above. Student and family data are linked to detailed information regarding the schools and residential locations among which the families choose. The focus is on metropolitan areas because opportunities for school and residential location choices are greatest in these areas and because advocates of greater choice often argue that education in urban areas would be the largest beneficiary of choice. New York was chosen because detailed information is available for both public and private schools and because metropolitan areas in New York are composed of many, typically 20 or more, public school districts. In such a setting, individuals are presented with a large choice set from which to select residences and schools.

Data come from households completing the 1990 Census of Population and Housing long-form, which includes information on whether each child attended public or private school. We are able to identify the Census block of residence for each household using restricted access files at the Bureau of the Census. The public school district for each residential location is then determined using a geographical mapping file that maps Census blocks into public school districts.

In contrast to the relatively small and homogeneous suburban school districts, urban districts typically are quite large. Owing to significant intra-district differences between urban public schools, district-level statistics are likely to be poor proxies for the local urban public school attributes relevant in both the public–private school and location choices of families. As a result, we map urban Census blocks into individual public school attendance areas.[7] In this way, our analysis of public–private school choice is based upon information regarding the exact urban public school alternative available to each student. The elementary school attendance areas are also used to represent the elemental "residential communities" within the set of urban localities.[8] Orfield (1994) argues that school attendance areas are useful in delineating neighborhoods, providing a sharper focus than the Census tracts typically employed in residential location research.

School attendance areas in suburban districts are not mapped because a preliminary analysis indicated that differences in school characteristics within suburban districts are relatively small. Instead, public school districts are used to define the suburban community or locational alternatives.[9] The public school option in each suburban location is defined to be a composite of all the public schools in the district, differentiated by school level (e.g., elementary).

Census data only indicate whether each student attends public or private school; there is no information for those attending private school regarding the particular private school, or type of private school, attended. However, we were able to obtain aggregate data from the New York Department of Education on the number of students living in each public school district that attend *each* private school.[10] Similar data disaggregated to public school attendance areas are employed for the city districts of Rochester and Syracuse. As discussed below, this aggregate data on private school enrollments are used along with school and Census data to estimate a model of private school choice.

Metropolitan areas are defined to include urban public school districts and suburban districts in a two-district ring around the urban district(s). Additional districts are included when the districts had characteristics similar to those falling within the two-district ring. This definition is somewhat more restrictive than the Office of Management and Budget definition of metropolitan statistical areas (MSA), which is defined in terms of entire counties. We were guided in this decision by our special interest in school choice within urban areas. We believe that the sample of households living in the two-district ring closely corresponds to the population that might possibly choose urban locations and schools. For example, more than 95 percent of the households with individuals working in the cities of Rochester and Syracuse live in school districts included in our sample. These workers reasonably could have lived in the central cities.

Conditional on living in a given metropolitan area, each household is assumed to jointly choose a particular residential location and a school for each child from the full set of alternatives. Reflecting their similarities, alternatives are grouped as follows. The locational alternatives are classified as being either urban ($m = 1$) or suburban ($m = 2$). Private schools are classified by type: Baptist-evangelical ($q = 1$), Catholic ($q = 2$), other religious ($q = 3$), and independent ($q = 4$). All private schools in the metropolitan area are assumed to enter the set of school alternatives available to each family, regardless of the family's residential location; parents have the option of living in one community and sending their children to private schools located elsewhere.

The full choice set for a particular metropolitan area is characterized as follows:

M represents the set of community types: urban ($m = 1$) and suburban ($m = 2$).

N_m represents the set of available communities of type m.

$\bar{N}_m$ represents the number of communities of type m.

Q represents the set of alternative private school types.
R_q represents the set of available private schools of type q.
$\bar{R}_q$ represents the number of private schools of type q.
S represents the complete set of school/location alternatives.

Each student living in a particular community has one public school alternative and the $\sum_{q\in Q}\bar{R}_q$ private school alternatives for the metropolitan area. With $\bar{N}_1$ urban locations and $\bar{N}_2$ suburban areas in which to live, there are a total of $(\bar{N}_1+\bar{N}_2)\left(1+\sum_{q\in Q}\bar{R}_q\right)$ elemental schooling alternatives within a metropolitan area. Table 2 shows the number of private elementary schools, by type, as well as the numbers of urban and suburban residential communities in each of the metropolitan areas.

The structure of our data is as follows. Each urban and suburban residential community is linked to data regarding the local public school alternative, other local government amenities (e.g., local tax and expenditure levels), housing and other community characteristics as well as distances from residences to each private school. This information along with data regarding the attributes of individual private schools[11] provides a detailed characterization of the school and residential choices available to families in each metropolitan area. The household-level data characterize students

Table 2. Available Private Elementary Schools and Residential Location Options by Metropolitan Area.

	Number of Private Elementary Schools by Category				Residential "Communities"	
	Baptist-Fundamentalist	Catholic	Other Religious	Independent	Urban	Suburban
Albany–Schenectady–Troy	9	40	4	7	29	30
Binghamton	5	12	2	1	7	11
Elmira	9	6	1	1	9	6
Jamestown–Dunkirk	5	3	5	0	11	13
Poughkeepsie	5	14	3	5	4	8
Rochester	19	45	9	6	33	25
Syracuse	7	29	2	2	24	22
Utica–Rome	3	18	1	2	27	21
Metropolitan average	7.8	20.9	3.4	3.0	18.0	17.0

and their families and identify residential location choices as well as whether each student attended public or private school. These data are supplemented with aggregate information regarding the number of students living in each public school district (or school attendance area) that attended each private school. Table 3a–c summarize the variables and their descriptive statistics.

4. SPECIFICATION AND ESTIMATION OF THE EMPIRICAL MODEL

With each family selecting a single alternative from a finite set of mutually exclusive options, the appropriate empirical specification is a random utility model, such as the nested multinomial logit model (NMLM) that we employ.[12] Consider a household having one school-age child. $U_{mn0} = \upsilon_{mn0} + \varepsilon_{mn0}$ is the family's utility associated with living in community n of type m and the student attending the public school alternative, 0. $U_{mnqr} = \upsilon_{mnqr} + \varepsilon_{mnqr}$ is the utility associated with living in community mn and the student attending private school r of type q. υ_{mn0} and υ_{mnqr} are the deterministic components of the two expressions. ε_{mn0} and ε_{mnqr} are assumed to be Gumbel random errors. Each family with school-age children is assumed to evaluate its finite set of mutually exclusive community/school options, S, and select the alternative that maximizes its utility. The alternative $mnqr$ is chosen if and only if $U_{mnqr} > U_s, \forall s \in S_{mnqr}$ where S_{mnqr} represents the set of all community/school alternatives, excluding the option shown in the subscript. Similarly, the public school option in community mn is selected if and only if $U_{mn0} > U_s, \forall s \in S_{mn0}$.

The branching in Fig. 1 reflects a particular NMLM random error structure. For example, the unmeasured attributes of communities are assumed to be more similar within a community type than across the community types. The following parameters reflect the assumed correlation structure of the error terms employed in the empirical analysis and shown in Fig. 1.[13]

μ_m, $m = 1,2$	reflects the similarity of communities of type m.
μ^S	reflects the similarity of public and private schools.
μ^*	reflects the similarity between the four types of private schools.
μ_q^*, $q = 1,2,3,4$	reflects the similarity of private schools of type q.

Since there is a single public school alternative for each location, $\mu_0^* = 1$.

Table 3a. Variable Definitions and Descriptive Statistics PrivateSchool-Choice Submodel.

		Mean (S.D.)
Household Attributes of Private School Students Entering $V_{..q}$		
ln(Income)	Mean natural logarithm of household income from all sources[a]	10.58 (0.45)
High school graduate	Proportion of households in which a parent graduated from high school[a]	0.94 (0.15)
College graduate	Proportion of households in which a parent graduated from college[a]	0.42 (0.31)
Minority	Proportion of households in which the head is either African-American or Latino[a]	0.13 (0.23)
White-collar	Proportion of households in which the head is a white-collar worker[a]	0.75 (0.27)
Catholic	Estimated proportion of household heads that are Catholic[b]	0.35 (0.14)
Baptist	Estimated proportion of household heads that are Baptist[b]	0.22 (0.13)
Private School Attributes Entering $V_{..qr}$		
ln(Tuition)	Natural logarithm of predicted school tuition[c]	6.91 (0.60)
Proportion minority	Proportion of students in school who are African-American or Latino[d]	
$\geq$0.05	Equals one if the proportion is at least 0.05, zero otherwise	0.48 (0.50)
$\geq$0.10	Equals one if the proportion is at least 0.10, zero otherwise	0.31 (0.46)
$\geq$0.15	Equals one if the proportion is at least 0.15, zero otherwise	0.21 (0.40)
$\geq$0.25	Equals one if proportion is at least 0.25, zero otherwise	0.16 (0.36)
$\geq$0.40	Equals one if proportion is at least 0.40, zero otherwise	0.11 (0.31)

Students/teacher	School mean number of students per teacher[d]	14.4 (4.74)
Mean reading	School mean score on 3rd grade reading exam[d]	36.2 (15.7)
Mean math	School mean score on 3rd grade math exam[d]	39.7 (17.2)
Percentage below srp read	Proportion of students in school below the State passing level (srp) on the 3rd grade reading exam[d]	0.08 (0.11)
Percentage below srp math	Proportion of students in school below the State passing level (srp) on the 3rd grade math exam[d]	0.03 (0.08)
Test dummy	Equals one if school is missing test data, zero otherwise[d]	0.15 (0.35)
Titles	Number of titles in school library[d]	4961 (4254)
School enrollment	Total school enrollment[d]	173.4 (114.5)
Private School Attribute Entering V_{mnqr}		
Distance	Mean distance from residences in location to each private school in metropolitan area (miles)[e]	10.3 (7.3)

[a]Public school district or school attendance area statistic for households of resident students attending private school, computed from the 1990 Census of Population and Housing long-form sample.

[b]Computed using data regarding ancestry and religion from the General Social Survey and ancestry codes of household heads in the 1990 Census of Population long-form sample.

[c]Information regarding tuition comes from a mail survey with telephone follow-up and the 1988 and 1992 editions of *Private Schools of the United States* published by the Council for American Private Education (1988, 1992). Predicted tuition is employed, based on regressions of actual tuition on school and regional characteristics. (Regression estimates are available from authors.)

[d]Computed using the Basic Education Database, New York State Education Department.

[e]Computed from geo-coded locations (longitudes and latitudes) of private schools and residences.

Table 3b. Variable Definitions and Descriptive Statistics Public-Private-Choice Submodels.

		Mean (S.D.)
Household Attributes of Students Entering $V_{..0}$		
ln(Income)	Natural logarithm of total household income from all sources[f]	10.476 (0.704)
High school graduate	Equals one if a parent graduated from high school, zero otherwise[f]	0.94 (0.24)
College graduate	Equals one if a parent graduated from college, zero otherwise[f]	0.33 (0.47)
White-collar	Equals one if a parent is in a white-collar occupation, zero otherwise[f]	0.71 (0.45)
Blue-collar	Equals one if a parent is in a blue-collar occupation, zero otherwise[f]	0.27 (0.44)
Household size	Number of members of household[f]	4.5 (1.2)
Married	Equals one if head is married, zero otherwise[f]	0.82 (0.38)
Female	Equals one if student is female, zero otherwise[f]	0.48 (0.50)
Public school teacher	Equals one if a parent taught in a public K-12 school, zero otherwise[f]	0.04 (0.20)
Private school teacher	Equals one if a parent taught in a private K-12 school, zero otherwise[f]	0.02 (0.13)
Public School Attributes Entering V_{mn0}		
Schools minority (srace)	Proportion of public school students who are African-American or Latino[d]	0.07 (0.14)
School minority 0–5	Equals srace if srace ≤ 0.05, zero otherwise	0.027 (0.019)
School minority 5–15	Equals srace if $0.05 <$ srace ≤ 0.15, zero otherwise	0.015 (0.033)
School minority15–30	Equals srace if $0.15 <$ srace ≤ 0.30, zero otherwise	0.013 (0.040)
School minority 30+	Equals srace if srace > 0.30, zero otherwise	0.016 (0.08)
Peer married	Proportion of children in the public school living in households where the household head is married[g]	0.80 (0.12)
Peer lunch	Proportion of children in the public school receiving free or reduced-price school lunches[d]	0.22 (0.19)
Peer poverty	Proportion of children in the public school living in poverty[g]	0.14 (0.12)
Peer income	Average family income of children attending the public school[g]	42,587 (12,509)

Peer college	Proportion of children in the public school who had at least one parent graduate from college[g]	0.31 (0.18)
Peer high school	Proportion of children in the public school who had at least one parent graduate from high school[g]	0.92 (0.09)
Peer white collar	Proportion of children in the public school who had at least one parent employed as a white-collar worker[g]	0.68 (0.15)
Peer blue collar	Proportion of children in the public school who had at least one parent employed as a blue-collar worker[g]	0.29 (0.13)
Safety1	Factor indicating extent of problem in district of students using offensive language or bullying (higher values less problem)[h]	4.30 (0.49)
Safety2	Factor indicating extent of problem with student violence against teachers (higher values less of a problem)[h]	4.25 (0.33)
Safety3	Factor indicating extent of problem with student use of drugs (higher value less of a problem)[h]	4.08 (0.37)
Titles in library	Number of titles in school library[d]	9199 (3552)
School enrollment	Total school enrollment[d]	504.1 (137.6)
Class size	Average size of a common branch class in the school[d]	22.6 (1.6)
Mean reading score	Mean score on the 3rd grade reading competency test[d]	42.1 (3.1)
Mean math score	Mean score on the 3rd grade math competency test[d]	49.4 (3.1)
Percentage below srp reading	Proportion of students below the State passing level (srp) on the 3rd grade reading exam[d]	0.093 (0.069)
Percentage below srp math	Proportion of students below the State passing level (srp) on the 3rd grade math exam[d]	0.013 (0.022)

[d]Computed using the Basic Education Database, New York State Education Department.

[f]Student- and household-level data from the 1990 Census of Population long-form survey.

[g]Public school district or school attendance area statistic for households of students attending public school, computed using 1990 Census data.

[h]Computed using a factor analysis of 13 questions on the Superintendent Survey for Crime and Safety in New York State Schools, 1992–1993.

Table 3c. Variable Definitions and Descriptive Statistics Location-Choice Submodels for Owners and Renters.

		Owners	Renters
Household Attributes Entering V_{mn}			
High school graduate	Equals one if a parent graduated from high school, zero otherwise[f]	0.97 (0.17)	0.85 (0.35)
College graduate	Equals one if a parent graduated from college, zero otherwise[f]	0.40 (0.49)	0.12 (0.32)
White-collar	Equals one if a parent is in a white-collar occupation, zero otherwise[f]	0.79 (0.41)	0.56 (0.50)
Blue-collar	Equals one if a parent is in a blue-collar occupation, zero otherwise[f]	0.21 (0.41)	0.39 (0.49)
ln(C + Income−cost)	Natural logarithm of total household income less total annual housing costs, including rents, utilities, and fees for renters and mean property taxes, utilities, fees, and other annualized costs for owners[f,i,j,k]	10.88 (0.45)	10.53 (0.37)
Location Attributes Entering V_{mn}			
Police expenditure	Per-capita police expenditure in municipality by county, city, town, and village[i]	167 (79)	166 (80)
Transportation expenditure	Per-capita transportation expenditure in municipality by county, city, town, and village[i]	190 (63)	191 (65)
Recreation expenditure	Per-capita recreation expenditure in municipality by county, city, town, and village[i]	80 (43)	78 (43)
Urban	Equals one if location is in city, zero otherwise	0.53 (0.50)	0.53 (0.50)
Neighborhood income	Mean income of households in location[j]	35,112 (11,214)	34,951 (11,037)
Neighborhood proportion owners	Proportion of households in location owning their homes[j]	0.58 (0.21)	0.58 (0.21)
Neighborhood crime rate	Rate of violent crimes in municipality[l]	52.8 (37.4)	50 (36)
Neighborhood-boarded up	Proportion of housing structures in location that are boarded up[j]	0.005 (0.009)	0.005 (0.008)
Neighborhood minority (nrace)	Proportion of location residents who are African-American or Latino[j]	0.13 (0.21)	0.12 (0.20)

Variable	Description		
Neighborhood minority 0–5	Equals nrace if nrace ≤0.05, zero otherwise	0.03 (0.02)	0.03 (0.02)
Neighborhood minority 5–15	Equals nrace if 0.05< nrace ≤0.15, zero otherwise	0.03 (0.04)	0.03 (0.04)
Neighborhood minority 15–30	Equals nrace if 0.15<nrace ≤ 0.30, zero otherwise	0.03 (0.06)	0.02 (0.05)
Neighborhood minority >30	Equals nrace if nrace >0.30	0.04 (0.12)	0.04 (0.11)
Housing Attributes Entering V_{mn}			
Rooms	Location's average number of rooms per housing unit[j]	6.4 (0.37)	4.4 (0.48)
Bedrooms	Location's average number of bedrooms per housing unit[j]	4.1 (0.18)	3.0 (0.29)
One-acre parcel	Proportion of housing units on parcels of at least one acre[j]	0.17 (0.19)	0.06 (0.09)
Age	Average age of housing structures in location[j]	52.4 (16.1)	46.7 (13.3)
Structure1	Proportion of single-family housing units[j]	0.81 (0.16)	0.18 (0.12)
Structure2a	Proportion of two- and three-unit housing structures[j]		0.60 (0.15)
Structure3	Proportion of structures having more than three units[j]		0.09 (0.09)
Structure2b	Proportion of structures having two or more units[j]	0.14 (0.17)	
ln(*n*units)	Natural logarithm of the number of housing units[j]	5.62 (1.06)	4.95 (0.92)
Room variance	Within-location variance in the number of rooms[j]	2.14 (0.52)	2.2 (0.63)
One-acre parcel variance	Within-location variance in lot size[j]	0.11 (0.08)	0.05 (0.06)
Age variance	Within-location variance in age of structures[j]	575 (253)	709 (225)
Number of observations		3703	1914

[f]Student- and household-level data from the 1990 Census of Population long-form survey.

[i]Tax and spending computed from Local Government Data Base, State Office of the Comptroller.

[j]Community averages for public school districts or attendance areas, computed using the 1990 Census of Population.

[k]Note that the average annual housing cost in some locations exceeds the incomes of some families. Adding the constant C allowed us to use the log specification. The parameter estimates in Table 8 correspond to C equaling \$20,000. These results are robust to alternative values of C as well as alternative variable specifications (e.g., including cost/income rather than ln(C + income−cost).

[l]Crime rates from New York State Criminal Justice Statistics.

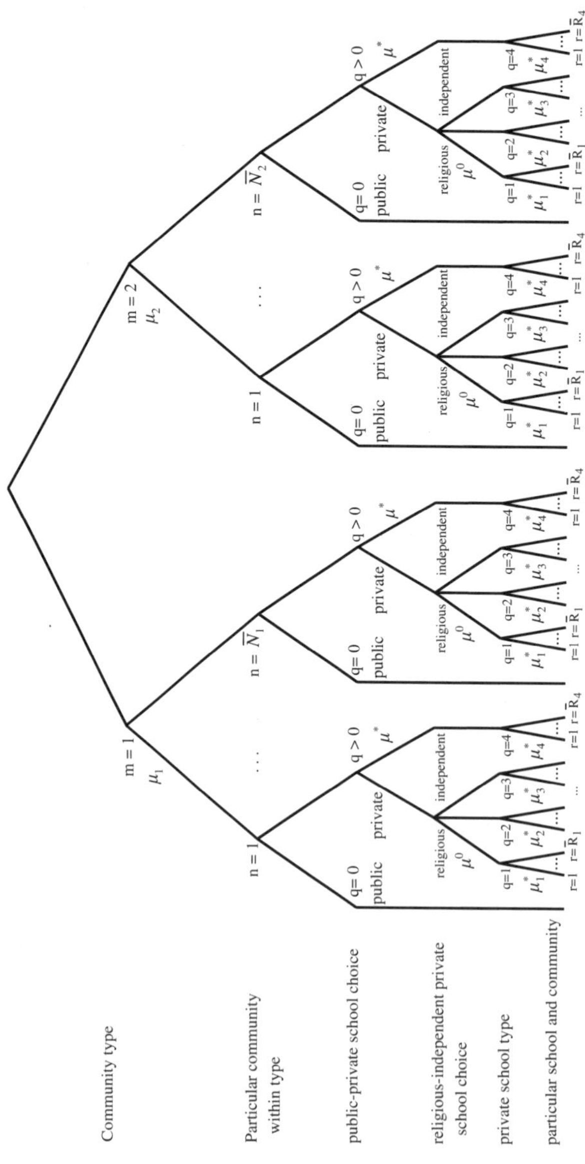

Fig. 1. Clusters of Alternatives.

The model is given empirical relevance through the specification of υ_{mn0} and υ_{mnqr} to be a function of school and community attributes, the bundle of other goods and services consumed by the household (e.g., housing and a composite of other goods) as well as sociodemographic variables proxying for tastes and preferences. The following decompositions are useful given the categories of the explanatory variables discussed below.

$$\upsilon_{mn0} = V_m + V_{mn} + V_{..0} + V_{mn0}$$
$$\upsilon_{mnqr} = V_m + V_{mn} + V_{..*} + V_{..q} + V_{..qr} + V_{mnqr}$$

V_m and V_{mn} include the non-school locational attributes which may affect the attractiveness of the community type and specific community. $V_{..0}$ and $V_{..*}$ are components of utility associated with the attractiveness of all public and private schools, respectively, unrelated to the community type, location, or particular school. $V_{..q}$ relates to all private schools of type q. $V_{..qr}$ relates to the attributes of the rth private school of type q that are independent of the student's residential location. V_{mnqr} relates to the attributes of the rth private school of type q that depend upon residential location. Variables reflecting the sociodemographics of households enter various components. For example, the relative attractiveness of public and the various types of private schools may differ depending upon the education, occupation, and religion of the household. In addition, a household's income net of the cost of living in a particular location will enter V_{mn}, reflecting expenditures on other goods and services. Each of the non-stochastic components of utility is assumed to be linear-in-parameter functions of the explanatory variables.

Even though the NMLM model can be specified in terms of the joint probability of a family living in a particular community and the student attending a particular school, an equivalent specification based on conditional probabilities has a simpler form useful in estimation.

4.1. Private School-Choice Submodel

The probabilities in the two school-choice submodels are conditional on the family living in a particular community (e.g., mn). Consider a family with a single student. The probability that the student attends private school r conditional on attending a private school of type q is $P(r|m,n,q,q>0) = \exp\left(V_{..qr} + V_{mnqr}\right)/\exp\left(H_{mnq}\right)$ where $H_{mnq} \equiv \ln\left(\sum_{r' \in R_q} \exp\left(V_{..qr'} + V_{mnqr'}\right)\right)$ is related to the systematic component of the maximum utility (i.e., the expected maximum utility) that the child would derive from attending the most attractive private school of type q.[14] The probability that the student attends a private schools of type q, conditional on the child attending a private school, is $P(q|m,n,q{>}0) = \exp\left(V_{..q} + \mu_q^* H_{mnq}\right) \big/ \exp(H_{mn^*})$ where $H_{mn^*} \equiv \ln\left(\sum_{q'=1}^{4} \exp\left(V_{..q'} + \mu_q^* H_{mnq}\right)\right)$. $V_{..*} + \mu^* H_{mn^*}$ is the systematic component of the maximum utility from the student attending a private school. It follows that the probability of a student attending private school qr conditional on the student both living in community mn and attending a private school is $P(q,r|m,n,q{>}0) = P(r|m,n,q,q{>}0)P(q|m,n,q{>}0)$.

Note that the components of the utility from schooling corresponding to all private schools, $V_{..*}$, and private schools of type q, $V_{..q}$, do not appear in the expression for $P(r|m,n,q,q{>}0)$ because the components are additive and common to all the schools of type q. Similarly, $V_{..*}$ does not enter $P(q|m,n,q{>}0)$ and V_m as well as V_{mn} do not enter either probability expression since the school choice probability is conditional on a residential location. More generally, variables which are the same for all the alternatives in a (nested) subset of alternatives do not affect the relative attractiveness of the alternatives in the subset, unless the variables are interacted with variables that differ across the alternatives or are interacted with coefficients which differ across the alternatives.

4.2. Public–Private-Choice Submodel

The probability that a student attends some private school, conditional on the family living in community mn, is $P(q{>}0|mn) = \exp(V_{..*} + \mu^* H_{mn^*})/ \exp(H_{mn})$. $H_{mn} \equiv \ln\left[\exp(V_{..*} + \mu^* H_{mn^*}) + \exp(V_{..0} + V_{mn0})\right]$ is the systematic component of the maximum utility from schooling, where the student optimally chooses between the full set of school options available to those living in community mn. Similarly, the probability that the student attends the public school alternative in community mn is $P(q=0|mn) = \exp(V_{..0} + V_{mn0}) / \exp(H_{mn})$. Here the public–private school choice depends upon the public school attributes, a composite of private school attributes measured by the inclusive value for private schools and the attributes of the student and her family.

4.3. Locational-Choice Submodel

The probability that a one-student family lives in location mn, conditional on the family living in a community of type m, is $P(n|m) = \exp\left(V_{mn} + \mu_m H_{mn}\right) / \exp(H_m)$. $H_m \equiv \ln \sum_{n' \in N_m} \exp\left(V_{mn'} + \mu_m H_{mn'}\right)$ is the systematic component of the maximum utility from the family living in a community of type m and the student attending the most attractive school alternative. The probability that the family lives in a location of type m is $P(m) = \exp(V_m + \mu_m H_m) / \sum_{m' \in M} \exp(V_{m'} + \mu_{m'} H_{m'})$.

The submodels of community location, public–private school choice and private school choice together characterize a general NMLM of residential and school choice. For example, the probability that a single-student household chooses to live in community n of type m and send the child to private school r of type q is $P(m, n, q, r) = P(q, r|m, n, q > 0)P(q > 0|mn)P(n|m)P(m)$.

The three submodels lend themselves to sequential estimation, which is common with NMLM. Rather than estimate the full model FIML, the parameters in the private school-choice submodel are estimated using data for private schools and private school students. Conditional on these estimates, the other parameters in the public–private-choice submodel are estimated. Conditional on these estimates, the remaining parameters in the submodel of community location are estimated. Again, the error structure does not imply that the location and school choice decisions are made sequentially. Rather, the assumed error structure implies the joint probability of location and school choice can be expressed as the product of conditional probability that both have relatively simple forms and can be used in sequential estimation.

The nature of our data necessitates using a variant of the sequential estimation method. Census data only indicate whether each student attends public or private school; for those attending private school, there is no information regarding the particular private school or type of private school attended. Thus, the full model cannot be estimated solely based on household-level Census data.

Since choice among private schools is an integral part of our broader model of school choice and is of interest in itself, we estimated the private school-choice submodel using aggregate data on the number of students living in each public school district (or school attendance area) that attend *each* private school in the metropolitan area. Household-level Census data are used to calculate mean attributes for the households of private school students living in each public school district (i.e., household attributes entering $V_{\cdot\cdot q}$ and distance to each private school, which enters V_{mnqr}). The private school-choice model is estimated using this information on mean attributes of the private school students by public school district of residence (or school attendance area) and the district-level enrollment counts for each private school. Effectively, a student-level model is estimated in which district-level means are used as proxies for the explanatory variables for each student.[15]

The estimated parameters in the model of private school choice are then used with student-level data to estimate the inclusive value reflecting the systematic component of the maximum utility from a student living in the *mn*th community attending a private school, H_{mn^*}. The estimated inclusive value for each student along with a variety of student-level data and information on the attributes of the local public school options are used to estimate the public–private school-choice submodel. In turn, the model of residential location is estimated.

The model described above is for single-child households. Two issues arise with multiple children. First, the public–private school choices for siblings are likely to be linked. Unmeasured household attributes that increase the likelihood of one student attending private school will often increase the likelihood of siblings attending private school – often of the same type, if not the same school. The school choices for siblings will also be linked through households' budget constraints. Second, the residential location decisions of families with multiple children may reflect differences in tastes due to the differences in household composition. Most pertinent here, the extent to which local school attributes affect the relative attractiveness of alternative residential locations may depend upon the number of children.

Our ability to account for the jointness of the school choice decisions for siblings is limited because aggregate data are used to estimate the private school-choice model; we have no information regarding which private schools siblings attend. The household-level Census data regarding whether siblings attend public or private school would allow the above public–private-choice submodel for individual students to be generalized to a household-level model for multiple children. However, the following analysis is based on the simpler model which implicitly assumes that the school choices of siblings are independent.

This independence assumption implies that the schooling inclusive value for each student should enter the utility expression for each location in the locational-choice submodel. Because the estimated schooling inclusive value for each sibling is the same,[16] entering an inclusive value for each child in a household with *c* children is equivalent to weighting the schooling inclusive value by *c*. Thus, for single and multiple child households $P(n|m) = \exp\left(V_{mn} + \mu_s c H_{mn}\right) / \exp(H_m)$ where $c = 1$ for a one-child household is a special case. In addition, V_{mn} would also differ for households with multiple children to the extent that these households place a different value on other locational attributes (e.g., housing and non-school local amenities) and expenditures on other goods. What is important is the weight placed on schooling relative to those on the other location-specific attributes. To allow for the possibility that the relative weighting differs with the number of children in school, the schooling inclusive value, H_{mn}, is entered in $P(n|m)$ interacted with dummy variables indicating whether the household had one, two, three, or more children in school. This specification imposes no structure on how the coefficient of H_{mn} varies with the number of students. Definitions and descriptive statistics of the variables employed in the estimation are presented in Tables 3a–c.

Most private school attributes enter $V_{..qr}$. These include tuition, proxies for school resources (e.g., class-size and titles), educational outcomes (test scores), and student-body attributes (e.g., racial composition). The coefficients for each of these variables are assumed to be the same across the private school types. Distance to a particular school enters V_{mnqr} since it is dependent upon residential location.

A variety of variables reflecting household attributes is assumed to affect the attractiveness of the various types of private schools and are entered in $V_{..q}$, $q = 1,2,3,4$. These variables include ln(income) and dummy variables reflecting whether at least one parent had a high school degree, a college degree, and/or a white-collar job. A dummy variable indicating whether the student is nonwhite is also included. A variable reflecting the likelihood of the head-of-household being Catholic is entered in $V_{..2}$ for Catholic schools and a variable reflecting the likelihood of being Baptist is entered in $V_{..1}$ for the Baptist-evangelical type.[17] Since all the variables entering $V_{..4}$ also entered $V_{..1}$, $V_{..2}$ and $V_{..3}$, the normalization $V_{..4} = 0$ is maintained with no loss of generality. Since the private school-choice submodel employs aggregate data in estimation, these variables reflect public school-attendance area or school district means for the household attributes of those students attending private school.

In the case of the location-dependent public school option, V_{mn0} includes class and school size, titles in library, reading and math test scores, three factors reflecting school discipline/crime problems,[18] as well as several proxies for the public school environment and student-body attributes (percent of students having a parent that graduated from college, percent coming from two parent households, percent receiving free or reduced price lunches, and percent of students that are African-American or Latino). The household-level socioeconomic variables entering $V_{..0}$ include the household's income and size as well as dummy variables reflecting whether at least one parent has a high school or college degree, a white-collar or blue-collar job, a job as a public school teacher and a job as a private school teacher.[19] A dummy variable is also included indicating if the child is female and whether parents are married. With the same socioeconomic variables assumed to enter $V_{..0}$ and $V_{..*}$, the normalization $V_{..*} = 0$ is maintained with no loss of generality. As a result, the coefficients for the variables entering $V_{..0}$ reflect how the variables affect the general attractiveness of public schools relative to that of private schools. Similar normalizations elsewhere imply similar interpretations.

The community attributes entering V_{mn} to characterize the mnth location include categories of non-school public expenditures and the community crime rate, as well as neighborhood attributes including the racial and socioeconomic composition of the local population (i.e., mean household income, proportion of owners and proportion of units boarded up). The utility associated with each community will also depend upon the household's underlying tastes and preferences, which we proxy using several household-level socioeconomic variables. However, these variables are not interacted with attributes that vary across communities so that the socioeconomic variables enter V_m rather than V_{mn}. Specifically, variables reflecting the education and occupation of parents are included in V_m to allow for such factors to affect the relative attractiveness of urban and suburban locations. With the same socioeconomic variables entering V_1, and V_2, the normalization $V_2 = 0$ is maintained with no loss of generality.

Even though not explicitly shown in Fig. 1 or discussed in the above description of our model, the link between residential location and housing choice needs to be taken into account. Just as the attractiveness of a community will depend upon the attributes of the local public school, its attractiveness will depend upon the price and other characteristics of the housing available in the community. Even though housing choice is not of special interest here, we account for inter-community differences in the prices, other characteristics and availability of housing, in order to avoid problems of omitted variables bias – especially regarding the estimated effects of locational attributes.[20]

Assuming a multinomial logit model of intra-location housing choice, let Z_{mn} represent a family's housing inclusive value associated with a particular community (i.e., the expected maximum utility from the housing choice in that community, taking into account the attributes of the housing stock there). This housing index enters V_{mn} as an explanatory variable, paralleling the treatment of H_{mn} for schooling.[21] If the utility function in the multinomial logit model of housing choice is linear in parameters, the housing inclusive value for a location can be written as follows:

$$Z_{mn} = \ln \sum_{j=1}^{J_{mn}} e^{\theta z_{mnj}} = \theta \bar{z}_{mn} + \lambda \left[\frac{1}{J_{mn}} \sum_{j=1}^{J_{mn}} e^{\theta(z_{mnj} - \bar{z}_{mn})} \right] + \lambda \ln J_{mn}$$

Here the mnth location has J_{mn} housing units where z_{mnj} is a vector characterizing the relevant attributes associated with the jth unit. θ is a vector of parameters and $\bar{z}_{mn}$ the vector of mean attributes for the mnth location. $\bar{z}_{mn}$ includes household income net of the mean annual cost of housing in the location, including property taxes. λ is the similarity coefficient corresponding to housing within locations. It can be shown that when the number of housing alternatives is large and the housing attributes approach a normal distribution with covariance Σ_{mn}, the housing inclusive value is a function of the mean and covariance of the housing attributes as well as the log of the number of housing units: $Z_{mn} = \ln \sum_{j=1}^{J_{mn}} e^{\theta z_{mnj}} = \theta \bar{z}_{mn} + \lambda \theta \Sigma_{mn} \theta' + \lambda \ln J_{mn}$.[22] Rather than (1) estimate a multinomial logit model of (intralocation) housing choice to obtain $\hat{\theta}$, (2) use $\hat{\theta}$ to calculate $\hat{Z}_{mn}$ for each household in each location, and (3) enter $\hat{Z}_{mn}$ as an explanatory variable in the location-choice model, we have directly included ln J_{mn} and mean housing attributes for each location in the model of location choice, along with the other locational attributes.[23] Even though we do not include all elements of Σ_{mn}, the variances for a number of the housing attributes are included. We are confident that the approach adequately accounts for housing attributes so as not to bias the estimated coefficients for other locational attributes.

5. EMPIRICAL RESULTS

Our estimates indicate that the public–private school choices and residential location choices of white parents directly contribute to the increasing racial segregation of elementary school students. In particular, we find that white parents are sensitive to student racial composition in their school and residential location decisions. Given our interest in the effect of student-body racial composition on these choices, it is important that the empirical analysis includes a full set of controls to minimize the possibility that the racial composition of schools is spuriously correlated with relevant, but unmeasured, school attributes. The estimated private-, public–private-, and location-choice submodels shown in Tables 4, 5 and 8 include numerous controls for individual, school, peer, and neighborhood variables, in addition to variables reflecting the racial compositions of schools and communities. (A note at the bottom of Table 4 summarizes how the estimated coefficients should be interpreted.) In general, the empirical results for all three submodels accord with a priori expectations. Even though the estimated model yields a variety of interesting insights relating to how tuition, academic quality and student–peers affect public and private school choice, the focus of this paper is on the effects of student-body racial composition.

Table 4. Private School NMLM Estimation Results[a].

	Baptist-Evangelical	Catholic	Other Religious	Independent
Constant	14.840**	21.143**	−7.137*	
	(7.69)	(6.72)	(−2.35)	
ln(Income)	−0.621**	−0.530**	1.489**	
	(−3.90)	(−2.14)	(5.62)	
High school graduate	−7.024**	−12.131**	−5.443**	
	(−5.44)	(−5.55)	(−3.86)	
College graduate	−0.624**	−1.306**	0.698	
	(−2.74)	(−3.70)	(1.65)	
Minority	0.936*	2.042**	0.833	
	(2.24)	(3.14)	(1.55)	
White collar	−1.499**	−0.801	−4.411**	
	(−4.30)	(−1.41)	(−8.89)	
Catholic		4.560**		
		(9.83)		
Baptist	−1.356**			
	(−3.34)			
Distance	−0.245**	−1.144**	−0.551**	−0.442**
	(−14.55)	(−13.98)	(−22.22)	(−17.52)
$(\text{Distance})^2$	−0.0019*	0.023**	0.0066**	0.0080**
	(−2.01)	(50.17)	(6.43)	(6.31)

School attributes			
ln(tuition)	−0.278**		
	(−9.27)	Mean reading	0.020**
Proportion minority			(4.95)
≥0.05	−0.046**	Mean math	−0.019**
	(−2.59)		(−7.82)

≥0.10	−0.183**	Percentage below srp read	−0.195
	(−6.32)		(−1.36)
≥0.15	0.005	Percentage below srp math	−0.569**
	(0.11)		(−3.08)
≥0.25	−0.255**	Test dummy	−0.147
	(−4.88)		(−0.890)
≥0.40	0.169**	Titles (1000s)	−0.000012**
	(3.59)		(−4.31)
Students/teacher	0.085**	School enrollment	0.011**
	(7.74)		(29.86)
$(\text{Students/teacher})^2$	−0.003**	$(\text{School enrollment})^2$	−0.000014**
	(−9.22)		(−22.85)
Similarity Coefficient		Log likelihood	−69,152.14
Catholic μ_2*	0.5838	No. of observations	7994
	(55.19)		

*Coefficient is statistically different from zero at the 0.05 level of significance.
**Coefficient is statistically different from zero at the 0.01 level of significance.
[a]As indicated in Table 3a, the variables here enter the utility expression corresponding to each private school alternative. For example, the estimated coefficient of ln(tuition) measures the effect that tuition has on the attractiveness (i.e., utility) of a school. As shown, the effect that distance has on the attractiveness of a school is allowed to vary across school types. The estimated coefficient associated with a household attribute and a particular school type reflects how that attribute affects the attractiveness of that type of school relative to that of independent schools, other things constant. For example, the attractiveness of Baptist-Evangelical schools is estimated to be lower relative to the attractiveness of independent schools as parents are better educated. An equivalent statement is that better educated parents are estimated to find independent schools relatively more attractive. The variables in Tables 5 and 8 have similar interpretations.

Table 5. Public–Private NMLM Estimation Results for Whites.

Household Attributes		School Attributes	
ln(Income)	1.387** (3.01)	School minority 0–5	−9.408** (−5.50)
ln(Income)^2	−0.082** (−3.69)	School minority 5–15	−5.934** (−4.01)
High school graduate	−2.144** (−12.62)	School minority 15–30	−1.711 (−1.84)
College graduate	−15.640** (−3.14)	School minority >30	−0.777* (−2.06)
White-collar	−0.535** (−2.80)	Peer married	0.716* (2.20)
Blue-collar	−0.091 (−0.48)	Peer-poverty	0.090 (0.36)
Household size	−0.146** (−7.96)	Safety1	0.121 (1.94)
Married	−0.369** (−4.84)	Safety2	−0.217* (−2.39)
Female	−0.090* (−2.10)	Safety3	0.059 (0.67)
Public school teacher	0.738** (6.14)	Titles in library	−0.0000127* (−2.28)
Private school teacher	−0.035 (−0.24)	School enrollment	0.0018* (2.08)
		(School enrollment)^2	−0.00000121 (−1.51)
		Urban	0.255* (2.34)

			College or more	Less than college
Constant	4.636 (1.11)	Peer college	1.273** (5.17)	0.099 (0.37)
		Class size	0.941** (2.63)	−0.375 (−1.30)
Similarity coefficent Private school, μ*	−0.160** (−13.08)	(Class size)^2	−0.023** (−2.93)	0.006 (1.00)
		Mean reading score	0.042 (1.26)	−0.011 (−0.40)
		Mean math score	−0.008 (−0.40)	0.035* (2.18)
		Percentage below srp reading	0.277 (0.24)	−1.407 (−1.62)
		Percentage below srp math	2.273 (1.02)	6.996** (4.20)
Log likelihood function	−7748.947	Number of observations	26683	

*Coefficient is statistically different from zero at the 0.05 level of significance.
**Coefficient is statistically different from zero at the 0.01 level of significance.

5.1. Results for the School-Choice Submodels

The racial composition of the public school alternative is entered in the utility expression associated with each public school as a continuous function of the proportion of the student body that is either African-American or Latino. Because the change in the attractiveness of a school alternative resulting from an increase in this proportion might differ depending on the initial racial mix, the variable is entered using a piece-wise linear spline. The parameter estimates imply that the attractiveness of the public school option, as viewed by whites, declines at a decreasing rate as the proportion of the student-body that is African-American or Latino increases. The estimated linkage between school racial mix and the probability of white students attending public school is shown in Fig. 2. Conditional on actual residential location and a given public school racial mix, the probability of each student attending the local public school option is calculated with all other school attributes and all individual student/family variables evaluated at their actual values. The predicted proportion (average probability) of white students attending the local public school is calculated separately for those living in urban and suburban settings, with the proportion of public

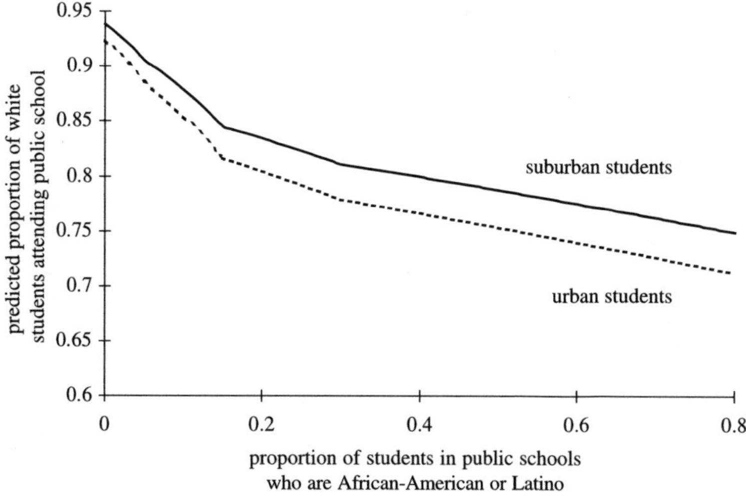

Fig. 2. Proportions of White Urban and Suburban Students Predicted to Attend Public School, Conditional on Actual Residential Choices.

school students that are African-American or Latino evaluated over the range of values shown. As shown in Fig. 2, a given change in the racial composition of the student body is estimated to have the largest effect when most students are white (i.e., the proportion of African-American and Latino students is small). When African-American and Latino students make up at least a large minority of the student body, changes in that proportion are estimated to have a relatively smaller effect on the public school choices of whites.

As shown in Fig. 2, the mean probability curves for urban and suburban whites differ somewhat. This is the result of differences between urban and suburban students and their families as well as differences in the attributes of urban and suburban public schools, as summarized in Table 6. Compared to students living in suburban communities, the parents of urban students

Table 6. Descriptive Statistics for Students and Their Local School Options for Urban and Suburban Locations.

	Urban	Suburban
Proportion of students attending public school	0.802	0.920
Parent's education		
Less than high school	0.125	0.048
High school	0.634	0.606
College or more	0.241	0.346
Parent's occupation		
White-collar worker	0.644	0.723
Blue-collar worker	0.302	0.260
Not in labor force	0.054	0.017
Household income	$35,570	$45,924
School attributes		
Total enrollment	469	512
Class size	22.6	22.7
Mean reading score	38.6	42.8
Mean math score	46.7	49.9
Student-body attributes		
Proportion African-American or Latino	0.285	0.026
Zcollege	0.178	0.333
Zmarried	0.611	0.838
Plunch	0.511	0.160

typically have less education, lower incomes and are more likely to be blue-collar workers, or not in the labor force. The public schools available to urban students are smaller, have lower test scores, and have student-peers whose parents are less educated as well as more likely to be single. Given these differences and the statistical significance of these variables in the school-choice model, it is somewhat surprising that the two curves do not differ by more; the effects of these variables, individually and as a group, are relatively modest, as the probabilities of urban and suburban students attending public school differ only by a few percent when the racial composition of schools is held constant. In contrast, the racial composition of the local public alternative has a much larger effect, as reflected in movements along each of the curves in the graph. In fact, the difference between the actual proportions of white urban and suburban students attending public schools (0.80 versus 0.92) largely results from differences in the racial compositions of the schools. The proportion of public school students who are either African-American or Latino is 0.29 in urban public schools, but only 0.03 in suburban public schools. To see this, consider the case of white suburban students represented by the solid line in Fig. 2. When three percent of suburban public school students are African-American or Latino, 92 percent of white suburban students are predicted to attend public school. In contrast, if students in suburban schools were 29 percent African-American and Latino, as is the case in urban schools, 81 percent of suburban white students are predicted to attend public school – very close to the 80 percent of urban whites who actually attend public schools. The racial composition of suburban schools appears to be key in explaining why relatively few white suburban families send their children to private school. As the following simulation shows, a related point holds for urban students.

Case A in Table 7 provides a point of reference where all attributes of urban public schools are evaluated at their metropolitan area's urban school means. In this case, 79.5 percent of white urban students are predicted to choose urban public schools. Case B is the hypothetical situation in which the urban schools in each metropolitan area had attributes that were the same as the area mean public school attributes available to suburban students. Under this scenario, it is estimated that 93.7 percent of all white students living in urban areas would attend public schools. This estimate is close to the percent of white suburban students actually choosing public schools (92 percent), which underscores the importance of school attributes as determinants of school choice.

In order to isolate the effects of student racial composition, consider case C in which the urban schools in each metropolitan area have student-body

Table 7. Proportions of White Students Living in Urban Settings Predicted to Attend Public School.

Case A	
Attributes of urban public schools set equal to the mean attributes of the metropolitan area's urban public schools	79.5
Case B	
All attributes of urban public schools set equal to the mean attributes of the metropolitan area's suburban public schools	93.7
Case C	
Racial attributes of urban public schools set equal to the mean attributes of the metropolitan area's suburban public schools with other attributes evaluated at the urban school means	91.4
Case D	
Non-racial attributes of urban public schools set equal to the mean attributes of the metropolitan area's suburban public schools with the racial attributes evaluated at the urban school means	83.8

racial mixes equal to the suburban area means, with other school variables equal to the urban area means. In this case, 91.4 percent of white urban students are estimated to choose urban public schools. Contrast this to case D where the racial composition of urban public schools is evaluated at the urban area means but other school variables are evaluated at the suburban area means. Here, only 83.8 percent of white urban students are predicted to choose urban public schools. These simulations indicate that the racial composition of public schools is key in explaining the difference between the patterns of public–private school choice found in urban and suburban settings.

Is the racial composition of schools really so important in the school choices of whites, or might the large estimated effect be due to an omitted-variables bias? Even though our empirical model of school choice includes a set of school and student-body attributes far richer than is typical in the school choice literature, it is possible that school racial composition is correlated with other relevant, but unmeasured, attributes of schools or their student bodies. An analysis of such possibilities is presented in Section 5.4, where the estimated effect of school racial composition is shown to be robust to alternative model specifications and estimation strategies (e.g., IV estimation). That analysis draws upon the following two sections.

5.2. Results for the Location-Choice Submodel

Reconsider Fig. 2. Over 90 percent of white students would select the public options if students were all white, whereas approximately 15 percent fewer whites would select the public sector if a majority of public school students were African-American or Latino. This 15 percent change,[24] as well as the simulated changes in Table 7, correspond to the situation where households' residential locations are unaffected by the changes in urban school attributes. Enrollment changes could be larger if the racial composition of schools affects residential location.

Parameter estimates for the models of residential location choice are shown in Table 8. Separate models are estimated for the samples of renters and owners who had moved within the last five years. As is common in the residential location literature, a sample of recent movers is used in estimation because the transaction costs associated with relocating could result in long-time residents not being optimally located. In an effort to control for life-cycle considerations, the analysis focuses on young families having no children in school beyond the fifth grade.

Since our focus is on how school attributes affect the residential choices of families, the estimated similarity coefficients for the schooling inclusive values are of central interest. The other location attributes are included as controls in an effort to isolate the direct effect of schooling. The estimated similarity coefficients for schooling are statistically significant, indicating that the attractiveness of the local public school option and the proximity to private schools are important determinants of location choice. Those variables that are statistically significant and quantitatively important in the public–private school-choice model are also important in determining the schooling inclusive value that, in turn, is relevant in locational choices.[25] Note that the effect of the school inclusive value on the attractiveness of a location does not appear to be systematically related to the number of children in the family.

The importance of residential location as a form of school choice can be demonstrated by extending the above simulation to account for residential choice. Consider Table 9. Case A again provides a point of reference where all attributes of the urban public schools in each metropolitan area are set equal to the area's urban public school means. The estimated proportion of white students in each of the four combinations of school and location types,

Table 8. Residential Location NMLM Estimation Results.

	Owners	Renters		Owners	Renters
Schooling similarity coefficients, μ^S			***Urban Dummies***		
School inclusive value – one child	0.704**	0.268**	Urban location	3.007*	8.057**
	(7.727)	(2.910)		(2.357)	(4.632)
School inclusive value – two children	1.068**	0.233*	High school graduate	−0.862**	−0.625**
	(9.595)	(2.222)		(−3.227)	(−3.274)
School inclusive value – more than two	0.685**	0.166	College graduate	0.264*	−0.107
	(2.757)	(1.067)		(2.271)	(−0.793)
Community type similarity coefficients			White-collar	−0.447	−0.240
Suburban locations, μ_2	1.087**	1.389**		(−0.739)	(−1.392)
	(8.077)	(4.037)	Blue-collar	−0.830	−0.379*
Urban locations, μ_1	1.072**	1.282**		(−1.356)	(−2.028)
	(7.720)	(3.738)			
Neighborhood attributes			***Housing attributes***		
ln(C+income—cost)	9.868**	7.013**	Number rooms	0.129	0.572*
	(13.715)	(4.186)		(0.516)	(2.200)
Per-capita police expenditure ($1000s)	3.259**	−2.822**	Number bedrooms	0.059	−0.020
	(3.229)	(−2.532)		(0.123)	(−0.049)
Per-capita transportation expenditure ($1000s)	0.065	−0.458	One-acre parcel	0.049	−0.241
	(0.132)	(−0.968)		(0.438)	(−0.908)
Per-capita recreation expenditure ($1000s)	−4.440**	0.216	Age	−0.077**	−0.028
	(−3.464)	(0.157)		(−4.045)	(−1.348)

Neighborhood income ($1000s)	0.044**	−0.0151**	Age^2	0.00070**	0.00023
	(7.455)	(−3.080)		(3.190)	(1.036)
Neighborhood proportion owners	−0.501	0.375	Structure1	0.973*	1.598**
	(−1.760)	(1.363)		(2.013)	(3.017)
Neighborhood crime rate	0.003	0.004	Structure2a		0.727*
	(1.047)	(1.721)			(2.159)
Neighborhood proportion board up	−5.832	−1.467	Structure3		−0.042
	(−0.729)	(−0.215)			(−0.103)
Neighborhood minority 0–5	2.312	−3.398	Structure2b	0.166	
	(1.056)	(−1.309)		(0.262)	
Neighborhood minority 5–15	1.735	−1.559	ln(*n*units)	1.009**	1.032**
	(1.081)	(−1.148)		(26.505)	(22.037)
Neighborhood minority 15–30	−3.682	−1.595	Room variance	0.052	−0.074
	(−1.945)	(−1.238)		(0.548)	(−1.266)
Neighborhood minority >30	−0.868	−3.83**	One-acre parcel variance	0.112	−0.341
	(−0.727)	(−4.362)		(0.438)	(−0.908)
			Age variance	0.00026	−0.00006
				(0.960)	(−0.434)
Log likelihood	−11156.01	−8152.43	Number of observations	3703	1914

*Coefficient is statistically different from zero at the 0.05 level of significance.
**Coefficient is statistically different from zero at the 0.01 level of significance.

Table 9. Mean Estimated Probabilities of School and Location Choice.

		Children of Homeowners			Children of Renters		
		Public Sector $P(m, q=0)$	Private Sector $P(m, q>0)$	Total $P(m)$	Public Sector $P(m, q=0)$	Private Sector $P(m, q>0)$	Total $P(m)$
Case A: Attributes of urban public schools set equal to the mean attributes of the metropolitan area's urban public schools	Urban location ($m=1$)	0.07	0.03	0.10	0.29	0.05	0.34
	Suburban location ($m=2$)	0.83	0.07	0.90	0.62	0.04	0.66
	Totals: $P(q=0)$ and $P(q>0)$	0.90	0.10		0.91	0.09	
Case B: All attributes of urban public schools set equal to the mean attributes of the metropolitan area's suburban public schools	Urban location ($m=1$)	0.21	0.02	0.23	0.40	0.02	0.42
	Suburban location ($m=2$)	0.71	0.06	0.77	0.55	0.03	0.58
	Totals: $P(q=0)$ and $P(q>0)$	0.92	0.08		0.95	0.05	
Case C: Racial attributes of urban public schools set equal to the mean racial attributes of the metropolitan area's suburban public schools	Urban location ($m=1$)	0.17	0.02	0.19	0.38	0.03	0.41
	Suburban location ($m=2$)	0.75	0.06	0.81	0.56	0.03	0.59
	Totals: $P(q=0)$ and $P(q>0)$	0.92	0.08		0.94	0.06	

as well as the implied marginal proportions, are shown separately for children of home owners and renters. In case B all attributes of urban public schools are set equal to the mean attributes of the metropolitan area's suburban public schools. If urban public schools had attributes like those of their suburban counterparts, the proportion of owner–children living in urban areas and attending public school would be three times as large, as compared to case A (0.21 versus 0.07). This increase largely reflects a reduction in the proportion of owners living in the suburbs and sending their children to public schools there (0.83 versus 0.71). The proportion of renter–children attending urban public schools is 0.4 in case B as opposed to 0.29 in case A. While still large, the change is relatively smaller than for owners. Note that the increase in urban public enrollment by renters comes from both the movement of renters from suburban to urban locations and urban students from private to urban public schools. Together, these large estimated changes in the distribution of children across the four school categories provide strong evidence that public school attributes are important determinants of the school and residential choices made by parents.

The importance of school racial composition in explaining the differences between cases A and B is shown in case C. Here, the racial attributes of urban public schools are set equal to the mean racial attributes for each area's suburban public schools, with all other attributes set equal to the urban means. The comparison shows that two-thirds or more of the estimated increase in the proportion of white students attending urban public schools can be explained by the change in the racial composition of urban public schools (e.g., of the total increase for the children of owners from 0.07 to 0.21, the change from 0.07 to 0.17 is attributable to race alone).

In formulating our model of school choice, we believe that the residential location decisions of households are potentially important. The relative importance of residential location choice as the means by which white parents react to the racial composition of urban public schools is shown in Fig. 3. Curve *M* corresponds to the curve for urban students shown in Fig. 2, with the exception that the proportion of white *urban* students attending public schools shown in Fig. 2 is multiplied by the proportion of white students living in urban areas, thereby obtaining the proportion of all white students attending urban public schools. Taking the residential locations of families as given, curve *M* only accounts for the effect that the proportion African-American and Latino has on the public–private school choices of urban whites. Curve *N* shows the proportion of all white students predicted to attend urban public schools when public–private and locational choices are allowed to respond to the racial mix of urban public schools. Here, all other

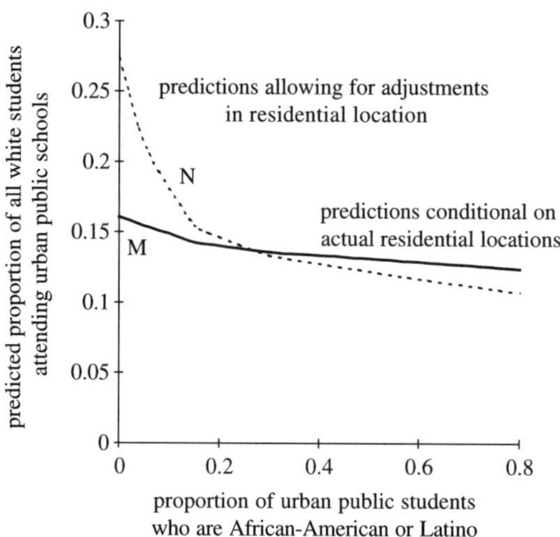

Fig. 3. Proportions of All White Students Predicted to Attend Urban Public Schools.

urban school attributes, all suburban school attributes, and all individual student/family variables are evaluated at their actual values. The steepness of *N* relative to *M* provides evidence of the important linkage between public school racial composition and the residential location decisions of whites, as *N* and *M* differ only in that the former accounts for the effect of the public school racial mix on residential choice but the latter does not. Again, the racial composition of urban public schools has its biggest impact on urban public school choice when the proportion of African-American and Latino students is low.

The above comparison provides strong evidence that residential location is the primary means by which families exercise school choice. Not only is residential choice relatively more important than private school choice, the absolute importance of private school choice is reduced when parents are able to optimally choose the school district in which to live. For example, suppose that parents have optimally chosen residential locations and schools but the proportion of public school students in each urban location that are African-American or Latino then increases by 0.10. Conditional on the initial residential locations remaining unchanged, the number of white students attending urban public schools is estimated to decrease by four percent, with those leaving transferring to private schools. When families are able to respond by choosing both residential locations and public–

private schools, the estimated number of white students attending urban public schools decreases by 23 percent. At the same time that the number of students transferring out of urban public schools is over five times larger, the total number of students remaining in urban locations and attending private schools is only one-fifth as large as when residential location is given. Suburban public schools and residences appear to dominate urban locations and private schools, when parents consider the alternatives to urban public schools and residences.

The importance of school choice through residential location, as compared to public–private school choice, is striking, but should be put into perspective. First, metropolitan areas in New York and other northeastern states have relatively large numbers of small public school districts. Metropolitan areas in other parts of the country typically have fewer districts of greater size, often as a result of school districts being coterminous with counties. Fewer public school alternatives to choose among may well result in a reduction in the importance of residential location relative to that of public–private school choice. This is consistent with the finding of Martinez-Vazquez and Seaman (1985) that more students attend private school in metropolitan areas having relatively fewer public school districts per square mile, other things constant. It is also important to note that our estimated models of residential location provide information regarding the locations that renters and owners would select if currently choosing. However, large transaction costs associated with moving will often result in families choosing to remain in dwellings and locations that would be suboptimal if such costs were not present. It follows that adjustments in the long-run equilibrium patterns of residential location resulting from changes in public school and other community attributes may well take many years. A substantial portion of the adjustment may occur when new cohorts of young couples initially choose locations.[26] To the extent that high transactions costs impede families' public school choice through residential location, public–private school choice will be relatively more important, at least in the short run.

Even with the above caveats, our findings make clear that the determinants and consequences of residential location choice need to be taken into account when considering school choice within the current institutional setting, as well as when evaluating various proposals intended to expand school choice.

5.3. A Schelling Model of Racial Sorting

Thus far, the focus has been on the impact that school racial composition has on the school choices made by whites. However, the proportion of whites attending urban public schools will in turn affect school racial composition. As discussed by Schelling (1971) and Clotfelter (1976), such feedback can have important implications such as racial tipping. Let B represent the total number of African-American and Latino students in a metropolitan area and β represent the proportion of those students attending urban public schools. Similarly, W represents the total number of white students in a metropolitan area and ω represents the proportion of those students that attend urban public schools. It follows that the proportion of urban public school students that are African-American or Latino is $\delta \equiv \beta B/(\beta B + \omega W)$. To simplify the analysis, suppose that β is constant and that all urban public schools have the same student-body racial mix ($= \delta$). It follows that the value of ω implies the proportion of urban public students that are African-American or Latino. The dashed line in Fig. 4 is such an identity, which can also be represented as $\omega \equiv \beta\big(B/W\big)\big((1-\delta)/\delta\big)$. Note that the position of the identity only depends upon β and B/W, with the curve in Fig. 4 corresponding to the Albany-Schenectady-Troy MSA. The solid line represents the estimated behavioral relationship between the proportion of white students that would choose to attend urban public schools and the schools' racial composition, again for Albany-Schenectady-Troy. This curve is like

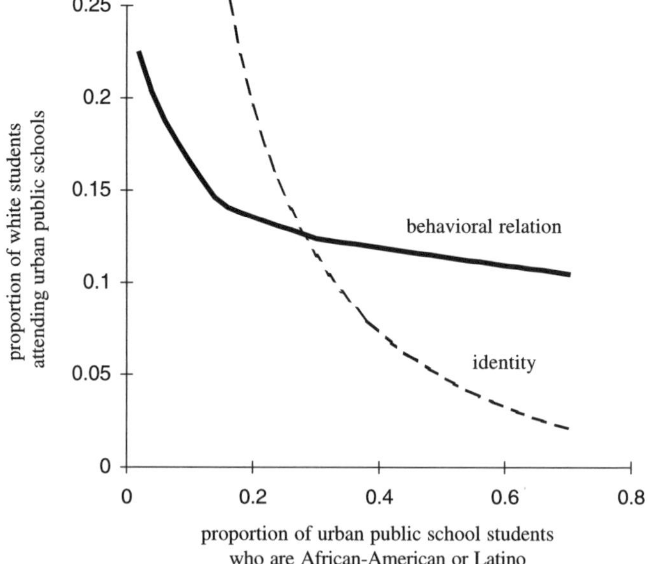

Fig. 4. Schelling Model of Racial Sorting.

curve N in Fig. 3 except that it corresponds to a particular MSA, rather than a composite of the eight MSAs. The equilibrium proportion of African-American and Latino students corresponds to the intersection of the behavioral relation showing school choice by whites and the identity linking the choices of white students to the racial mix of urban public schools.[27]

Note that an increase in B/W results in the identity in Fig. 4 shifting up, or to the right, and, in turn, a reduction in the equilibrium number of whites selecting urban public schools. Such a comparative static analysis is closely linked to the early work of Clotfelter (1976) who used data for 84 metropolitan areas to estimate the reduced-form relationship between the (equilibrium) proportion of whites attending private school and the racial composition of students in the metropolitan area (B/W). Our analysis differs in two respects. First, we are able to distinguish between "white flight" to private schools and flight associated with whites moving to the suburbs. Second, we have estimated a student-level model of school choice, which implies the behavioral relation in Fig. 4.[28] This, in turn, implies a reduced-form relation between the equilibrium level of ω and B/W similar to that estimated by Clotfelter.

Our model also allows us to consider how the distribution of white students is affected by other factors, holding B/W constant. Starting with the initial equilibrium at point R in Fig. 5, suppose that there is a shift up in the behavioral relation of the proportion of white students wanting to attend urban public schools, given δ. This might be due to urban public schools improving in academic quality. Note that the ultimate increase in the equilibrium proportion of white students attending urban public schools exceeds the vertical distance between Q and R at the initial racial mix. This follows from the fact that the initial increase in the number of whites attending urban public schools results in a reduction in the proportion of urban public school students that are either African-American or Latino, which leads to a further increase in the number of whites in the urban public sector, and so on. The initial (exogenous) increase in the proportion of white students attending urban public schools is 0.05 in the example and the increase in the equilibrium proportion of white students attending urban public schools is 0.06 (= 0.186–0.126). The ultimate change is 20 percent larger as a result of this feedback. The magnitude of the feedback effect depends upon the slope of the behavioral relation relative to the slope of the identity, the feedback effect being larger as this ratio of slopes is larger. Albany-Schenectady-Troy is chosen for Fig. 5 because the 20 percent feedback effect is typical, with three MSAs having smaller feedback effects and four having larger feedbacks. The feedback effects range from 4 to 50 percent of the exogenous

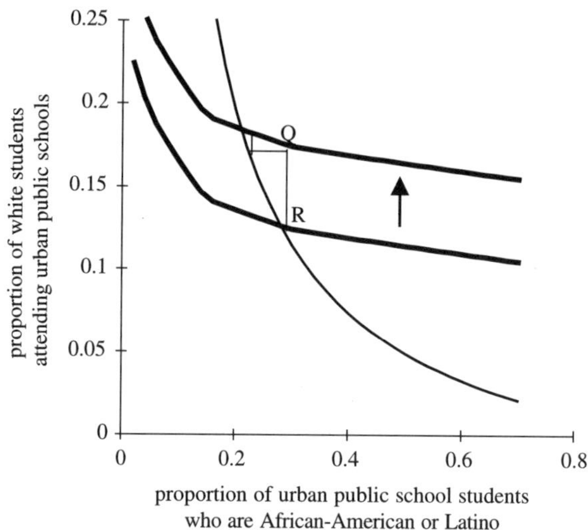

Fig. 5. A Change in the Equilibrium Racial Composition of Urban Public Schools.

change. The magnitude of the effect is negatively correlated with the ratio of African-American and Latino students to white students in the metropolitan area. With the exception of Poughkeepsie, the feedback effects were smaller in the larger MSAs.

In reality, the dynamics of school choice and changes in the equilibrium distribution of students across schools is more complicated than the model in Fig. 5. First, a complete model would account for the potentially important school and location choices of African-American and Latino families. Second, an exogenous increase in the number of white students attending urban public schools likely would alter non-racial student-body attributes correlated with race. The distribution of student test scores and other measures used by parents to proxy academic quality would likely change as well. Ultimately, property values and political outcomes determining the local resources allocated to public education likely would change. Thus, the total feedback resulting from such an exogenous change will differ from the feedback directly related to racial preferences discussed above. However, these other feedbacks are likely to complement, or amplify, the direct racial effects.

Even though the empirical results presented here do not provide a complete framework for considering policy simulations and comparative static analyses within a broadly defined education system, they are relevant to the theoretical and simulation models employed by Benabou (1996), Nechyba

(1996), Epple and Romano (1998), Manski (1992) and others. Such models crucially depend upon assumptions regarding the determinants of the school and location choices made by parents, assumptions that can be evaluated in light of the above empirical findings. In particular, our results indicate that the direct effects of student-body attributes on school-related choices warrant greater attention.

5.4. Robustness of the Estimated Effect of School Racial Composition

Given the provocative nature of the estimated effect of school racial composition, careful scrutiny is warranted. In particular, one might question whether the large estimated effect is due to an omitted-variables bias. Such a bias could arise if there were school and student-body attributes known by, and pertinent to, parents when choosing among schools that are not accounted for in our analysis. However, the relevant question is not whether there are such omitted variables – there always are. Rather, is it likely that such omitted variables could explain the large estimated effect of school racial composition? We address this issue by considering an expanded set of explanatory variables and employing alternative estimation strategies.

The first three columns of Table 10 show a subset of the parameter estimates for models having the same student, school, and racial composition variables. The three specifications differ with regard to the other variables characterizing the attributes of the student body. Model 1 includes no student-body attributes, other than racial composition. Model 2 is the model described earlier and reported in Table 5. This model includes information regarding the proportion of students in each school having a parent who graduated from college (peer-college), the proportion of students living in poverty, measured by the proportion of students receiving free or reduced price lunches (peer-lunch), and the proportion of students from two-parent households (peer-married). The third model includes all the variables in the second as well as the proportion of students having a parent who graduated from high school (peer-high school), the proportions of students having parents who are white- and blue-collar workers (peer-white-collar and peer-blue-collar, respectively), the average income of parents (peer-income) and a variable measuring the proportion of the students living in poverty as defined and measured by the Census Bureau using 1990 Census of Population data (peer-poverty).

Comparison of the estimated coefficients and *t*-statistics for the racial composition variables across the three models shows that the individual parameter estimates are quite robust. Since the four parameters together

Table 10. Public–Private School Choice Model Parameter Estimates Based on Alternative Specifications and Estimation Strategies.

	Model 1	Model 2	Model 3	Model 4	Model 5	Model 6
School minority 0–5	−8.69	−9.408	−8.77			−5.226
	(−5.166)	(−5.497)	(−5.006)			(−2.386)
School minority 5–15	−7.27	−5.934	−5.787			−5.599
	(−5.072)	(−4.011)	(−3.801)			(−3.455)
School minority 15–30	−1.458	−1.711	−2.281			−1.623
	(−1.912)	(−1.842)	(−2.398)			(−1.579)
School minority 30+	−0.505	−0.777	−0.591			−0.286
	(−1.411)	(−2.062)	(−1.521)			(−0.707)
School minority 0–15				−7.162	−8.101	
				(−8.917)	(−4.586)	
School minority 15+				−0.952	−2.918	
				(−3.189)	(−3.728)	
Urban	0.205	0.2552	0.2025	0.289	0.301	
	(2.019)	(2.343)	(1.818)	(2.706)	(2.031)	
Peer married		0.7158	1.4491	0.696	0.590	0.3796
		(2.199)	(3.66)	(2.155)	(1.688)	(1.133)
Peer lunch		0.0901	−0.155	0.1212	0.696	−0.141
		(0.357)	(−0.59)	(0.485)	(2.087)	(−0.501)
Peer college (college or more)		1.2731	1.837	1.261	1.580	1.3293
		(5.172)	(5.027)	(5.128)	(5.879)	(5.22)
Peer college (less than college)		0.099	0.656	0.077	0.488	0.1507
		(0.368)	(1.793)	(0.287)	(1.607)	(0.545)
Peer high school			−0.665			
			(−1.161)			
Peer white-collar			−0.336			
			(−0.372)			
Peer blue-collar			−0.246			
			(−0.293)			
Peer income			−9E-06			
			(−1.71)			
Peer poverty (Census)			0.527			
			(0.988)			
Log likelihood	−7769	−7749	−7742	−7750		−7719

determine a piece-wise linear spline, it is instructive to consider the splines as a whole. They are plotted in Fig. 6 as having a common intercept in order to focus on differences in the estimated marginal effect of school racial composition. By going from the model with no student-body attributes other than racial composition (model 1) to the model with measures of parents' educational attainment, family structure, and poverty (model 2), the

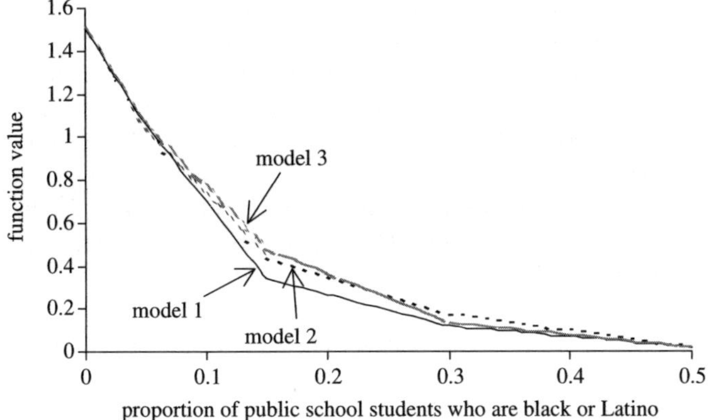

Fig. 6. Estimated Splines Showing the Marginal Effect of School Racial Composition.

estimated effect of student-body racial composition is reduced, as one would expect. However, the magnitude of the change is quite small. Expanding the set of student-body attributes further (model 3) has even less of an effect on the estimated spline. The estimated effect of changes in racial composition is little affected whether there are no other student-body attributes included, a basic set of attributes or a much-expanded set.

With regard to the possible scope for omitted variables, we believe that the student-body and school variables included broadly reflect the kinds of information parents are likely to have and consider when making school choices. The included variables provide a rich set of controls for student and school quality and are likely to be correlated with a variety of other school and student-body attributes. Nonetheless, there are variables that parents may know, for which we have no direct information, e.g., school leadership, or curricular orientation. Even though our model does not include these variables, we would expect that they would be correlated with other included variables, such as test scores, class size, or family characteristics. Suppose they are not. Omitted variable bias would require that these variables be highly correlated with race, not correlated with the other student-body attributes included and have an effect on school choice that is larger than the combined effect of the currently included variables. This seems quite unlikely.

In an effort to explore the issue of omitted-variable bias further, we estimated a public–private school-choice model for African-American students. If student-body racial composition were proxying unobserved school or student-body attributes, rather than a direct effect of race, the racial-composition variables might well have estimated effects in the model for African-American students similar in magnitude and significance to those estimated for whites. This is not the case; the school racial composition variables in the model estimated for African-American students are close to zero and statistically insignificant. For a related discussion see Lankford and Wyckoff (2005).

It is also relevant to note that our initial analysis employed data for Buffalo, along with data for the eight metropolitan areas studied here. The results of that estimation are nearly identical to those presented here. Several factors caused us to question whether the large estimated effect of race is an anomaly linked to Buffalo. The Buffalo City School District has court-ordered busing and many of its school attendance areas draw students from multiple non-contiguous groupings of blocks. Minority students make up large portions of the student bodies in Buffalo's public schools and households in the Buffalo metropolitan area make up about 40 percent of our sample. As a result, it is possible that the racial composition of schools proxies the concerns of white parents in Buffalo regarding busing or the configuration of attendance areas, rather than race per se. Owing to this possibility, the Buffalo metropolitan area was dropped from our analysis. However, there was no meaningful change in the estimated effect of school racial composition.

The large estimated effect of school racial composition could also be the result of a "reflection problem" similar to that discussed by Manski (1993). Rather than the proportion of white students attending a public school being a function of the school's racial composition, the racial composition of the school merely could be a reflection of the proportion of white students choosing the public alternative. Such a possibility is shown in Fig. 7 which is similar to Fig. 4 except that the proportion of whites attending the public school is assumed to be unaffected by school racial composition. Let line AA' represent the initial relationship between the proportion of white students choosing to attend the public alternative and the racial composition of the public school. Suppose that there are unobservables common to all the white students living in the urban district or common to the urban schools (e.g., unmeasured aspects of school quality) that affect school choice. Let BB' represent the behavioral relation when this unobserved factor results in a higher portion of white students choosing the public alternative. The example shows that the equilibrium proportion of students in the public school who are African-American or Latino will be higher as the equilibrium proportion of white urban-public students choosing to attend the school is lower. Even though school racial composition does not directly affect the school choices of whites, school racial composition and the school

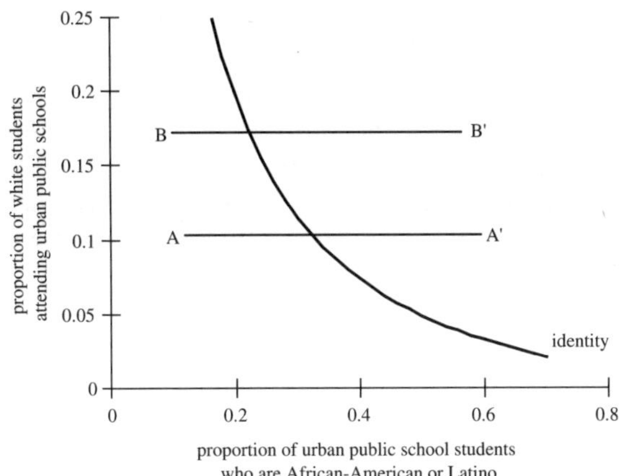

Fig. 7. Example of a Reflection Problem.

choices of whites would be positively correlated. In effect, school racial composition would be proxying for the common unobserved factor causing the shift in the aggregate behavioral relationship.[29]

As noted by Manski, the difficulty of sorting out the linkages between demand (or supply) for a good and the good's price is the most common reflection problem considered by economists. Is the quantity demanded affected by price or is price merely a reflection of the quantity demanded, or both? When estimating the demand for a good, the standard method for dealing with this issue is to use an IV approach in which the market price is instrumented using exogenous determinants of supply and demand. The approach we use is similar.

Reconsider Fig. 4. Just as exogenous shifts in the supply curve can be used to deal with the potential reflection problem when estimating a demand function, exogenous shifts in the school–racial–composition identity can be used to deal with the reflection problem in our analysis of school choice. As noted above, the racial identity depends upon the proportion of minority students in the metropolitan area or, equivalently, the ratio of minority to white students in the metropolitan population. It follows that the equilibrium racial composition of the public school alternative(s) will vary with the racial composition of students in the metropolitan area. Assuming that families do not move between metropolitan areas as a result of the metropolitan-wide racial composition of students, this racial composition will be exogenous to the residential and school choices of white parents. It follows that the metropolitan-wide measure can be used as an instrument for the actual racial composition of public schools. Exogenous factors affecting the proportion of white students attending public schools can be used in a similar way.

Such an IV approach is used to investigate both whether there is a reflection problem and the robustness of the racial composition effect more generally. The set of instruments includes the proportion of white students in the metropolitan area who are Catholic, the proportion having a college educated parent, and the proportion of all students in the metropolitan area who are either African-American or Latino.[30] The model is identical to that in Table 5, with the exception that the racial-composition spline is restricted to have a single kink at 0.15. This is done to reduce the number of (spline) parameters needed to be estimated based on inter-metropolitan variation in the three variables.

The IV estimates are shown as model 5 in Table 10. Model 4, estimated by maximum likelihood ignoring the potential reflection problem, is the same as model 2 (as well as that in Table 5) with the exception that a one-kink spline is employed to allow comparison. The IV estimates of the racial composition effect, being slightly larger in magnitude, indicate that the large estimated effect is not due to the reflection problem. Note that the IV estimates also are relevant to the issue of omitted variables generally. Only to the extent that any remaining omitted variables are correlated with the inter-metropolitan variation in the racial composition of the student population could the IV estimator of the racial composition effect be biased.

At the same time that the robustness of the ML (multinomial logit) and IV estimates allay concerns of a reflection problem, the striking similarity of the two sets of estimates raises another issue. With the IV estimation relying on differences in the overall student racial composition between metropolitan areas, it is possible that these differences and the inter-metropolitan differences in the racial composition of urban public schools are proxies for unobserved differences between these areas? This issue warrants attention as 48 percent of the variance in the racial composition of the urban public schools in our sample is explained by the between-metropolitan-area variance. For suburban public schools, 31 percent of the variation in student-body racial composition is explained by the between-metropolitan variation. We address the issue by estimating the effect of school racial composition using the within-area variation in school racial composition. The effects of between-metropolitan-area differences is netted out by generalizing the model of public–private school choice in Table 5 (model 2 in Table 10) to include a set of dummy variables reflecting the urban and suburban areas in *each* metropolitan area.[31] The estimated effect of school racial composition for this "fixed-effect" specification is shown in model 6 of Table 10. With the race coefficients changing little and remaining statistically significant, there is clear evidence that the estimated effect of school racial composition is not merely the result of inter-metropolitan differences in racial composition proxying for unobserved differences across these areas.

In summary, even though it is not possible to rule out the possibility that the estimated effect of school racial composition is due to spurious correlation, the scope for such an explanation is quite limited. The omitted variables would have to be highly correlated with school racial composition yet be uncorrelated with the variety of other student-body attributes included. At the same time, the omitted variables would have to have an effect on school choice that exceeded that of the combined school and student-body attributes included in the analysis. Furthermore, the omitted variables would have to be highly correlated with the inter-metropolitan variation in the racial composition of the populations of *all* students as well as the intra-area variation in the racial composition of urban and suburban public schools. Finally, the unobserved factors would have to be important for the school choices of white parents but not important for African-Americans. The striking robustness of the estimated effect of school racial composition and these implied restrictions provide strong evidence that student-body racial mix has a large direct effect on the school choices of whites.

Even if one accepts this conclusion, important questions remain regarding the sources of the effect. It may be the case that some white parents do not want their children to associate with any African-American or Latino students. However, other factors could be more important. Even if parents are only concerned with academic matters when choosing among schools, the lack of information regarding, and the difficulty in assessing, school quality might result in the easily observed racial composition of schools being used as a signal for academic quality. Race might also be used as a proxy for the tastes and preferences of other students and their parents (e.g., attitudes toward education and other matters). Parents may want their children to attend schools in which a large majority of the students come from families with similar backgrounds. The policy implications of these explanations differ greatly. For example, if the lack of information is a major consideration, the dissemination of more information regarding school quality (e.g., school report cards) could lead to school racial composition being less important. Similarly, efforts to encourage parents to look beyond race in assessing school quality as well as the educational goals and attitudes of other parents and students might also help.

Questions regarding the relative importance of these and other explanations for the large effect of school racial composition warrant future research. However, econometric identification issues regarding sorting out the relative importance of various explanations are substantially more problematic than the ones that arise here in estimating the total direct effect.

6. CONCLUDING REMARKS

Our estimates suggest that the school choices afforded to parents through private school choice and residential location importantly affect the racial segregation of schools. Segregation can result indirectly from school choice decisions reflecting the education and incomes of students' own parents as well as the non-race attributes of student peers. For example, because African-Americans, on average, have relatively less education and lower incomes, some degree of segregation will result from better-educated parents sending their children to schools having strong academic programs or schools having student-peers with better educated parents. Such indirect links could be important. However, we believe that the school choice estimates presented in this paper show a striking direct link. Whites confronted with urban public schools with even moderate concentrations of African-Americans or Latinos are much more likely to opt for private schools or choose suburban public schools. When they do choose private schools they choose those with lower concentrations of nonwhites. In combination, the effect is to make schools more racially segregated. As a result of this sorting directly related to race, urban public schools, which already having substantially higher concentrations of nonwhites than their suburban counterparts, have become even more segregated. This sorting helps explain the changing patterns shown in Table 1.

The effects of student-body attributes on school choice and the resulting sorting of students have implications that go beyond those related to goals of racial diversity. First, an important consideration is that educational outcomes will be affected by this sorting to the extent that the educational achievement of individual students depends on the abilities and attributes of student peers.[32] In addition, the effect of school choice on residential patterns is important given recent findings concerning the effect that segregation has on minorities, in terms of schooling, employment, and single parenthood.[33] Second, given the importance of local finance in public education, the impacts that sorting through residential location has on the distribution of educational resources across public school districts will likely be significant. These differences in educational resources are likely to be especially important given that the sorting of students may result in those public districts having relatively few resources also having disproportionately large numbers of students with special needs. Third, the school choice debate has continued with little empirical evidence regarding the factors that are key determinants of school choices by parents (e.g., academic considerations, tuition, and distance). The importance of student-body socioeconomic attributes in school choice, relative to the importance of school academic attributes, raises serious questions regarding the ultimate effect of expanded school choice. Fourth, discussions regarding expanding parents' school choice options need to be grounded in an understanding of the full consequences of parental school choice within the current educational system. Given the importance of residential choice within the current educational system, it is possible that families living in suburbs will be little affected by policies intended to expand school choice options. Furthermore, policies that break the link between residential location and the public school alternative might, in the long-run, affect residential location decisions as much as the general attributes of the schools students attend. Fifth, the self-selection demonstrated in our research may have important implications for research addressing efficiency comparisons across schools and the Tiebout bias potential in demand studies of local public goods. Finally, the fact that the residential and school choices of white families have impeded efforts to achieve greater racial integration is a clear indication of the importance of choices by parents and students more generally. Discussions regarding alternative educational policies need to take into account how the policies would affect the behavior of students and their families, as such behavior can result in policies having consequences far different from those intended.

NOTES

1. The Theil coefficient is a measure of inequality that can be decomposed, similar to variance decompositions. See Allison (1978) for a discussion of the Theil coefficient and its decomposition. We decompose total inequality into that which occurs within individual sectors (here defined to be urban public schools, suburban public schools and private schools) and that occurring between sectors.

2. Rivkin (1994) and Clotfelter (1999) find that most of the racial segregation that currently exists in public schools results from the location decisions of households among school districts, and not from insufficient effort to integrate schools within districts. Orfield (1994) argues that the relatively small sizes and large numbers of school districts in northeastern metropolitan areas allow Tiebout shoppers to more easily choose bundles of preferred locational characteristics.

3. In recent years public school choice through open-enrollment plans and magnet schools has increased. However, the single public school option for the vast majority of students is determined by the residential location of the family. In this institutional setting, public–private school choice and residential location remain the primary means by which parents exercise school choice. See note 7.

4. Aggregate data are employed by Clotfelter (1976), Downes (1993), Erekson (1982), Gemello and Osman (1984), Gustman and Pidot (1973), Hamilton and Macauley (1991), Martinez-Vasquez and Seaman (1985), Schmidt (1992), Sonstelie (1979, 1982), and West and Palsson (1988). Student-level data are employed in research by Bayer et al. (2003), Coleman, Hoffer, and Kilgore (1982), Hoxby (1996), Kirby and Darling-Hammond (1988), Lankford and Wyckoff (1992, 2001), Lankford, Lee, and Wyckoff (1995), Long and Toma (1988), and Noell and Myers (1983). Numerous studies of the relative performance of Catholic and public schools also model public–private school choice, in order to account for self-selection in the estimation of treatment effects. See Figlio and Stone (1999) and Neal (1997) for recent examples.

5. See Clotfelter (1976), Downes (1993), and Sonstelie (1982).

6. Epple and Romano (1996) analyze the case where there is a private alternative to a publicly provided service whose quantity is determined by majority voting. Just as the existence of a private alternative can affect individuals' voting and the politician equilibrium, such private alternatives can affect the residential location decisions of households and the Tiebout equilibrium. See Nechyba (1996).

7. A complication arises when public school districts do not use neighborhood school attendance boundaries exclusively to determine enrollment (e.g., magnet schools). In our sample of districts, some degree of public school choice was available in Rochester and Syracuse in 1990. However, because the open enrollment plans were established to achieve desegregation, the choices available to parents were quite limited. For example, whites living in school attendance areas having relatively "too few" whites in the local public school had no public school choice. A similar statement holds for Blacks attending schools in which they were underrepresented. Furthermore, those eligible for and applying to particular schools were selected through lotteries. In such an environment, a family's residential location largely determined the local public school option. Owing to the complexity of the public choice environment and the fact that nearly all students attend neighborhood schools, we have chosen to model the local public school option to be the school for the neighborhood attendance area. The research assistance of Michael Collins, Frank Papa and Lester Rhee, as well as the assistance of officials in each of the urban districts, is greatly appreciated.

8. Middle and high school attendance areas typically encompass multiple elementary attendance areas so that public school students in several elementary attendance areas attend the same middle school. In a few cases more than one middle or high school draws students from a single elementary school attendance area. In such a case, a complete characterization of the location/public school choice set would reflect all possible elementary–middle–high school combinations, which would include many elementary school attendance areas and partitions of others. The following analysis does not account for such partitioned elementary attendance areas.

9. Public school districts in New York can cross all other jurisdictional boundaries. For example, there are school districts that draw students from portions of multiple villages, towns, and counties. In effect, Tiebout-shoppers face a smorgasbord from which to select various combinations of towns, villages and school districts. Given the complexity of these jurisdictional alternatives, we have chosen to define the locational geography in terms of school districts. However, average property taxes and expenditure for other local governments are taken into account.

10. The data on private school enrollments by public school district of residence came from state aid forms submitted by school districts to the State Education Department.

11. Information regarding tuition was obtained using a mail survey with telephone follow-up and the 1988 and 1992 editions of *Private Schools of the United States* published by the Council for American Private Education (1988, 1992).

12. Useful introductions and summaries of the commonly used NMLM are provided by Ben-Akiva and Lerman (1985) and Borsch-Supan (1987).

13. The diagram should be interpreted as nothing more than a visual representation of the alternatives in groups possibly having correlated errors. A sequential decision-making process (e.g., a family chooses a community and then a school option) is not assumed and should not be inferred from the diagram. Rather, households are assumed to jointly choose residential locations and schools; that is, households choose among the twigs at the bottom of the diagram.

14. More formally, $V_{..*} + V_{..q} + \mu_q^* H_{mnq} = E[\max_r (V_{..*} + V_{..q} + V_{..qr} + V_{mnqr} + \varepsilon_{mn}(qr)) | m, n, q] - \gamma / \mu_q^*$ where γ is Euler's constant.

15. The model characterizing $P(q, r | m, n, q > 0)$ is estimated using the Nlogit FIML option in LIMDEP 7.0 for aggregate data with weights reflecting the number of private school students in each school district.

16. Because the model of public–private school choice estimated includes a dummy variable for the sex of the student, the implied inclusive value will differ for boys and girls. However, the effect of sex is estimated to be quite small quantitatively, and so this difference will be ignored.

17. See Lankford and Wyckoff (1992) for a summary of the method used to proxy religion.

18. The New York State Department of Education surveyed school district superintendents on issues of safety and security in their schools during the 1992–1993 school year. Responses to 13 categorical responses for elementary schools were used in a factor analysis to construct three factors relating to school safety. For a complete description of the survey see New York State Education Department (1994).

19. The omitted categories are less than a high school education, not in the labor force and not an elementary or secondary school teacher, respectively.

20. Many studies focus on the choice of housing characteristics, ignoring residential location. Other studies do not model the choice of specific housing units, focusing more on the non-housing aspects of residential choice (e.g., location choice). These studies often model the joint selection of residential location and related choices such as mode of transportation. Our analysis is similar in that we estimate a joint model of residential location and school choice.

21. For example, see Quigley (1985).

22. See Ben-Akiva and Lerman (1985) for a discussion and references.

23. See Lerman (1979) for an application of this method.

24. Whether this is viewed as being a large change depends upon one's perspective. Such a 15 percent reduction in the proportion of white students attending public school translates into a tripling of the number of whites attending private school.

25. The expression for H_{mn} shown above makes this clear.

26. This scenario is consistent with the pattern of change summarized for New York in Table 1 where the (relative) increase in suburban public school enrollment of white students was accompanied by reductions in their enrollments in both urban public and private schools.

27. As shown in Fig. 4, the equilibrium is both unique and stable. Even though this is necessarily the case with the probabilistic choice model employed (see Miyao, 1978), deterministic choice models such as those employed by Schelling often have both multiple and unstable equilibria.

28. Our estimated model of location choice could also be used to construct the relation between the proportion of whites choosing to live in urban (or suburban) settings and the racial mix of neighborhoods, similar to the behavioral relation in Fig. 4. Clark (1991) employs opinion survey data to estimate such relations in order to study the residential segregation model of Schelling. To our knowledge, no one has used an estimated model of residential location to infer the link between location choice and neighborhood racial mix.

29. It is pertinent to note that the reflection or reverse causation here results from assuming the change in the unobserved factors has differential effects on the proportions of white and minority students wanting to attend the public alternative. In the example given, the factor resulting in change in the behavioral relation for whites (AA' to BB') was implicitly assumed to have no effect on the proportion of minority students wanting to attend the public alternative, β. This follows from the assumption that the curve reflecting the racial identity $\omega \equiv \beta(B/W)\big((1-\delta)/\delta\big)$ did not shift. If, instead, the change in the unobserved factors affected white and minority students symmetrically, the shift in the identity would be such that the equilibrium racial composition would remain unchanged. There would be no reflection problem.

30. To allow for the linkages between these variables and school racial composition being different for urban and suburban settings, these variables are interacted with an urban dummy variable. The set of instruments also includes all the student, school and student-body variables in Table 5, the exception being those variables measuring school racial composition. A GMM estimation strategy is used to obtain the IV estimates of the logit model. See Lee (1996, pp. 108–113).

31. We are ignoring the variance between urban and suburban schools because the urban dummies in the public–private school-choice model effectively nets out the effect of this variation.

32. Questions remain regarding the magnitudes and nature of such peer effects. See the empirical papers by Evans, Oates, and Schwab (1992) and Rivkin (1997) as well as the theoretical work of Manski (1993).

33. See Borjas (1995) as well as Cutler and Glaeser (1997).

ACKNOWLEDGMENTS

The research reported in this paper was supported by an American Statistical Association/National Science Foundatoin/Census Bureau Research Fellowship and a grant from the Spencer Foundation. The authors thank a number of people at the Census Bureau for their support and advice, especially Doug Hilmer, Bob Kominski, and Paul Siegel. We are also grateful to the New York State Education Department and the New York State Office of the State Comptroller for data. We have benefited from comments by Dale Ballou, Eleanor Brown, Paul Courant, Tom Downes, Bill Duncombe, Dan Goldhaber, Caroline Minter Hoxby, Steve Rivkin, Kim Rueben, John Yinger, and seminar participants at Union College, Syracuse University and a University at Albany and Binghamton University video-conference. The views expressed, and any errors, are attributable to the authors.

REFERENCES

Allison, P. (1978). Measures of inequality. *American Sociological Review*, *43*(6), 865–880.

Bayer, P., McMillan, R., & Rueben, K. (2003). *What drives racial segregation: New evidence using Census Micro-Data*. Working Paper.

Benabou, R. (1996). Equity and efficiency in human capital investment: The local connection. *Review of Economic Studies*, *63*, 237–264.

Ben-Akiva, M., & Lerman, S. (1985). *Discrete choice analysis: Theory and application to travel demand*. Cambridge: MIT Press.

Borjas, G. J. (1995). Ethnicity, neighborhoods, and human-capital externalities. *American Economic Review*, *85*(3), 365–390.

Borsch-Supan, A. (1987). *Econometric analysis of discrete choice*. New York: Springer.

Clark, W. A. V. (1991). Residential preferences and neighborhood racial segregation: A test of the Schelling segregation model. *Demography*, *28*(1), 1–19.

Clotfelter, C. (1976). School desegregation, "tipping," and private school enrollment. *Journal of Human Resources*, *11*(1), 28–50.

Clotfelter, C. (1999). Public school segregation in metropolitan areas. *Land Economics*, *75*(4), 487–504.

Coleman, J., Hoffer, T., & Kilgore, S. (1982). *High school achievement: Public, catholic, and private schools compared*. New York: Basic Books.

Council for American Private Education. (1988, 1992). *Private schools of the United States*. Washington, DC: Council for American Private Education.

Cutler, D. M., & Glaeser, E. L. (1997). *Are Ghettos good or bad? Quarterly Journal of Economics*, *112*(3), 827–872.

Downes, T. A. (1993). *On estimating individual demands for local public goods from aggregate data: The case of schooling*. Mimeo.

Epple, D., & Romano, R. E. (1996). Ends against the middle: Determining public service provision when there are private alternatives. *Journal of Public Economics*, *62*, 297–325.

Epple, D., & Romano, R. (1998). Competition between private and public schools, vouchers and peer group effects. *American Economic Review*, *88*(1), 33–62.

Erekson, O. H. (1982). Equity targets in school finance, tuition tax credits, and the public–private choice. *Journal of Education Finance*, *8*, 436–449.

Evans, W. N., Oates, W. E., & Schwab, R. M. (1992). Measuring peer group effects: A study of teenage behavior. *Journal of Political Economy*, *100*(5), 966–991.

Figlio, D., & Stone, J. (1999). Are private schools really better? In: S. Polachek (Ed.), *Research in labor economics* (Vol. 18). Stanford, CT: JAI Press.

Gemello, J. M., & Osman, J. (1984). Estimating the demand for private school enrollment. *American Journal of Education*, *92*, 262–279.

Gustman, A., & Pidot, G. (1973). Interactions between educational spending and student enrollment. *The Journal of Human Resources*, *8*(1), 3–23.

Hamilton, B. W., & Macauley, M. K. (1991). Determinants and consequences of the private–public school choice. *Journal of Urban Economics*, *29*(3), 282–294.

Harris, L. (1976). *The issue: Quality of life*. The Harris Survey, November 8.

Hoxby, C. M. (1996). The effects of private school vouchers on schools and students. In: H. F. Ladd (Ed.), *Holding schools accountable: Performance-based reform in education* (pp. 177–208). Washington, DC: The Brookings Institution.

Kirby, S., & Darling-Hammond, L. (1988). Parental school choice: A case study of Minnesota. *Journal of Policy Analysis and Management*, *7*, 506–517.

Lankford, H., Lee, E., & Wyckoff, J. (1995). An analysis of elementary and secondary school choice. *Journal of Urban Economics*, *38*, 236–251.

Lankford, H., & Wyckoff, J. (1992). Primary and secondary school choice among public and religious alternatives. *Economics of Education Review*, *11*(4), 317–337.

Lankford, H., & Wyckoff, J. (2001). Who would be left behind by enhanced public school choice? *Journal of Urban Economics*, *50*(2), 288–312.

Lankford, H., & Wyckoff, J. (2005). Why are schools racially segregated? Implications for school choice policies. In: J. T. Scott (Ed.), *School choice and diversity: What the evidence says* (pp. 9–26). New York: Teacher College Press.

Lee, J. (1996). *Methods of moments and semiparametric econometrics for limited dependent variable models*. New York: Springer.

Lerman, S. R. (1979). Neighborhood choice and transportation services. In: D. Segal (Ed.), *The economics of neighborhood* (pp. 83–118). New York: Academic Press.

Long, J., & Toma, E. (1988). The determinants of private school attendance, 1970–1980. *Review of Economics and Statistics*, *70*, 351–356.

Manski, C. (1992). School choice (vouchers) and social mobility. *Economics of Education Review*, *11*(4), 351–369.

Manski, C. (1993). Identification of endogenous social effects: The reflection problem. *Review of Economic Studies*, *60*, 531–542.

Martinez-Vazquez, J., & Seaman, B. (1985). Private schooling and the Tiebout hypothesis. *Public Finance Quarterly*, *13*(3), 355–368.

Miyao, T. (1978). A probabilistic model of location choice with neighborhood effects. *Journal of Economic Theory*, *19*(2), 347–358.

Neal, D. (1997). The effects of Catholic secondary schooling on educational achievement. *Journal of Labor Economics*, *15*(1), 98–123.

Nechyba, T. (1996). *Public school finance in a general equilibrium Tiebout world: Equalization.programs, peer effects and private school vouchers.* Working Paper no. 5642. National Bureau of Economic Research.

Nechyba, T., & Strauss, R. (1998). Community choice and local public services: A discrete choice approach. *Regional Science and Urban Economics, 28*(1), 51–73.

New York State Education Department. (1994). *A study of safety and security in the public schools of New York state*, Albany.

Noell, J., & Myers, D. (1983). *The demand for private schooling: An empirical analysis.* Working Paper. Office of Planning, Budget, and Evaluation, U.S. Department of Education.

Orfield, G. (1994). *Metropolitan school desegregation: Schools and urban change. In: Round tables on regionalism.* Social Science Research Council, U.S. Department of Housing and Urban Development, December 8–9, pp. 1–32.

Quigley, J. M. (1985). Consumer choice of dwelling, neighborhood and public services. *Regional Science and Urban Economics, 15*, 41–63.

Rivkin, S. (1994). Residential segregation and school integration. *Sociology of Education, 67*, 279–292.

Rivkin, S. (1997). *The estimation of peer group effects.* Mimeo. Department of Economics, Amherst College.

Schelling, T. C. (1971). Dynamic models of segregation. *Journal of Mathematical Sociology, 1*, 143–186.

Schmidt, A. (1992). Private school enrollment in metropolitan areas. *Public Finance Quarterly, 20*(3), 298–320.

Sonstelie, J. (1979). Public school quality and private school enrollments. *National Tax Journal, 32*(Suppl.), 343–353.

Sonstelie, J. (1982). The welfare cost of free public schools. *Journal of Political Economy, 90*, 794–808.

U.S. Department of Education. (1983). *Office of educational research and improvement.* Parents and school choice: A household survey.

West, E., & Palsson, H. (1988). Parental choice of school characteristics: Estimation using statewide data. *Economic Inquiry, 26*(4), 725–740.

BEYOND ACHIEVEMENT: ENROLLMENT CONSEQUENCES OF CHARTER SCHOOLS IN MICHIGAN

Eugenia F. Toma, Ron Zimmer and John T. Jones

ABSTRACT

One of the biggest public school reform movements in the past decade has been the passage of charter school laws. Forty states and Washington, DC have approved legislation that allows charter schools to operate within their jurisdictional boundaries. The academic research thus far has focused on where charter schools have been located and the achievement consequences of the schools. This paper addresses a direct effect of charter schools by examining their enrollment consequences. We find that in Michigan approximately 17 percent of the students who enroll in charter schools were previously enrolled in private schools and approximately 83 percent move from the traditional public schools.

1. INTRODUCTION

One of the most important reform movements in the K-12 public school system over the past decade has been states' passage of charter school laws and the subsequent establishment of charter schools. Forty states and

Improving School Accountability: Check-Ups or Choice
Advances in Applied Microeconomics, Volume 14, 241–255

ISSN: 0278-0984/doi:10.1016/S0278-0984(06)14009-2

Washington, DC have approved legislation that allows charter schools to operate within their jurisdictional boundaries. Since the first charter law passed in 1991, individuals and institutions have responded by opening over 3,500 charter schools and enrolling nearly 1 million students nationwide.

The academic research relating to charter schools has primarily addressed two major questions. One avenue of research has examined the political economy issues surrounding the passage of charter school laws (Stoddard & Corcoran, 2005) and the subsequent location or supply of charter schools (Glomm, Harris, & Lo, 2005). The second and larger strand of research has focused on the achievement effects of charter schools both on the charter-enrolled students and on students in the traditional public schools (Bettinger, 2005; Buddin & Zimmer, 2005; Bifulco & Ladd, 2005; Sass, 2005; Booker, Gilpatric, Gronberg, & Jansen, 2004; Hanushek, Kain, & Rivkin, 2002; Hoxby & Rockoff, 2004; Zimmer et al., 2003; Solmon, Paark, & Garcia, 2001).

Like all school reform efforts, charter school legislation presumably is intended to improve performance in the public school system. Scholars and the public view charter laws as ones that were passed to free schools from the bureaucratic burdens of traditional public schools, to stave off more radical school voucher proposals, to provide choice to particular segments of the population who might otherwise leave the system or be poorly served by the system, or to introduce competition between schools.

While the aim of charters may be to increase support for the public schools, few scholars have directly addressed the consequences of charters beyond looking at the achievement effects. We propose to do so by looking at enrollment patterns. In particular, we look at a single state, Michigan, over a five-year period involving rapid growth of charter schools and look in some detail at enrollment in charter schools vis-à-vis other school types. As part of this analysis, we examine the effect charter schools have on private school enrollment. Whether charter schools can attract students from private schools is an important question because if they can, the public burden of educating students may increase as these schools will bring in students who previously exerted little demand on public resources. We hypothesize that individuals choose charter schools if they anticipate greater satisfaction from this school type than from others, regardless of whether they are traditional public or private schools. Empirically, we find that almost one-fifth of the enrollment in the Michigan charter schools comes from the private sector while over four-fifths comes from traditional public schools.

2. REFORM IMPLICATIONS

Since the 1970s, there have been many school reform efforts that have directly or indirectly affected enrollment in the public education system. One reform that has received a great deal of scholarly attention, as well as attention by state courts and legislatures, has been the shift in financing of schools from local property tax bases to more centralized state sources of funding. The literature is lengthy and somewhat inconclusive regarding the long-term effects of the shift in financing methods on the voter–taxpayers' support for public schools. Several scholars have argued that the decline in financial support for California public schools and the increase in private school enrollment are attributable to the *Serrano v. Priest* court case that overturned the local property tax as the base for financing public schools (Sonstelie, 1979, 1995; Downes & Schoeman, 1998). Fischel (1992) argues that any shift in financing away from localities weakens the link between school quality and property values and, therefore, results in less support for the publicly provided good.

Nechyba (2003) has raised conceptual questions about the net effect of centralized financing. While caps on spending in high-income districts presumably weaken the public's support for schools in those districts and lead to increase in private enrollment, low-income districts may gain from the change and increase public school enrollment. Furthermore, because centralized financing weakens the relationship between housing quality and school quality, persons may sort into areas where they previously would have chosen not to live and create additional pressure for higher-quality public schools. While scholars have given significant attention both conceptually and empirically to the intended and unintended consequences of centralization of funding (Fischel, 1989, 1992; Theobald & Picus, 1991; Murray, Evans, & Schwab, 1998; Downes & Schoeman, 1998; Moser & Rubenstein, 2002; Zimmer & Jones, 2005), they have given less attention to whether the major structural reform of the 1990s, the advent of charter schools, increases or decreases various forms of support for public schools. As we will describe below, the establishment of charter schools should influence taxpayer demand for the public schools and influence support for private sector schooling.

To understand how charter schools might affect the taxpayers' support for the public schools, it is useful to describe some of the institutional features of charter laws. Charter schools are publicly financed schools that operate outside the regulations of the traditional public schools. The extent to which the regulations are loosened varies by state and according to the type of charter law that has been passed.[1] Charter schools cannot charge tuition and are funded on a per-pupil formula that varies across states from as low as 50 percent of the traditional funding base to about 80 percent (Finn, Manno, & Vanourek, 2000). Also of importance, charter schools rarely receive public funding for capital expenses. Rather, the chartering organization typically assumes responsibility for locating and financing capital structures and for their maintenance over time.

In a study examining where charter schools have been located, Glomm et al. (2005) found that greater district heterogeneity in race and adult education was associated with greater numbers of charter schools. Furthermore, districts in which more private schools were located and districts that had greater amounts of spending on special education also had more charter schools. Others (Booker, Zimmer, & Buddin, 2005) note that charter schools tend to locate disproportionately in poor performing districts. Studies such as this imply that charter schools arose as a means of satisfying demands that were not being met by the traditional public schools for at least some segment of the population.[2] Stoddard and Corcoran (2005) looked across states and across schools districts and found that weak student performance (on SATs) and demographic heterogeneity were related to greater support for and enrollment in charter schools.

The studies examining the location of charter schools suggest the advent of new school types should increase taxpayers' demand for public schools. To illustrate more precisely the effects of charter schools on demand for public schooling, consider the following simple description typically used to illustrate the household choice between public and private school types. Suppose each household h has one child and that child can attend private school, P, or a traditional public school, T.[3] Each household chooses its school type i from these options in its residential district.[4] The household utility from any school type depends on its tastes and preferences for the school type relative to a composite package of consumption goods, X_h. Household utility can be expressed as

$$U_{hi} = U(P,\ T,\ X_h,\ \varepsilon_{hi}) \tag{1}$$

where ε_{hi} is a scalar composite of all relevant but unmeasured factors influencing utility. The inclusion of this disturbance term will capture both unmeasured school-specific characteristics and the perception of these characteristics by the household. For the household, the budget constraint is

$$I_h = tP + \tau_h B_h + X_h \tag{2}$$

where t is the private school tuition, τ the household's tax price for the publicly provided schooling, and B the household's tax base. From the household's perspective, the tax rate for public schooling is independent of its decision to enroll in either the public or private school options. It can, of course, completely avoid expenditures on private schools with a decision to enroll in public schools, but it will still pay the public school bill under the private school option. Households choose the school alternative *i* only if the utility it derives from that school type is greater than any of the other *k* alternatives, or $U_{hi} > U_{hk}$. To attend private school, households must receive marginal utility that exceeds that of the public schools by at least the amount of the private tuition.

Now, suppose we introduce another school type so that the household chooses between private schools, traditional public schools, and the new charter schools.[5] The utility function is now given by

$$U_{hi} = U(P,\ T,\ C,\ X_h,\ \varepsilon_{hi}) \tag{3}$$

where *C* represents charter schools. Of great significance, the household's budget constraint remains unchanged. Because the tax price to the household is the same for charter and traditional public schools, the household will choose between the public types independently of the tax price.

If the charter schools, previously unavailable in the public sector, provide a product that better matches the tastes of the household, utility from the charter school increases relative to that of the traditional public school and the household will enroll its child in the new charter option, ceteris paribus. Furthermore, households that previously chose the private sector may receive sufficient added utility from the charter schools to switch enrollment from the private sector to the public one.

As we aggregate from the household to the community, there will be long-run implications for the education sector that go beyond enrollment. Recall that financing the operations of charter schools occurs at a percentage of the cost of traditional schools and that expenditures for capital are typically excluded. So while students in charter schools conceptually lower the cost of providing public schooling, the alternatives offered by charter schools presumably increase demand for schooling provided in the public sector. The relative magnitude of these changes will determine the ultimate effect on the budgetary outlays for public schooling and the household's tax price for the public schools.[6]

While there are competing effects on the long-run budgetary consequences of charter schools, the enrollment effects discussed above can occur in the short run. If charter schools offer a schooling alternative that taxpayers view as sufficiently superior to their status quo choice, they will switch to the charters. Significantly, enrollment in the charter schools comes from either the traditional public schools or the private sector.[7] Because the choice to attend charter schools is made at the household level, enrollment behavior serves as a revealed preference for charter schools vis-à-vis other school types.

3. CHARTER SCHOOLS IN MICHIGAN: DATA

The remainder of this paper focuses on the state of Michigan. This is a particularly interesting state in terms of charter schools, because it was one of the first states to pass legislation allowing charter schools (1993), and its charter laws are among the strongest of the states. According to the Center for Education Reform, Michigan scores approximately 45 on a 50-point scale of strength of charter laws. Arizona and the District of Columbia had equally strong laws under this ranking. Although school districts technically can begin charter schools, the voting rules for approval by districts are sufficiently binding that few districts have done so.[8] The rules allow, however, universities and other organizations, both for-profit and nonprofit, to seek charter approval. For the school year 2005–2006, approximately 85,000 students attend 220 charter schools in Michigan. Our analysis examines the effect charter schools have on public support in the years from 1994–1995 through 1998–1999, which is a period of strong charter school growth as shown in Table 1.

Charter schools in Michigan, like in other states, do not charge tuition but rather receive funding based on per-pupil enrollment. They are required to hire certified teachers, must administer the Michigan accountability tests (MEAP), and abide by the health and safety codes of other public schools. If the school oversubscribes, the schools grant entrance through random selection. Unlike the traditional public schools, however, charter schools in Michigan can renew their charters only with adequate student academic performance.

To examine the effects of charter schools in Michigan, we look at the universe of school districts and charter schools[9] over the five academic years 1994–1995 to 1998–1999.[10] Data came from a variety of sources. *Michigan*

Table 1. Charter Schools in Michigan.

School Year	Number of Charter Schools
1994–95	8
1995–96	43
1996–97	79
1997–98	108
1998–99	138

School Report (MSR) is one of our main sources from which school district identification codes, enrollments, and district race/ethnicity percentages for the academic years 1994–1995 to 1998–1999 were retained. From the enrollment data, we calculate the annual percentage growth of public school enrollment for each county and use this variable to control for student growth that may affect the types of schooling options within each county.

We also collected the breakdown of local, state, and federal revenue from Michigan's 1014 report.[11] From this report, we constructed a variable measuring the proportion of state funding for each district and charter school across the state over time. This variable acts as a control for the impact that centralized funding may have on school choice from Michigan's Proposal A in 1994.[12]

Local economic conditions that affect unemployment rates and income levels directly affect decision making. County unemployment rates for each year are used to control regional variations in economic factors. These rates are merged at the county level by year and are accessible from the Michigan Department of Career Development website.[13] Information on population income comes from the Internal Revenue Service's data series, "County Income Data."[14] From these data, we retain the reported county gross income and divide it by the number of reported county returns.[15] This produces an estimate of the average tax filer's gross income for each county for each year. These data are then merged with the other data by county and year to control for preferences for different types of schools to the extent schooling preferences are correlated with income.

Finally, we collected private school enrollment from the National Center for Education Statistic's Private School Universe Survey.[16] This survey is administered in even years and thus enrollment in odd years is unobserved. To increase the usefulness of these data, we impute the missing observations with averages of the previous and successive even years. This approach assumes private school enrollment trends linearly between years, which may not be the case; however, it is not an unreasonable method to preserve the degrees of freedom. Table 2 shows the mean and standard deviation for the variables across the five school years.

4. EMPIRICAL MODEL

The remainder of this paper examines the enrollment consequences of the introduction of charter schools in Michigan. While others have looked at the consequences of charter schools on achievement scores of students, the

Table 2. Descriptive Means from 1994–1995 through 1998–1999 School Years.

Variables	Observations	Mean	S.D.
Percent countywide private enrollment	3186	8.84	4.622
Percent countywide charter enrollment	3186	0.21	0.745
Percent countywide traditional public enrollment	3186	90.95	4.807
Average countywide yearly student growth rate	2456	0.650	1.867
Unemployment rate	3201	4.60	1.942
Real gross income per tax filer ($000)	3201	39.99	9.211
Proportion district-wide black enrollment	3127	8.81	22.454
Proportion district-wide white enrollment	3127	85.75	23.653
Proportion district-wide Hispanic enrollment	3127	2.72	5.579
Proportion district-wide American-Indian enrollment	3127	1.84	6.588
Proportion state revenue	3140	79.04	16.036

enrollment effects are a direct measure of whether charter schools enhance competition among schools and whether the competition is among public and/or private schools.

The requirement of mandatory schooling creates an enrollment identity that partitions the school-aged population between public or private educational institutions. This identity is disrupted with the introduction of a third education alternative, charter schools, that may siphon a portion of the population away from the two alternatives. Exploiting the effect of the exogenous introduction of charter schools on this enrollment relationship allows a direct means of estimating charter schools' impact on public and private school enrollments. Because there may be unobservable differences between parental and student characteristics, we use a district/charter school fixed effect approach that controls for time invariant unobservable characteristics. Formally, the model is estimated by

$$\begin{aligned}\text{PRIVATE}_{dt} = {} & \alpha_0 + \alpha_1\text{CHARTER}_{dt} + \alpha_2 Zc_t \\ & + \alpha_3 X_{dt} + \alpha_4\text{YEAR} + \mu_{dt} + \varepsilon_{it}\end{aligned} \tag{4}$$

where c and d represent county c, and district or charter school d in year t in the model. Charter schools are identified in the data as their own districts.[17] PRIVATE is the percent of a county's total enrollment in private schools for all districts; CHARTER the percent of the county's enrollment in charter schools for each county district; Z a vector of county level variables that are expected to influence enrollment and can be measured annually; X a vector of district level variables that are expected to influence enrollment and that can be measured annually; μ represents district/charter school fixed effects; and ε the error term. Independent variables included in the Z vector are annual enrollment growth rates, GROWTH, by county; unemployment rate, UNEMPLOYMENT; and average real income, INCOME. Independent variables included in the X vector are percent of the population that is black, BLACK; percent that is Hispanic, HISPANIC; and percent Native American, NATIVE AMERICAN (percent white is the omitted category); and percent of total school revenues derived from the state, STATE REVENUE. We also include a year time trend variable, YEAR.

For the enrollment variables, we used county-level data rather than district data because charter schools do not restrict enrollment to the designated district of residence.[18] Similarly, the distance from a student's residence to the private school influences private school enrollment but is not restricted to the public school district boundaries. In Michigan, counties contain multiple school districts and it is reasonable to assume students could travel across these districts to choose either charter or private schools. For other variables, including racial characteristics and the proportion of revenue received from the state, we used district data because variances across the districts within the counties should lead to greater precision in our estimates.

The data set for purposes of analysis is restricted to the set of observations (2,390) for which we have a full sample. Table 3 presents the enrollment results from estimating the above equation. An increase in the proportion of public school students who are in charter schools is significantly and

Table 3. Effects of Charters on Percent Private Enrollment.

Independent Variables	Coefficients	*t*-Statistics
Charter	−0.17*	−2.46
Income	0.01	0.57
Black	−0.02*	−2.01
Hispanic	0.01	1.04
Native American	−0.01	−0.51
State revenue	0.00	1.17
Growth	0.05*	5.19
Unemployment	−0.01	−0.43
Time	−0.16*	−14.16
Constant	8.92*	11.87
N	2390	
Prob. $>F$	0.000	

*Indicates significance at the 0.05 level.

**Indicates significance at the 0.1 level.

negatively related to the proportion of total enrollment in private schools.[19] More specifically, the coefficient on PRIVATE indicates that approximately 17 percent of charter school enrollment over this period is pulled from the private sector. Put in perspective, the significance of this estimate becomes quite large. Slightly more than 8 percent of the students in Michigan were enrolled in private schools over this period of time; with 17 percent of charter enrollment derived from this 8 percent, the effects on the private sector could be quite large.

To provide a slightly different perspective on this, we re-estimated the above model but substituted numbers of students enrolled in the private and charter schools for the percent of students enrolled. Table 4 reports the results. The estimated coefficient on the charter enrollment variables suggests that private schools will lose one student for every three students gained in the charter schools. Taken together, the estimates in Tables 3 and 4 indicate that not only are charter schools having a statistically significant effect on private schools but an effect that is economically meaningful.

Other economic factors also affect the private schools as indicated by the above regressions. The annual enrollment growth rate is positive, as expected, in both regressions and is statistically significant in the first regression. Also of interest, YEAR is significant and negative in both regressions, suggesting that private school enrollment has diminished over time, ceteris paribus. Of the racial variables, only proportion black is significant and has a negative effect.

Table 4. Effects of Charters on Numbers of Private Students.

Independent Variables	Coefficients	*t*-Statistics
Charter	−0.31*	−13.49
Income	2.93	−0.19
Black	−45.16*	−4.21
Hispanic	2.23	0.26
Native American	11.49	0.61
State revenue	0.22	0.06
Growth	5.02	0.53
Unemployment	−5.27	−0.18
Time	−105.79*	−9.01
Constant	9386.61*	11.94
N	2390	
Prob. > *F*	0.000	

*Indicates significance at the 0.05 level.

**Indicates significance at the 0.1 level.

Table 5. Effects of Charters on Numbers of Public Students.

Independent Variables	Coefficients	*t*-Statistics
Charter	−0.30*	−3.49
Income	−1.52	−0.03
Black	216.47*	5.35
Hispanic	86.93	2.74
Native American	−68.86	−0.97
State revenue	1.72	0.12
Growth	99.13*	2.76
Unemployment	10.93	0.10
Time	821.44*	18.57
Constant	56625.45*	−19.12
N	2390	
Prob.>*F*	0.000	

*Indicates significance at the 0.05 level.
**Indicates significance at the 0.1 level.

The above regression results indicate that charter schools are competitors to private schools, but how do charter schools impact traditional public schools? Although the results in Table 2 can give us part of the answer, we can also directly estimate the magnitude of the effect similar to that in Table 3. In particular, we change the dependent variable of the regression model from private school enrollment to traditional public school enrollment and re-estimate the parameters.[20] The parameter estimate on charter school enrollment indicates the magnitude of the substitutability between charter schools and traditional public schools. Table 5 presents the results. The Charter enrollment coefficient shows that the traditional public schools lose one student for every three students added to charter schools. In absolute numbers, the charter schools draw enrollment from public schools at nearly the same rate as they do from private schools.[21]

The signs on the remaining estimates are intuitively appealing and attest to the accuracy of the model. Again, annual enrollment growth rate positively and significantly affects numbers of students in traditional public schools, as do both the percent of black students and percent of Hispanic students.

5. CONCLUSIONS

The history of charter schools is still very young in the U.S. There has been a surprising amount of work on the consequences of charter schools in terms of student achievement on standardized tests. The consequences have varied by state and study but there is not agreement at this point regarding the achievement consequences of charter schools.

This paper suggests that there are other dimensions or margins on which charter schools should be evaluated. Taxpayer preferences for the public schools are likely to be first demonstrated through enrollment decisions. Our results for Michigan suggest that charter schools are generating immediate competitive effects for both traditional public schools as well as for private schools. The finding that charter schools are attracting significant numbers of students from the private sector has long-run consequences for the financing of public schools. While charter schools are financed at a fraction of the cost of traditional schools, the public sector expenditures for education will not necessarily decline if the public school student base expands with the development of charter schools. Using the "vote with your feet" criterion, charter schools appear to have increased support for the public school system in Michigan. In future work, we plan to extend the work across states. Much remains to be done.

NOTES

1. See Stoddard and Corcoran (2005) for a full description of the types of charter laws across the states as well as an analysis of the determinants of the type of law passed.
2. See Stoddard and Corcoran (2005) for a detailed analysis of the political economy of the passage of charter school laws.
3. Households can also choose home schools but we do not consider them in this paper because of lack of data. Often these models separate private religious and private secular schools. See Houston and Toma (2003), Lankford, Lee, and Wyckoff (1995), Lankford, and Wyckoff (1992), and Long and Toma (1988).
4. While the public school must be within the district of residence, the private school can be located outside the public district boundaries. We shall address this in the empirical section.
5. Charter schools, like private ones, may be chosen outside the boundaries of the residential public school district.
6. This paper will not examine the financial consequences of charter schools. Rather, we focus on enrollment effects for a single state. Across states, the consequences may vary depending on the particulars of the funding formulae for the charter schools.
7. Although not allowed in this model, empirically charters can also generate enrollment from new growth in their jurisdiction.
8. For the district to establish a charter school, there must be majority approval by the school board in Michigan.
9. In Michigan, charter schools are treated as their own school districts.

10. We chose these years because 1995 is the first year of significant enrollment in charter schools in Michigan. Beginning in 2000, other factors such as No Child Left Behind complicate the issues discussed here.

11. http://www.state.mi.us/mde/reports/B1014/index.html.

12. We have also restricted our data to post Proposal A years.

13. http://www.michlmi.org/web_nav/Unemployed/frame.htm.

14. http://ftp.fedworld.gov/pub/irs-soi/prodserv.pdf.

15. When dollar values are used in the regression they are based on real 1994 dollars.

16. http://nces.ed.gov/surveys/pss/.

17. In Michigan, charter schools are considered their own district. Thus, the district fixed effects controls for time invariant characteristics across districts and charter schools simultaneously.

18. MSA would perhaps be preferable, but we do not have these data at this point of time. Note that we also estimated the model using district-level data and found quite similar results to those presented in this paper.

19. Plank and Sykes (1999) looked at aggregate numbers in the first year of charter schools in Michigan and found that private school enrollment decreased as charter school enrollment increased.

20. We also estimated percentage of enrollment to verify our results and confirmed that approximately 83 percent of charter enrollment comes from the traditional public schools.

21. The charter schools may be attracting other students from population growth or home schooling. These data do not allow us to determine alternative sources of attraction.

ACKNOWLEDGMENTS

We thank Eric Brunner, J. S. Butler, participants in the Martin School's Institute for Federalism & Intergovernmental Relations workshop, and participants at the 2005 meeting of the Southern Economic Association for comments. We also thank Doug Carr for assistance with data.

REFERENCES

Bettinger, E. P. (2005). The effect of charter schools on charter students and public schools. *Economics of Education Review*, *24*(2), 133–147.

Bifulco, R., & Ladd, H. (2005). The impacts of charter schools on student achievement: Evidence from North Carolina. Available at: <http://www.pubpol.duke.edu/people/faculty/ladd/SAN04-01.pdf>; accessed September 2, 2004.

Booker, K., Gilpatric, S., Gronberg, T. J., & Jansen, D. W. (2004). *Charter school performance in Texas*. Private Enterprise Research Center Working Paper. Texas A&M University.

Booker, K., Zimmer, R. W., & Buddin, R. (2005). *The effects of charter schools on school peer composition*. RAND Working Paper. Available at: http://www.rand.org/publications/WR/WR306/.

Buddin, R., & Zimmer, R. W. (2005). A closer look at charter school student achievement. *Journal of Policy Analysis and Management*, *24*(2), 351–372.

Downes, T. A., & Schoeman, D. (1998). School financing reform and private school enrollments: Evidence from California. *Journal of Urban Economics*, *43*, 418–443.

Finn, C. E., Manno, B. V., & Vanourek, G. (2000). *Charter schools in action*. Princeton, NJ: Princeton University Press.

Fischel, W. A. (1989). Did serrano cause proposition 13? *National Tax Journal*, *42*, 465–473.

Fischel, W. A. (1992). Property taxation and Tiebout model: Evidence for the benefit view from zoning and voting. *Journal of Economic Literature*, *30*, 171–177.

Glomm, G., Harris, D., & Lo, T.-F. (2005). Charter school location. *Economics of Education Review*, *24*(4), 451–457.

Hanushek, E. A., Kain, J. F., & Rivkin, S. G. (2002). The impact of charter schools on academic achievement. Available at: <http://edpro.stanford.edu/eah/papers/charters.aea.jan03.PDF>; accessed September 2, 2004.

Houston, R. G., Jr., & Toma, E. F. (2003). Home schooling: An alternative school choice. *Southern Economic Journal*, *69*(4), 920–935.

Hoxby, C. M., & Rockoff, J. E. (2004). *The impact of charter schools on student achievement*. Working Paper. Harvard University.

Lankford, R. H., Lee, E. S., & Wyckoff, J. H. (1995). An analysis of elementary and secondary school choice. *Journal of Urban Economics*, *38*, 236–254.

Lankford, R. H., & Wyckoff, J. H. (1992). Primary and secondary school choice among public and religious alternatives. *Economics of Education Review*, *11*, 317–337.

Long, J., & Toma, E. F. (1988). The determinants of private school attendance. *Review of Economics and Statistics*, *70*, 351–357.

Moser, M., & Rubenstein, R. (2002). The equality of public school district funding in the United States: A national status report. *Public Administration Review*, *62*(1), 63–72.

Murray, S. E., Evans, W. N., & Schwab, R. M. (1998). Education finance reform and the distribution of educational resources. *The American Economic Review*, *88*(4), 789–812.

Nechyba, T. J. (2003). Fiscal federalism and private school attendance. *International Economic Review*, *44*(1), 179–204.

Plank, D. N., & Sykes, G. (1999). How choice changes the education system: A Michigan case study. *International Review of Education*, *45*(5/6), 385–416.

Sass, T. R. (2005). *Charter schools and student achievement in Florida*. Working Paper. Florida State University.

Solmon, L., Paark, K., & Garcia, D. (2001). Does charter school attendance improve test scores? The Arizona results. Goldwater Institute Center for Market Based Education, Phoenix, AZ. Available at: <http://www.goldwaterinstitute.org/pdf/materials/111.pdf>; accessed September 2, 2004.

Sonstelie, J. (1979). Public school quality and private school enrollments. *National Tax Journal*, *32*, 343–353.

Stoddard, C., & Corcoran, S. (2005). *The political economic of school choice: Support for charter schools across states and school districts*. Working Paper presented at the AEFA annual conference.

Theobald, N. D., & Picus, L. O. (1991). Living with equal amounts of less: Experiences of states with primarily state-funded school systems. *Journal of Educational Finance*, *17*(1), 7–32.

Zimmer, R., Buddin, R., Chau, D., Daley, G., Gill, B., Guarino, C., Hamilton, L., Krop, C., McCaffrey, D., Sandler, M., & Brewer, D. (2003). *Charter school operations and performance: Evidence from California*. Santa Monica, CA: RAND Coproration.

Zimmer, R., & Jones, J. (2005). The impact of Michigan's move towards centralized funding on local bond referenda. *Southern Economic Journal*, *71*(3), 534–544.

THE LABOR MARKET IMPACT OF SCHOOL CHOICE: CHARTER COMPETITION AND TEACHER COMPENSATION

Lori L. Taylor

ABSTRACT

Charter schools have the potential to enhance competition in the public education sector. As such, they could have a particularly significant impact in the labor market for teachers. This study uses data on more than 312,000 teachers from 483 urban Texas school districts to explore the impact of charter school competition on the compensation of teachers at traditional public schools. The analysis suggests that once charter enrollments reach critical mass, increasing competition from charter schools increases salaries for all but the most experienced teachers.

Charter schools are an increasingly popular type of school reform. During the 1994–1995 school year, there were roughly 100 charter schools in the United States; 10 years later there were more than 3,300.[1] Forty states and the District of Columbia have some form of charter school law on the books.

Improving School Accountability: Check-Ups or Choice
Advances in Applied Microeconomics, Volume 14, 257–279

ISSN: 0278-0984/doi:10.1016/S0278-0984(06)14010-9

One reason for the popularity of charter schools – at least among economists – is their potential to enhance the degree of competition in education. Charter schools are publicly funded schools that compete for enrollments with traditional public schools. Charter schools do not have the residency requirements of traditional public schools, so students need not change their residence to be able to attend a charter school. Charter schools also tend to be less heavily regulated than traditional public schools, which may make them more effective competitors than other public schools.

Increased competition from charter schools may have a particularly significant impact in the labor market for teachers. The economics literature implies that school districts have market power in both the labor and the product markets.[2] If teacher labor markets are oligopsonistic, then charter school entry could lead to higher salaries for school district personnel, ceteris paribus.[3] However, if monopoly power in the product market generates economic rents, there are few parties to whom those rents might be dissipated besides school district personnel. To the extent that teachers have been able to appropriate a share of the economic rents generated by the market power of school districts, the entry of charter schools could lead to lower salaries.[4]

This study uses individual data on more than 312,000 teachers from 483 urban Texas school districts to explore the impact of charter school competition on the compensation of teachers at traditional public schools. The analysis suggests that once charter enrollments reach critical mass, increasing competition from charter schools increases salaries for all but the most experienced teachers.

THE THEORY OF TEACHER LABOR MARKETS

The elementary and secondary education industry in the United States is often highly concentrated. More than 30 percent of U.S. educational markets are served by a single public school district, and there are many more that are served by only a handful of educational providers.[5]

There are contrasting theoretical models concerning the impact of such concentration on teacher salaries. Boal and Ransom (1997) lay out a classic, Cournot model of oligopsony, which can be directly applied to the educational labor market. In the oligopsony model, each school district chooses an employment level to maximize its revenue function, given the employment level of all other providers in the market. As a result, wages are a function of market concentration, the (employment-weighted) average marginal revenue product per worker, and the elasticity of labor supply.

Assuming that labor supply is not perfectly elastic, and holding constant labor supply and the market-wide demand for labor, oligopsony in the education market implies that wages fall as market concentration increases.

The education market has more than one potential dimension of market power, however. The same territorial exclusivity that could give rise to oligopsony power in the market for educator labor could also give rise to oligopoly power in the market for education services. In locations where there is only one potential employer of teachers, there is also only one provider of educational services. School districts have the potential to earn rents in either the product or the labor market, and few residual claimants on those rents. There are no shareholders or capital owners per se. Plausibly, the parties most likely to capture any rents are the school district employees.

Blanchflower, Oswald, and Sanfey (1996) develop a model in which employees share in any rents earned by the firm. Wages in an industry are a function of expected opportunity wages outside the industry, industry rents per worker and the worker's relative bargaining power. Applying this model to education implies that teacher wages are an increasing function of school district rents (if any). To the extent that competition from charter schools reduces those rents, it should also reduce teacher compensation.

As discussed in Taylor (2006), the two competing models – oligopsony and rent-sharing – support very similar reduced-form equations for educator compensation. Let **Z** be a vector of factors other than market concentration that determine marginal revenue of school districts (primarily the determinants of local education demand and the educational technology), **A** be a vector of community characteristics that determine the prevailing wage (primarily cost of living and amenity differentials) and U be the local unemployment rate. Assuming that market concentration (H) is one of the sources of economic rents under the rent-sharing scenario, and that the elasticity of educator labor supply is a function of the determinants of expected opportunity wages, then

$$w_{\text{oligopsony}} = f(H, Z, A, U) \tag{1a}$$

and

$$w_{\text{rent-sharing}} = g(H, Z, A, U, \phi) \tag{1b}$$

where ϕ is an indicator of the worker's relative bargaining power.

The most obvious difference between the two reduced-form equations is that the rent-sharing equation has an extra term for the educator's relative bargaining power.[6] However, for the purposes of this analysis, the most important distinction between the two equations is the very different partial derivative with respect to market concentration (H). Holding constant the determinants of marginal revenue and labor supply (**Z** and **A**, respectively), the expected partial derivative of $w_{\text{oligopsony}}$ with respect to H is negative while the expected partial derivative of $w_{\text{rent-sharing}}$ with respect to H is positive. Thus, the growth of charter schools could either raise or lower teacher salaries, depending on which model best explains educator compensation.

USING TEXAS AS THE TEST CASE

Texas represents an attractive laboratory for exploring the relationship between charter competition and teacher compensation. Texas has been in the vanguard of the charter school movement. Texas adopted a charter school law in 1995, authorizing the creation of 20 charter schools. Sixteen charter schools opened their doors in the 1996–1997 school year and another three opened the following year. The number of charters tripled during the 1998–1999 school year (to 61), and expanded to 190 for the 2003–2004 school year. However, despite such explosive growth, charter schools remain a very small part of the educational market in Texas. During the 2003–2004 school year, 60,748 of the 4.3 million public school students in Texas attended charter schools, and 3,675 of the nearly 300,000 Texas teachers worked in charter schools.

Texas also contains a wide range of potential market structures within a single state's policy environment. There are more than 1,000 traditional, independent school districts in Texas. The Dallas metropolitan area alone has 71 such districts. Furthermore, Texas public school districts cover the gamut of school district sizes. There are 147 traditional Texas districts with less than 150 students and two districts (Dallas Independent School District and Houston Independent School District) with more than 150,000 students. The large number of districts of both types – traditional and charter – makes it easier to isolate the effect of charter schools from the impact of Tiebout competition among traditional public schools.

Finally, much of the variation in teacher compensation reflects the premia paid for individual-specific characteristics like experience or educational attainment. Because the distribution of teacher characteristics is likely to vary across labor markets, it is important to control for such characteristics when estimating the effect of charter competition on teacher compensation. Texas collects detailed information on the earnings, demographics and job characteristics of its school district personnel. As such, analysis of Texas data again permits the researcher to better isolate the impact of charter schools.

Texas Charter Schools

Any examination of Texas charter schools quickly reveals that they are not representative of Texas schools as a whole. Texas charter schools tend to be disproportionately urban. Of the 190 charter schools accepting enrollments in 2003–2004, 178 were located in one of 26 metropolitan areas. As a result, 97 percent of the students in Texas charter schools are urban. In contrast, only 86 percent of the students in traditional public school districts are urban.

Not only are they disproportionately urban, but charter schools are also disproportionately concentrated in major urban areas. More than half of the charter schools accepting enrollments in 2003–2004 were located in either the Houston, Dallas or San Antonio metropolitan areas. Fifty-nine percent of the charter school enrollments were in Houston or Dallas, and three of the state's smaller metropolitan areas had no charter school enrollments.

Even among the urban schools of Texas, charter schools stand out. During the 2003–2004 school year, Texas charter schools in urban areas served a student population that was disproportionately black and low income. Black students represented less than 15 percent of enrollment at traditional public schools, but 40 percent of enrollment at charter schools. Sixty-three percent of charter school students but 52 percent of traditional school students in urban areas were identified as economically disadvantaged.

The share of Hispanic students in charter schools was somewhat lower than the share of Hispanic students in traditional public schools (41 percent instead of 45 percent), but charter schools served dramatically fewer students with limited English proficiency (9 percent instead of 16 percent). Given that most Texas students with limited English proficiency are Hispanic, the pattern suggests that charter schools disproportionately attract English-speaking Hispanics.

Texas Educational Markets

Because Texas charter schools are so geographically clustered, it seems appropriate to focus on urban school districts when examining the labor market impact of charter schools. Given such a focus, a key element of the analysis will be the definition of education markets. One obvious strategy is to equate education markets with metropolitan areas. Chambers (1995, 1997) and Taylor (2006) have used this approach. Alternatively, one could argue that a labor market is defined by a reasonable commuting distance, and therefore that the relevant education market for each school district is the district itself plus all districts within a given radius. Beck (1993) and Merrifield (1999) used this approach and argued that 25 miles represents a reasonable commuting distance. Because there are only 26 Texas metropolitan areas, this analysis will use the latter approach.

Where available, the latitude and longitude of each Texas campus were taken from the National Center For Education Statistics' Common Core Database (CCD). The CCD contains latitude and longitude data on 77 percent of Texas campuses with enrollments in 2002–2003. The remaining campuses were assigned latitudes and longitudes according to the zip codes at their street address.[7] These data on latitude and longitude were used to calculate the distance in miles from one campus to another for all Texas campuses.

When isolating the effect of charter school competition on wages, it is important to control for variations in Tiebout competition among traditional public schools. Therefore, this analysis will use two measures of market concentration. The first is a Herfindahl-based index of competition among traditional public school districts (TDCOMP). For each district, TDCOMP is one minus the sum of squared enrollment shares for all traditional public school districts with at least one campus within a 25-mile radius of a campus from the district in question.[8] In other words, TDCOMP is one minus the Herfindahl index of enrollment concentration for each education market. When there is no competition among traditional public school districts in a market, TDCOMP equals zero. If a market were perfectly competitive, TDCOMP would be equal to one.

The second measure of market concentration is the market share for charter schools (CHARTSHR). CHARTSHR is defined as the total charter school enrollment within a 25-mile radius of any campus from the district in question, divided by the total public school enrollment (charter plus traditional) for all districts with at least one campus within the same geographic area.

Table 1 presents descriptive statistics for the two measures of market concentration. The first panel describes the two measures for all metropolitan areas in Texas. The second and third panels describe the two measures for the Dallas and Houston metropolitan areas, respectively.

As the table illustrates, there is considerable variation in market concentration across urban school districts. TDCOMP ranges from perfect concentration (TDCOMP = 0) almost to perfect competition (TDCOMP = 1). The mean TDCOMP, which drifted slightly upward from 2000 through 2004, implies the competitive equivalent of six equal-sized school districts. On average, TDCOMP is higher in the Dallas and Houston metropolitan areas

Table 1. Descriptive Statistics for Market Concentration in Education.

Variable	Year	Number of Teachers	Mean	Std. Dev.	Minimum	Maximum
All metropolitan areas						
TDCOMP	2000	207,751	0.823	0.123	0.000	0.930
TDCOMP	2001	215,056	0.826	0.124	0.000	0.932
TDCOMP	2002	222,018	0.828	0.123	0.000	0.933
TDCOMP	2003	226,114	0.832	0.122	0.000	0.936
TDCOMP	2004	229,454	0.835	0.122	0.000	0.938
CHARTSHR	2000	207,751	0.696	0.371	0.000	2.578
CHARTSHR	2001	215,056	0.994	0.528	0.000	3.504
CHARTSHR	2002	222,018	1.195	0.549	0.000	2.892
CHARTSHR	2003	226,114	1.321	0.582	0.000	3.546
CHARTSHR	2004	229,454	1.471	0.669	0.000	3.472
Dallas metropolitan area						
TDCOMP	2000	38,019	0.895	0.069	0.272	0.930
TDCOMP	2001	39,883	0.899	0.067	0.275	0.932
TDCOMP	2002	41,390	0.902	0.066	0.298	0.933
TDCOMP	2003	42,921	0.904	0.064	0.322	0.936
TDCOMP	2004	43,620	0.908	0.062	0.331	0.938
CHARTSHR	2000	38,019	0.811	0.287	0.000	1.242
CHARTSHR	2001	39,883	1.169	0.420	0.000	2.121
CHARTSHR	2002	41,390	1.408	0.460	0.000	2.389
CHARTSHR	2003	42,921	1.594	0.542	0.000	3.043
CHARTSHR	2004	43,620	1.828	0.602	0.000	3.472
Houston metropolitan area						
TDCOMP	2000	53,029	0.867	0.055	0.494	0.915
TDCOMP	2001	53,776	0.874	0.055	0.489	0.914
TDCOMP	2002	56,555	0.875	0.054	0.479	0.913
TDCOMP	2003	58,546	0.880	0.055	0.475	0.915
TDCOMP	2004	59,539	0.884	0.051	0.495	0.917
CHARTSHR	2000	53,029	0.951	0.308	0.000	1.301
CHARTSHR	2001	53,776	1.411	0.467	0.000	1.949
CHARTSHR	2002	56,555	1.544	0.506	0.000	2.133
CHARTSHR	2003	58,546	1.589	0.519	0.000	2.254
CHARTSHR	2004	59,539	1.678	0.546	0.000	2.183

than in other Texas metropolitan areas, but even these markets have at least a few districts that face relatively little competition within a 25-mile radius.

There is also considerable variation over time and space in charter school competition. Charter school enrollment has grown rapidly, and the share of charter school enrollment has grown accordingly. On average, the share of charter school enrollment has more than doubled since 2000, although it remains below 2 percent.

Charter school enrollment, as a share of total public school enrollment within a 25-mile radius, ranges from 0 to nearly 3.5 percent. In 2000, nearly one quarter of Texas urban school districts (118 of 483) did not have a charter school within a 25-mile radius; in 2004, there were 89 urban districts that still faced no charter school competition. Most metropolitan areas – including Dallas, Houston and San Antonio – contain at least one district with no charter schools within 25 miles.

Texas Payroll Data

Texas collects detailed information on the earnings, demographics and job characteristics of its school district personnel. The personnel files indicate salary, years of experience, educational attainment, gender, ethnicity, effective days worked, school assignment and the district of employment. In addition, the teacher records include indicators for job assignments (math, science, health and P.E., computer or special education), and for the percentage of time each individual spends teaching in a field for which he or she holds a Texas state teaching certificate.

Table 2 presents descriptive statistics on the 312,935 teachers used in this analysis. The analysis data set includes all individuals with complete data who worked as a teacher at least half time for a traditional, urban school district during at least one of the five school years from 1999–2000 through 2003–2004.[9]

As the table illustrates, the teachers in Texas' urban public schools are disproportionately White, non-Hispanic females. Average experience is near the national norm, but Texas teachers are much less likely to hold an advanced degree than their counterparts in other states. (The most recent national data indicate that 47 percent of public school teachers nationwide have graduate degrees; in Texas urban school districts, only 25 percent of teachers have such degrees.) On average urban Texas teachers spend more than 25 percent of their teaching time in a field for which they are not certified.

THE ESTIMATION

This analysis is based on the reduced-form versions of the oligopsony and rent-sharing models presented in Eqs. (1a) and (1b). Thus, the teacher wage level in a market is a function of market concentration (TDCOMP and CHARTSHR), the other determinants of the marginal revenue product of school districts (**Z**), and the determinants of expected opportunity wages

Table 2. Descriptive Statistics for Teachers in Traditional Urban School Districts.

	Mean	Std. Dev.	Minimum	Maximum
F.T.E. monthly salary	$4,006	754.257	$2,424	$9,890
Black	0.092	0.289	0	1
Hispanic	0.185	0.388	0	1
Asian/ Indian	0.011	0.105	0	1
Male	0.216	0.412	0	1
Years of experience	11.647	9.529	0	50
No degree	0.006	0.079	0	1
MA	0.240	0.427	0	1
Ph.D.	0.005	0.071	0	1
New hire	0.168	0.374	0	1
Percent time in field of certification	0.749	0.398	0	1
Teaching assignment				
Math	0.139	0.346	0	1
Science	0.123	0.328	0	1
Health and P.E.	0.106	0.308	0	1
Computers	0.014	0.117	0	1
Special education	0.064	0.245	0	1
High school	0.499	0.500	0	1

Note: There are 1,100,393 observations covering 312,935 individual teachers in the data set.

(A and U). In turn, the wages received by an individual teacher are a function of the teacher wage level, teacher-specific characteristics and district-specific characteristics that could give rise to compensating differentials.

Formally, the specification can be expressed as

$$\ln(W_{idjt}) = \alpha + H_{jt}\beta_H + Z_{jt}\beta_Z + A_{jt}\beta_A + U_{jt}\beta_U + D_{dt}\delta + T_{it}\gamma + \varepsilon_{idjt} \quad (2)$$

where the subscripts i, d, j and t stand for individuals, districts, labor markets and time, respectively, $\mathbf{H}_{jt}$ is a vector of market concentration indicators, $\mathbf{D}_{dt}$ is a vector of district-specific characteristics that could give rise to compensating differentials and $\mathbf{T}_{it}$ is a vector of individual-specific characteristics. Because previous research has found a nonlinear relationship between market concentration and teacher compensation (Taylor, 2006), $\mathbf{H}_{jt}$ includes not only TDCOMP and CHARTSHR, but also their squares. Following the literature on teacher compensation, the dependent variable ($\ln(W_{idtj})$) is the logarithm of full-time-equivalent monthly salary.

The **Z** vector contains market-level characteristics other than concentration that determine the marginal revenue product of school districts. Likely candidates include factors describing the education technology and the local demand for education. Cost function analyses (e.g. Gronberg, Jansen, Taylor, & Booker, 2004) indicate that scale is a primary determinant of the educational technology, so the **Z** vector includes the log of enrollment. Meanwhile, education demand is frequently modeled as a function of the tax price of education and voter demographics (e.g. Hoxby, 2001). Following Hoxby (2001), I define the tax price of education as the additional tax revenue a district must generate to be able to spend an additional dollar on education.[10] Data on voter demographics in each school district – median income, the percent of the adult population with a high school diploma but no college degree, the percent of the adult population with at least a bachelors' degree, the percentage of households with school age children and the percentage of residents over 65 – come from the 2000 Census School District files. The **Z** variables are weighted averages of these characteristics across all school districts in the labor market.[11]

The expected wage is a function of the local unemployment rate (U) and the prevailing wage in a labor market (A). I use the NCES Comparable Wage Index (CWI) to measure the prevailing wage for college graduates in each Texas school district (Taylor & Fowler, 2006). The CWI measures the wage level for college graduates who are not educators in each of 800 labor markets nationwide. It is based on the Individual Public Use Microdata from the 2000 census and the Bureau of Labor Statistics' (BLS) Occupational Employment Survey. Data on local unemployment rates in each metropolitan area and county also come from the BLS. As with the **Z** vector, the CWI and U used in this analysis are weighted averages across all school districts in the labor market.

The **D** vector captures any district-specific compensating differentials. A district with a student body that is perceived as unusually challenging to teach will likely have to pay a premium to staff its classrooms. On the other hand, districts with low enrollments are likely to have small class sizes as well, allowing them to hire at a modest discount. Similarly, given commuting costs and typical rent gradients, districts near the center of a metropolitan area may have to pay a premium to attract teachers while districts on the urban fringe may be able to hire at a modest discount. To control for such effects, the **D** vector includes student demographics (the percentage of students who are economically disadvantaged, limited English proficient, and Anglo), school district size (the log of district enrollment and indicator variables for the Dallas and Houston Independent school districts)[12] and three indicators of district location – the average distance from the center of the closest metropolitan area, the share of rural enrollments within a 25-mile radius and the share of micropolitan enrollments within a 25-mile radius.

ENDOGENEITY ISSUES

Caroline Hoxby illustrated the importance of treating competition among school districts as endogenous, using topographic information as the exogenous source of variation (Hoxby, 1994, 2000). Although Hoxby's analysis has come under fire recently (e.g. Rothstein, 2004), her basic observation remains unassailable; the amount of competition facing a school district may not be exogenous.

Unfortunately, Hoxby's preferred instrument – the physical location of rivers and streams – is not well suited to Texas. The boundaries of Texas school districts are more a byproduct of political history than of natural barriers. Furthermore, natural barriers are largely irrelevant to charter school competition. Therefore, other instruments must be found.

Instruments for Traditional Tiebout Competition

Accepting that the pattern of district boundaries in Texas is largely given by history, any endogenous variation in TDCOMP arises from differences in the rate of enrollment growth among traditional public schools. Because uneven enrollment growth should reflect the availability and distribution of undeveloped land in the market, I include as instruments the average share of undeveloped land in the education market and the share of undeveloped land in the largest school district in the education market (both lagged one year). Markets with a greater share of undeveloped land, holding constant the share of undeveloped land in the largest district, should be more competitive because they have more of a residential fringe.

Instruments for Charter Competition

Any endogenous variation in CHARTSHR arises from the location decisions of charter schools. Therefore, the determinants of charter location should be appropriate instruments for CHARTSHR.

Charter schools are public schools and cannot formally earn profits, but they can dissipate rents to their own personnel in the form of wages or working conditions. As a consequence, their locational decisions should mirror those of profit maximizing firms. Therefore, I follow Grosskopf, Hayes, and Taylor (2004) and model charter location decisions as a function of a market's profit potential.

Potential charter school profits (π_i) can be defined as

$$\pi_i = \sum P_i Q_i - C(Q_1, \ldots Q_N) \tag{3}$$

where P_i is the amount of revenue generated by each student of type i, Q_i the number of students of type i that a charter school is able to attract, N the total number of student types, and C the cost of providing educational services to that mix of students.

In Texas, charter school revenue per student (P_i) is a function of the revenue characteristics of the student's home district and the programmatic needs of the individual student,

$$P_i = P(\tau_i, W_i) \tag{4}$$

where τ_i is a measure of M&O tax revenue per full-time-equivalent student in the regular education program[13] and $\boldsymbol{W}_i$ is a vector of indicators for whether the student participates in the compensatory education program (COMPED), the special education program (SPECIAL ED), the vocational education program (VOTECH), the BILINGUAL education program or the gifted and talented program (GIFTED). Students in each of those programs generate additional revenue above and beyond that available per student in regular instruction.

The number of students of type i that a charter school can attract (Q_i) will depend on an array of market characteristics (M_i). Following Grosskopf et al. (2004), that array includes the average percent of Black, Hispanic and other students who are failing the statewide standardized tests (FAILBLACK, FAILHISP and FAILELSE, respectively), the total number of public school students in the market (DENSITY), the share of students who are BLACK, and HISPANIC, the number of traditional public school districts with campuses within the radius (CHOICES) and the crow-flies distance from the center of the radius to the center of the metropolitan area (DISTANCE).

Meanwhile, the cost of providing educational services will depend on factor prices (ω_i) and the programmatic characteristics of the students. Housing costs are a significant determinant of the cost of living, and variations in the cost of living are important determinants of wage variations, so I use the fair market rent on a two bedroom apartment (as measured by the U.S. Department of Housing and Urban Development) to proxy for labor cost variations (ω).

Because the amount of charter competition in any educational market should be a function of the market's profit potential, the reduced-form model of charter competition becomes[14]

$$\text{CHARTSHR}_i = f(\tau_i, W_i, M_i, \omega_i) \tag{5}$$

Eq. (5) demonstrates that CHARTSHR should be a function of the profit potential of the education market. However, it is reasonable to believe that the introduction of a charter school will alter market characteristics. To ensure that the instruments for CHARTSHR are exogenous, I measure them with a five-year lag.[15] Thus, the instruments for charter competition in 1999–2000 are market characteristics from 1994–1995, the year that Texas adopted its charter school law and two years before the first charter school opened its doors.

Table 3 illustrates the explanatory power of Eq. (5). As the table illustrates, the profit potential of a local market – even lagged five years – can explain

Table 3. The Determinants of Charter Competition.

	Coefficient Estimate	Robust Standard Error
Dependent variable: CHARTSHR		
Fair market rent	−0.1774	0.2111
Failblack	−0.0268	0.0113**
Failhisp	0.0197	0.0068***
Failelse	0.0368	0.0107***
Black	0.0492	0.0085***
Hispanic	0.0226	0.0052***
M&O revenue	0.0000	0.0001
Compensatory education	−0.0132	0.0062**
Bilingual	−0.0217	0.0042***
Special education	0.0013	0.0211
Vocational/technical	−0.0115	0.0066*
Gifted	0.0220	0.0119*
Density	0.0000	0.0000***
Traditional choices	0.0195	0.0017***
fy2000	−0.9168	0.1611***
fy2001	−0.4996	0.1118***
fy2002	−0.2394	0.0662***
fy2003	−0.0626	0.0414
Constant	0.5495	1.5279
Number of observations	2,414	
R^2	0.6496	

Note: The OLS regression is weighted by the number of teachers from each district in the estimation sample.
*Significant at 10 percent level;
**Significant at 5 percent level;
***Significant at 1 percent level.

much of the variation in the charter enrollment shares. There is little evidence that variations in the basic revenue per pupil are sufficient to influence charter competition; the effect of M&O revenue, while positive, is not statistically significant. However, there is a consistent pattern to the relationship between the charter competition and the programmatic participation of students. A high concentration of compensatory education or bilingual education students is negatively associated with charter competition.[16]

THE RELATIONSHIP BETWEEN COMPETITION AND WAGES

Using the determinants of uneven enrollment growth and charter location as instruments for TDCOMP, CHARTSHR and their squares, yields the IV model of Eq. (2) presented in Table 4. A Durbin–Wu–Hausman test easily rejects ordinary least squares in favor of this two-stage least squares specification.[17] Because most of the independent variables – including the competition measures – do not vary within labor markets each year, the observations within any given labor market may not be independent. The standard errors have been adjusted to reflect such clustering.

As the table illustrates, both indicators of competition have a significant – and nonlinear – relationship with teacher compensation. Wages fall as the Herfindahl index of traditional school competition rises, but only up to a point. Once TDCOMP exceeds 0.56, wages begin to rise with competition. Similarly, once charter schools reach 0.77 percent of market enrollment, a growing charter share is associated with rising teacher wages.

The estimation in Table 4 suggests that a lack of competition among traditional school districts generates economic rents, which lead to higher teacher salaries. It provides much less evidence of rent sharing in markets with little or no charter competition. The coefficient on CHARTSHR, while negative, is far from significant. The corresponding F statistic is only 1.37, which is not significantly different from 0 at any conventional level of significance.

An alternative interpretation of the evidence is that charter school competition must reach critical mass in a market before it can have a detectable influence on teacher compensation. Researchers examining the relationship between competition and school efficiency frequently find evidence of threshold effects (e.g. Borland & Howsen, 1993; Grosskopf, Hayes, Taylor, & Weber, 2001; Zanzig, 1997).

Table 5 explores possible threshold effects in the relationship between charter competition and teacher compensation. The five alternative models

Table 4. The Effect of Charter Competition on Teacher Salary.

	Coefficient Estimate	Robust Standard Error
CHARTSHR	−0.0355	0.0303
CHARTSHR, squared	0.0232	0.0114**
TDCOMP	−0.5227	0.2097**
TDCOMP, squared	0.4692	0.1424***
Tax price	0.0344	0.0224
Average district size (log)	0.0157	0.0077**
Average income (log)	−0.0375	0.0436
Percent school age	0.1663	0.1522
Percent over 65	−0.2059	0.2105
Percent high school graduates	0.0033	0.1547
Percent college graduates	−0.0838	0.1451
Unemployment rate	−0.0070	0.0037*
Comparable wage index	0.0357	0.0668
District characteristics		
District enrollment (log)	0.0147	0.0024***
DISD	0.0055	0.0085
HISD	−0.0376	0.0095***
Percent low income	0.0039	0.0337
Percent L.E.P.	−0.0162	0.0371
Percent white	−0.0341	0.0257
Miles to metro center	0.0000	0.0003
Rural share	−0.0837	0.0493*
Micropolitan share	0.0066	0.0417
Number of observations	1,108,715	
R^2	0.8816	

Note: The dependent variable is log of full-time-equivalent monthly salary. The model also includes years of experience and its square, percent time teaching in a field for which the teacher was certified, and indicators for gender, ethnicity (Black, Hispanic and Asian/Indian), educational attainment (no college degree, MA and Ph.D.), classroom assignment (math, science, health and physical education, computer and special education), assignment to a high school, and first year in the district. The four competition indicators (CHARTSHR, TDCOMP and their squares) are treated as endogenous. The robust standard errors are adjusted for clustering by school district.

*Significant at 10 percent level;

**Significant at 5 percent level;

***Significant at 1 percent level.

presented in Table 5 differ from the baseline model in Table 4 only in that the quadratic specification of CHARTSHR has been replaced with a piecewise-linear specification. All five piecewise-linear models allow changes in CHARTSHR below a designated threshold to have a different marginal

Table 5. Threshold Effects in Charter Competition.

	Coefficient Estimate	Robust Standard Error
Competitive threshold = 0.25 Percent		
CHARTSHR $\leqslant$0.25	−0.2222	0.0820***
CHARTSHR $\geqslant$0.25	0.0391	0.0116***
R^2		0.8805
Prob > F, $\beta_{\text{CHARTSHR}\leqslant 0.25} = 0, \beta_{\text{CHARTSHR}\geqslant 0.25} = 0$		0.0005
Competitive threshold = 0.50 Percent		
CHARTSHR $\leqslant$0.50	−0.0663	0.0374*
CHARTSHR $\geqslant$0.50	0.0340	0.0115***
R^2		0.8819
Prob > F, $\beta_{\text{CHARTSHR}\leqslant 0.50} = 0, \beta_{\text{CHARTSHR}\geqslant 0.50} = 0$		0.0058
Competitive threshold = 0.75 Percent		
CHARTSHR $\leqslant$0.75	−0.0151	0.0256
CHARTSHR $\geqslant$0.75	0.0319	0.0119***
R^2		0.8827
Prob > F, $\beta_{\text{CHARTSHR}\leqslant 0.75} = 0, \beta_{\text{CHARTSHR}\geqslant 0.75} = 0$		0.0278
Competitive threshold = 1.00 Percent		
CHARTSHR $\leqslant$1.00	−0.0004	0.0221
CHARTSHR $\geqslant$ 1.00	0.0332	0.0128***
R^2		0.8828
Prob > F, $\beta_{\text{CHARTSHR}\leqslant 1.00} = 0, \beta_{\text{CHARTSHR}\geqslant 1.00} = 0$		0.0332
Competitive threshold = 1.25 Percent		
CHARTSHR $\leqslant$1.25	0.0027	0.0206
CHARTSHR $\geqslant$1.25	0.0408	0.0165**
R^2		0.8825
Prob > F, $\beta_{\text{CHARTSHR}\leqslant 1.25} = 0, \beta_{\text{CHARTSHR}\geqslant 1.25} = 0$		0.0270

Note: All specifications are identical to the instrumental variables model in Table 4 except CHARTSHR which is piecewise linear. The robust standard errors are adjusted for clustering by school district.

*Significant at 10 percent level;

**Significant at 5 percent level;

***Significant at 1 percent level.

effect than changes in CHARTSHR above the designated threshold. The various models explore thresholds at 0.25 percentage point intervals from 0.25 to 1.25 percent.

A negative coefficient on either section of CHARTSHR suggests rent sharing. As the table illustrates, only the first model provides evidence of rent sharing that is significant at the 5 percent level. The remaining models suggest threshold effects, not rent sharing. Because all of the models indicating threshold effects fit the data better than the one rent-sharing model, it is difficult to conclude that charter competition erodes teacher rents. It is much more likely that charter competition has threshold effects, and that once charter competition reaches the threshold value, increases in charter competition erode the oligopsony power of school districts.[18]

Thus, the patterns of teacher compensation suggest that both oligopsony power and rent sharing are at play in the market for Texas teachers. In markets where TDCOMP exceeds 0.56 or CHARTSHR exceeds 0.77, the oligopsony effect dominates, and wages rise with competition. However, in markets where TDCOMP is below 0.56, rent sharing best explains the pattern of compensation.

Most teachers work in the oligopsonistic part of the distribution. The baseline, quadratic model indicates that school districts in markets where the charter school share is one standard deviation above the urban average pay 2.2 percent more than districts in markets where the charter school share is one standard deviation below the average. Similarly, districts in markets where TDCOMP is one standard deviation above the urban average pay 6.3 percent more than districts in markets that are one standard deviation less competitive than average. In 2004, 82 percent of urban teachers in Texas worked in markets where an increase in charter share would increase compensation, and 95 percent worked in markets where an increase in competition in at least one dimension would increase compensation.

Intriguingly, the relative magnitude of the coefficients suggests that an increase in charter school competition has a much greater impact on teacher compensation than would a comparable increase in Tiebout competition among traditional public school districts. To illustrate this point, consider the change in charter school enrollment shares between 2000 and 2004. On average, the charter share more than doubled (from 0.696 to 1.471). However, if the charter schools had been classified all along as traditional public schools, their growth in enrollments would have increased the average TDHERF by no more than 0.003.[19] Thus, the model predicts that the increase in charter share since 2000 increased urban teacher salaries in Texas by 1.1 percent on average, while a comparable increase in Tiebout competition among traditional public schools would have increased salaries by only 0.1 percent.

The finding that markets with a larger charter share have higher wages, ceteris paribus, is particularly interesting in light of the compensation patterns of charter schools. As discussed in Taylor (2005), Texas charter schools pay generally lower wages than traditional public school districts. On average, teacher wages in Texas charter schools are 7.5 percent lower than one would expect, given the observable characteristics of charter schools and employees. In large part, this differential arises because, compared with traditional public schools, charter schools in Texas pay a much smaller premium for teacher experience, and no premium for advanced degrees (Taylor, 2005).

Because the wage gap between charter schools and traditional public schools increases with teacher experience, charter school competition might have differential impacts according to the experience level of the teachers. To explore this possibility, I divided teachers into five groups – those with fewer than five years of experience, those with 5–9 years of experience, those with 10–14 years of experience, those with 15–19 years of experience and those with at least 20 years of experience – and reestimated the quadratic version of Eq. (2). The median, urban teacher has nine years of experience, so the first two groups can be thought of as relatively inexperienced teachers, while the latter three groups can be thought of as relatively experienced teachers. Table 6 presents the coefficient estimates, while Fig. 1 traces out the implied relationships between charter competition and compensation, holding all other characteristics constant.

As both the table and the figure illustrate, there are significant differences across experience groups. For beginning teachers (those with less than five years of experience) the relationship between charter competition and wages is unambiguous. Markets with a greater share of charter school teachers pay higher starting salaries, ceteris paribus.[20] For highly experienced teachers (those with at least 20 years of experience), the relationship is also unambiguous: the wages of highly experienced teachers are unaffected by competition from charter schools. Teachers in the middle of the experience distribution, benefit from charter competition only when the charter share is above a competitive threshold.

The pattern of compensation strongly suggests that relatively inexperienced teachers have the most to gain from charter school competition. In 2004, more than 93 percent of relatively inexperienced, urban teachers worked in markets where charter school entry would raise teacher wages, while only 39 percent of relatively experienced teachers worked in such markets. Furthermore, moving from a market that is one standard deviation below average in charter share to a market that is one standard deviation above average is associated with a 3 percent increase in salary for relatively inexperienced teachers, but at most a 1.7-percent increase in salary for relatively experienced teachers.

Table 6. The Effects of Competition by Years of Experience.

	Coefficient Estimate	Robust Standard Error
Less than 5 years of experience		
CHARTSHR	0.0043	0.0376
CHARTSHR, squared	0.0083	0.0142
TDCOMP	−0.8719	0.3053***
TDCOMP, squared	0.6742	0.2107***
Number of Observations		337,941
Prob > F, $\beta_{\text{CHARTSHR}} = 0$, $\beta_{\text{CHARTSHR, squared}} = 0$		0.0904
Prob > F, $\beta_{\text{TDCOMP}} = 0$, $\beta_{\text{TDCOMP, squared}} = 0$		0.0019
5–9 years of experience		
CHARTSHR	−0.0494	0.0365
CHARTSHR, squared	0.0326	0.0136**
TDCOMP	−0.2610	0.2541
TDCOMP, squared	0.2899	0.1718*
Number of observations		222,890
Prob > F, $\beta_{\text{CHARTSHR}} = 0$, $\beta_{\text{CHARTSHR, squared}} = 0$		0.0013
Prob > F, $\beta_{\text{TDCOMP}} = 0$, $\beta_{\text{TDCOMP, squared}} = 0$		0.0133
10–14 years of experience		
CHARTSHR	−0.0519	0.0349
CHARTSHR, squared	0.0287	0.0121**
TDCOMP	−0.2601	0.2113
TDCOMP, squared	0.2825	0.1442*
Number of observations		152,722
Prob > F, $\beta_{\text{CHARTSHR}} = 0$, $\beta_{\text{CHARTSHR, squared}} = 0$		0.0024
Prob > F, $\beta_{\text{TDCOMP}} = 0$, $\beta_{\text{TDCOMP, squared}} = 0$		0.0077
15–19 years of experience		
CHARTSHR	−0.0540	0.0345
CHARTSHR, squared	0.0275	0.0117**
TDCOMP	−0.4956	0.2314**
TDCOMP, squared	0.4507	0.1602***
Number of observations		130,982
Prob > F, $\beta_{\text{CHARTSHR}} = 0$, $\beta_{\text{CHARTSHR, squared}} = 0$		0.0119
Prob > F, $\beta_{\text{TDCOMP}} = 0$, $\beta_{\text{TDCOMP, squared}} = 0$		0.0014
20 or more years of experience		
CHARTSHR	−0.0282	0.0374
CHARTSHR, squared	0.0174	0.0128
TDCOMP	−0.4132	0.2414*
TDCOMP, squared	0.4031	0.1693**
Number of observations		255,858
Prob > F, $\beta_{\text{CHARTSHR}} = 0$, $\beta_{\text{CHARTSHR, squared}} = 0$		0.1937
Prob > F, $\beta_{\text{TDCOMP}} = 0$, $\beta_{\text{TDCOMP, squared}} = 0$		0.0090

Note: All specifications are identical to the instrumental variables model in Table 4, but run on a restricted data set. The robust standard errors are adjusted for clustering by school districts.
*Significant at 10 percent level;
**Significant at 5 percent level;
***Significant at 1 percent level.

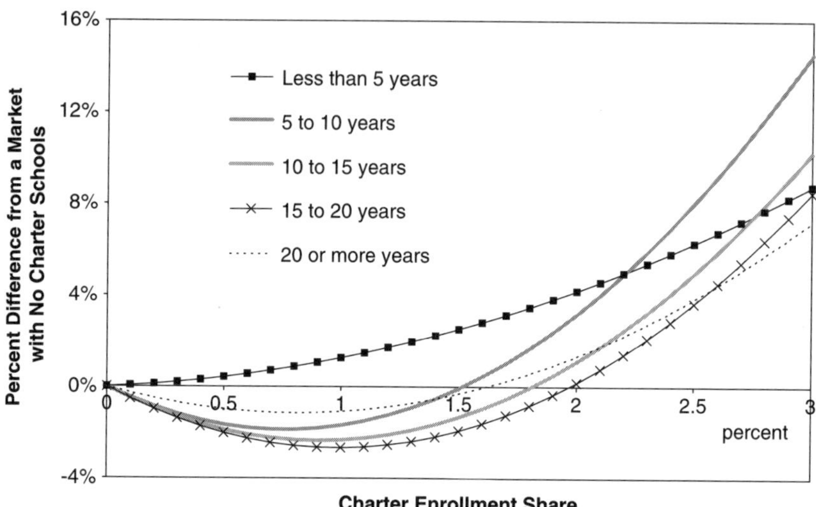

Fig. 1. The Effects of Charter Competition on Wages by Years of Experience.

Relatively inexperienced teachers may have more to gain from charter school competition because they are more likely to accept charter school jobs. Charter schools pay much smaller premia for experience than do traditional public schools, and hire much less experienced teachers (Taylor, 2005). On average, charter school teachers in Texas have less than half the teaching experience of teachers in urban, traditional school districts. One interpretation of the estimation results is that traditional school districts are not concerned about losing their highly experienced teachers to charter schools.

CONCLUSIONS

Charter schools are an increasingly important source of educational competition. One market in which their competitive influence is strong is in the market for teacher labor. Analysis of teacher labor markets in Texas suggests that teacher wages are highly sensitive to charter school competition. Furthermore, the compensation patterns in Texas suggest that competition from charter schools has a much greater impact on teacher compensation than does a comparable change in Tiebout competition among traditional public schools.

The impact on teacher salaries depends on the degree of charter school competition in the market. Charter school competition must reach critical mass in a market before it can have a detectable influence on teacher compensation. However, that competitive threshold is low. In most urban markets, the growth of charter schools is expected to raise salaries for all but the most experienced teachers.

NOTES

1. http://www.edreform.com/_upload/ncsw-numbers.pdf.
2. For a survey of the literature on market concentration and education, see Taylor (2000).
3. For example, see Boal and Ransom (1997), Luizer and Thornton (1986), Merrifield (1999) or Vedder and Hall (2000).
4. For example, see Blanchflower et al. (1996) or Hildreth and Oswald (1997).
5. According to the National Center for Education Statistics' F-33 school finance files for the 2002–2003 school year, 805 of the 2593 U.S. education markets are served by a single local education agency. Education markets are defined as the CMSA for all districts in a CMSA and as the county for all other districts.
6. If ϕ does not vary systematically across labor markets, the equations are observationally equivalent.
7. Using zip codes to identify geographic location can be problematic if the zip code area is large. Comparing the latitude and longitude assigned by CCD to those implied by zip codes indicates that the average difference between the two locational indicators is less than 3 miles, but that it can reach 25 miles in some sparsely populated areas.
8. Campuses with fewer than five students in enrollment and hospital campuses are not included when identifying districts with a campus within the competitive radius.
9. Records with missing or anomalous data were excluded. For example, teachers with zero years of experience for six years running have been excluded from the analysis. A handful of teachers with more than 50 years of experience have also been excluded. Teachers who had administrative duties have also been excluded.
10. The tax price is calculated from the statutory provisions of the Texas school finance formula as a function of school district wealth, student demographics and Texas' cost of education index. The cost of education index indicates differences in the predicted cost of hiring teachers in 1989. For more on Texas' cost of education index, see Alexander et al. (2000).
11. The labor market averages are averages of the characteristics in each school district within a 25-mile radius (the same definition of labor market used to calculate TDCOMP), weighted by each district's share of teacher employment in that market.
12. The Dallas and Houston Independent School Districts (ISDs) are notable outliers with 2004 enrollments of 160,000 and 211,000 students, respectively. Dallas ISD is more than twice as large as the next largest school district in the state.

13. This element of the charter school funding formula after 2002 is a weighted average of the home district's M&O tax revenue and the state average M&O revenue per pupil in regular instruction.

14. Note that profit maximization is not the only charter objective function that will yield this reduced-form equation. For example, charter competition would depend on the same set of factors if charter schools were attempting to maximize enrollments subject to a budget constraint.

15. Relying on a five-year lag ensures that the salary panel does not overlap with the panel of instruments. The most recent values used in the charter competition equation come from 1998–1999, one year before the first salary observations.

16. One interpretation of this pattern is that the finance-formula weights for low income and bilingual students are not sufficient to cover the expected costs of serving these populations.

17. The test statistic is 4.94 with 4 and 482 degrees of freedom.

18. Booker, Gilpatric, Gronberg, and Jansen (2004) find that competition from charter schools improves the performance of traditional public schools once the market penetration of charter schools reaches a similarly low threshold.

19. Between 2000 and 2004, the Herfindahl index of traditional school competition increased by 0.012 (from 0.823 to 0.835), while a Herfindahl index of total competition increased by 0.015 (from 0.825 to 0.840).

20. Although the model with both CHARTSHR and its square yields insignificant coefficients on both terms, alternative models with only one charter competition term (either CHARTSHR or its square but not both) yield a coefficient for the charter competition term that is positive and significant at the 5 percent level.

REFERENCES

Alexander, C. D., Gronberg, T., Jansen, D., Keller, H., Taylor, L., & Treisman, P. U. (2000). *A study of uncontrollable variations in the costs of Texas public education*. (Summary Report Prepared for the 77th Texas Legislature). Charles A. Dana Center, University of Texas at Austin, Austin, Texas. Retrieved May 19, 2005, from http://www.utdanacenter.org

Beck, P. M. (1993). *Monopsony in the market for public school teachers in Missouri: The static and dynamic impact of salaries and employment*. Ph.D. Dissertation, University of Missouri, Columbia, MO.

Blanchflower, D. G., Oswald, A. J., & Sanfey, P. (1996). Wages, profits and rent-sharing. *Quarterly Journal of Economics*, *61*, 227–252.

Boal, W. M., & Ransom, M. R. (1997). Monopsony in the labor market. *Journal of Economic Literature*, *35*, 86–112.

Booker, K., Gilpatric, S. M., Gronberg, T. J., Jansen, D. W. (2004). *The effect of charter competition on traditional public school students in Texas*. Private Enterprise Research Center Working Paper #411.

Borland, M. V., & Howsen, R. M. (1993). On the determination of the critical level of market concentration in education. *Economics of Education Review*, *12*, 165–169.

Chambers, J. G. (1995). Public school teacher cost differences across the United States: Introduction to a Teacher Cost Index (TCI) [online] Retrieved November 22, 1999, from http://nces.ed.gov/pubs/96344cha.htm

Chambers, J. G. (1997). *Geographic variations in public school costs*. Washington, DC: U.S. Department of Education, National Center for Education Statistics.

Gronberg, T. J., Jansen, D. W., Taylor, L. L., & Booker, K. (2004). School Outcomes and School Costs: The Cost Function Approach (report prepared for the Texas Joint Select Committee on Public School Finance, Austin). Retrieved May 19, 2005, from http://www.tlc.state.tx.us/roadmap/tsfp/reports.htm

Grosskopf, S., Hayes, K. J., & Taylor, L. L. (2004). Competition and efficiency: The impact of charter schools on public school performance (manuscript).

Grosskopf, S., Hayes, K. J., Taylor, L. L., & Weber, W. L. (2001). On the determinants of school district efficiency: Competition and monitoring. *Journal of Urban Economics*, *49*, 453–478.

Hildreth, A. K. G., & Oswald, A. J. (1997). Rent-sharing and wages: Evidence from company and establishment panels. *Journal of Labor Economics*, *15*, 318–337.

Hoxby, C. M. (1994). *Does competition among public schools benefit students and taxpayers?* NBER Working Paper #4979.

Hoxby, C. M. (2000). Does competition among public schools benefit students and taxpayers? *American Economic Review*, *90*, 1209–1238.

Hoxby, C. M. (2001). All school finance equalizations are not created equal. *Quarterly Journal of Economics*, *116*, 1189–1231.

Luizer, J., & Thornton, R. (1986). Concentration in the labor market for public school teachers. *Industrial and Labor Relations Review*, *39*, 573–584.

Merrifield, J. (1999). monopsony power in the market for teachers: Why teachers should support market-based education reform. *Journal of Labor Research*, *20*, 377–392.

Rothstein, J. (2004). Does Competition among Public Schools Benefit Students and Taxpayers: Comment, manuscript.

Taylor, L. L. (2000). The Evidence on Government Competition. Federal Reserve Bank of Dallas Economic and Financial Review.

Taylor, L. L. (2005). Teacher Cream Skimming: Do Charter Schools Attract the Most Effective Teachers? manuscript.

Taylor, L. L. (2006). *Competition and teacher compensation*. Bush School Working Paper #624.

Taylor, L. L., & Fowler, W. J., Jr. (2006). A comparable wage approach to geographic cost adjustments (NCES 2006–321). U.S. Department of Education. Washington, DC: National Center for Education Statistics.

Vedder, R., & Hall, J. (2000). Private school competition and public school teacher salaries. *Journal of Labor Research*, *21*, 161–168.

Zanzig, B. R. (1997). Measuring the impact of competition in local government education markets on the cognitive achievement of students. *Economics of Education Review*, *16*, 431–441.